Alfred Barry

Some lights of Science on the Faith

Eight Lectures Preached before the University of Oxford in the Year 1892

Alfred Barry

Some lights of Science on the Faith
Eight Lectures Preached before the University of Oxford in the Year 1892

ISBN/EAN: 9783337252625

Printed in Europe, USA, Canada, Australia, Japan

Cover: Foto ©Lupo / pixelio.de

More available books at **www.hansebooks.com**

THE BAMPTON LECTURES
FOR MDCCCXCII

Oxford
HORACE HART, PRINTER TO THE UNIVERSITY

Some Lights of Science on the Faith

EIGHT LECTURES

PREACHED BEFORE THE UNIVERSITY OF OXFORD
IN THE YEAR 1892

On the Foundation of the late Rev. John Bampton, M.A.
Canon of Salisbury

BY

ALFRED BARRY, D.D., D.C.L.

CANON OF WINDSOR, LATE PRIMATE OF AUSTRALIA

London
LONGMANS, GREEN, AND CO.
AND NEW YORK: 15 EAST 16TH STREET
1892

EXTRACT

FROM THE LAST WILL AND TESTAMENT

OF THE LATE

REV. JOHN BAMPTON,

CANON OF SALISBURY.

—— "I give and bequeath my Lands and Estates to the "Chancellor, Masters, and Scholars of the University of Oxford "for ever, to have and to hold all and singular the said Lands or "Estates upon trust, and to the intents and purposes hereinafter "mentioned; that is to say, I will and appoint that the Vice- "Chancellor of the University of Oxford for the time being shall "take and receive all the rents, issues, and profits thereof, and "(after all taxes, reparations, and necessary deductions made) "that he pay all the remainder to the endowment of eight "Divinity Lecture Sermons, to be established for ever in the "said University, and to be performed in the manner following:

"I direct and appoint, that, upon the first Tuesday in Easter "Term, a Lecturer may be yearly chosen by the Heads of Col- "leges only, and by no others, in the room adjoining to the "Printing-House, between the hours of ten in the morning and "two in the afternoon, to preach eight Divinity Lecture "Sermons, the year following, at St. Mary's in Oxford, between "the commencement of the last month in Lent Term, and the "end of the third week in Act Term.

Extract from Canon Bampton's Will.

"Also I direct and appoint, that the eight Divinity Lecture Sermons shall be preached upon either of the following Subjects—to confirm and establish the Christian Faith, and to confute all heretics and schismatics—upon the divine authority of the holy Scriptures—upon the authority of the writings of the primitive Fathers, as to the faith and practice of the primitive Church—upon the Divinity of our Lord and Saviour Jesus Christ—upon the Divinity of the Holy Ghost—upon the Articles of the Christian Faith, as comprehended in the Apostles' and Nicene Creed.

"Also I direct, that thirty copies of the eight Divinity Lecture Sermons shall be always printed, within two months after they are preached; and one copy shall be given to the Chancellor of the University, and one copy to the Head of every College, and one copy to the Mayor of the city of Oxford, and one copy to be put into the Bodleian Library; and the expense of printing them shall be paid out of the revenue of the Land or Estates given for establishing the Divinity Lecture Sermons; and the Preacher shall not be paid, nor be entitled to the revenue, before they are printed.

"Also I direct and appoint, that no person shall be qualified to preach the Divinity Lecture Sermons, unless he hath taken the degree of Master of Arts at least, in one of the two Universities of Oxford or Cambridge; and that the same person shall never preach the Divinity Lecture Sermons twice."

PREFACE

The Lectures, as here printed, are substantially those actually delivered, with some additional passages, either omitted in delivery for the sake of brevity, or subsequently inserted, where clearness seemed to require it.

I have only two prefatory remarks to make upon them.

First, that they embody an attempt to take some general view of the present relation of Science in its largest sense to the Christian Faith; as illustrated by examples of its bearing, confirmatory, elucidatory, or critical, on the substance of the Creed of Christendom, witnessing of Christ Himself. It is only too obvious that such an attempt, necessarily involving brevity of treatment, is liable also to the danger of superficiality. For it must indicate lines of thought, which it is impossible to follow out with anything like exhaustive completeness; it will probably touch on important controversies without ability to discuss them fully and thoroughly. Perhaps it may seem to savour of too great self-confidence, as dealing with a vast question as a whole, while men of high ability and learning have thought it enough to devote themselves to the study of single parts. But I venture to think that there is in our own days some danger of over-specialization, losing in the elaborate examination of each part the general proportion and cumulative force of the whole. In regard to these special studies, while we listen respectfully to the teaching of experts, there is still some value in what is in this aspect a lay opinion—standing (so to speak) further back from the picture, on which various hands are employed, and thus able to gain some conception of the general idea, and the mutual relation and proportion of the various parts. Perhaps what is true of all subjects is especially true of the Christian Faith, which necessarily has points of contact on all sides with the various forms of human knowledge, and of the Christian Evidence, which depends so largely upon a cumulative strength of combined witness, infinitely greater than the mere sum of the forces of its various elements. How far the attempt may have been successfully made is another question. No one is (I suppose) so keenly alive to the defects of a work, and its failure to reach even his own ideal, as the author. But I am convinced that the general idea itself is sound, and perhaps not without some special appropriateness to present conditions of thought.

Next, I can well understand that the view here taken of the relation of Science to Religion may seem too Optimistic. But there are two kinds of Optimism

—the Optimism which ignores difficulties, and the Optimism, which, seeing difficulties, yet sees, or trusts to see, through them. It should be impossible for any thinking man in days like our own to fall into the first. If I have unwittingly done so, and cried, 'Peace, where there is no peace,' it is a serious error. Certainly our Lord Himself seems to foretell the continuing, perhaps the increasing, existence of stumbling-blocks in the way of faith, as the world grows older. We seem to see already what He foreshadows to us—a growing intensity of conflict of first principles of good and evil, of truth and error, in proportion as old barriers of law and convention give way before modern boldness and exuberance of energy. But the higher form of Optimism is surely implied in Christianity itself. The Cross, while it is the symbol of conflict, is the symbol also of victory. If Christ is Himself the Truth, then, sooner or later, all real discoveries of truth must harmonize themselves with His Word; as all phases of intellectual and moral vitality must be taken up into His indwelling Life.

It appears to me—whether rightly I know not—that this principle is now being recognised more fully on both sides of the great antithesis. Science, while it pursues its special developments more exhaustively than ever, yet seems more and more alive to the need of correlating them all in some large philosophy of Being; more inclined to acknowledge that the moral insight of the soul, whatever may have been its origin and course of development, has a co-ordinate function with pure intellectual research, in discovering the inner secret of that philosophy; perhaps more deeply sensible that the search brings us into the presence of mystery, and forces upon us the alternative of Agnosticism or Faith. Theology, clearing and simplifying her fundamental principles, not that she may relax her grasp of them, but that she may hold them more firmly, is thus able to be more receptive of other forms of Truth, to enter into the harmony of what we ordinarily call the Natural and the Supernatural, and to understand that the Spirit of Truth, who is, according to our Lord's promise, to 'abide with us for ever,' has His witness to the world in all that tells it of truth and righteousness, as well as His higher witness to the faith of the Church, guiding it more and more into all the Truth of God in Christ.

In that conviction these pages are written, as a humble contribution to this larger idea of the Revelation of God. May He, through their imperfection, grant to some minds a glimpse of His perfect Truth!

A. B.

WINDSOR,
October 24, 1892.

CONTENTS

LECTURE I.

LAW LEADING TO CHRIST.

                                                                                PAGE

I. Definition of Law, its defect and its value. Application to the Scientific 'Reign of Law' 1–7

II. Protest against the Idolatry of Law; recognition of its true function in leading to the higher Truth; its relation to the Province of Faith 7–13

III. A. The Search of Science into a First Cause, as known in degree through its works; its result in an expectancy, satisfied only by Theism; the ultimate alternative between Agnosticism and Christian faith 13–22

III. B. The Scientific method of Induction, through Observation, Intuition, Verification; the element of faith involved, especially in the second stage. Analogy to the Christian theory of the knowledge of God, as revealed through inspired men, and perfected in Christ . . . 22–30

III. C. The relation of Science to the substance of the faith, not in its mysteries themselves, but in their manifestation; as (1) Confirmatory: Heredity and Mediation, Evolution and the 'new Creation'; (2) Elucidatory: the Universe and the universal Headship of Christ, Social Science and Christian unity; (3) Critical: Criticism and the Supernatural, Criticism and Holy Scripture . . 30–39

IV. Conclusion 39–42

LECTURE II.

HEREDITY AND MEDIATION.

                                        PAGE

I. The Christian doctrine of Mediation, in relation to inherited evil and independently of that relation. Difficulties of Individualism, intellectual and moral, in accepting it   43–47

II. The Scientific assertion of Solidarity and Heredity. The reality of the force of Heredity, modified by environment, balanced by individuality; not a Determinism, but a Predisposition 47–56

III. The reality of 'Original Sin' and its relation to Original Righteousness; its power as a Predisposition to evil; exaggerations of it—as the sole Heredity, as a rigid Determinism, as an inheritance of guilt—not parts of the true Christian doctrine 57–65

IV. The Mediation of the 'Second Adam,' touching man's whole nature; a principle of spiritual Heredity, extending through all time; its analogy, with difference, to the Natural Law. Its Predisposition to good, not the Determinism of the Calvinistic theory; its universal scope of power; the Pentecostal regeneration of humanity; the need of individuality in reception 65–81

V. The argument here of Analogy, not identity, between the Natural and the Supernatural. The evidence of experience, as the preparation for faith . . . 81–86

LECTURE III.

EVOLUTION—NATURAL AND SUPERNATURAL.

I. The Law of Evolution: (*a*) not implying an immanent Cause only, and not anti-Theistic; accepting and enlarging Teleology, and so a witness for a God 'above and through all'; (*b*) not properly identical with Darwinism; present scientific opinion on the subject 87–102

II. The developments of Evolution in the distinct Provinces of being; in the Inorganic world; in the world of Organic life; in the world of Humanity—in all a theory of Order, not Cause; relation of each to a Supreme Will; an Analogy, with difference, running through all . 102–122

III. The Christian Faith in this relation: (*a*) The Creation, broadly an Evolution under the Supreme Mind, traced simply in the lower worlds, clearly in the world of Humanity. (*b*) The Manifestation of Christ, in itself a Divine mystery, yet visibly a 'new Creation,' crowning and transcending the Natural Order, working by a spiritual Evolution, in the race and in the individual; a new and Diviner power of the Spirit, preparing for a future Dispensation at the Second Advent . . 122–137

LECTURE IV.

CHRIST AND ALL CREATION.

I. The Universal Headship of Christ: naturally less prominent, when the earth seemed the centre of the Universe, and then recognised mainly in the spiritual sphere. The knowledge of the vastness of the Universe, bringing some bewilderment and inclination to Pantheism, and demanding some expansion of the idea of Christ, as the Head . . 138–149

II. The Christian Revelation, mainly regarding humanity, gradually extended beyond it: its ancient relation to Gnostic Cosmology and Dualism; the corresponding modern relation to extended Natural Science or theory . . 149–155

III. The Headship over all Creation: the teaching of St. Paul in the Philippians, Ephesians, Colossians; the teaching of the Epistle to the Hebrews; the doctrine of the WORD in St. John, in its two-fold meaning of Transcendence and Immanence; the truth drawn out, as by S. Athanasius 155–162

IV. The same Truth, in relation to modern Science: the degree of our knowledge as to the Universal Headship, and the bearing of the Incarnation on all Creation . . 162–169

V. Its lessons: of consecration of our enlarged knowledge; of reverence to the majesty of Christ; of the finding of God, and the finding of man, in Him 169–175

LECTURE V.

CHRIST AND HUMAN SOCIETY.

                                                           PAGE

I. Unity of humanity in Christ: its relation to Social Science, and the demand of a 'Social Gospel' . . . 176–180

II. The history of Social conditions: the old Absolutism; the reaction of Individualism; the free unity needed for the future 180–190

III. The Christian theory of unity, of each soul with God in Christ, of all souls with one another in Him: its analogy to the Laws of the Physical system; its illustration in the 'Great Commandment'—the love of self, and love of man, harmonized in subordination to the Supreme Love of God 190–194

IV. This theory embodied: (*a*) in the Creation of a Catholic Church, one in Christ, diffused all over the world; (*b*) in the regeneration of the natural unities of family, neighbourhood, nation, race 194–205

V. The Christian Socialism: centred in God; working mainly not through Law, but through the Spirit; trusting in moral forces; applying not only to the Church, but to the natural unities. Defects in popular Christian teaching; need not only of interest, but of thought . 205–217

LECTURE VI.

CRITICISM AND THE SUPERNATURAL.

I. Characteristics of true Criticism, practical and scientific, and its spiritual conditions in dealing with Christianity 218–223

II. The true functions of Criticism, first to distinguish the essence of a thing, then to test it 223, 224

III. The actual Christianity in the Catholic Church, its unique power, and its foundation on Truth, the ideal Christianity, centred in Holy Scripture; both resting on Christ Himself, as the Life and the Light; the witness to this rest on Christ, from historical and literary Science . 224–231

IV. Christianity Natural: the present position of the argument from Analogy; the acceptance of Christianity, as the crown of the Natural Order 231–235
V. Christianity, Supernatural or Miraculous: changes of phases of Criticism and its present form; the development of a Divine Law in Miracle, as a two-fold sign of Will, Divine and yet working through man; as related to other elements of Revelation; as concentrated in the Manifestation of Christ. 235–248
VI. The Critical test, of the actual witness to Christ, of the character of Christ Himself, of His own self-disclosure, of the province of faith; and its presentation of the great alternative 248–257

LECTURE VII.
CRITICISM AND HOLY SCRIPTURE.

I. What is Scripture in itself? Its variety as an epitome of human literature; its unity, subjective in Inspiration, objective in its relation to the Manifestation of God in Christ. Drawbacks and advantages of this function of Biblical Criticism 258–268
II. How has Scripture grown to be what it is? The growth of the Canons, and the growth of the individual books. The enquiry to be without prejudice; the question of the miraculous to be faced; external and internal evidence to be balanced. The experience of past New Testament Criticism; the questions now really at issue in Old Testament Criticism; the analogy between the two . 268–282
III. What is the basis of Scriptural Authority? The distinction between Revelation and Inspiration, indicated in human experience and in the Old Testament, known fully by the word of the Lord Jesus Christ; the actual relation between the two. The right and hopeful enquiry is into the reality of Scriptural Revelation, as directly or indirectly 'the word of eternal life' from Christ . 282–292
IV. The essentials of such Revelation. Is it sufficient? The question answered by examination of the doctrine in itself, and in its fruits, anticipating the further enquiry, Is it true? 292–296

LECTURE VIII.

TRUTH IN REVELATION.

I. The essentials of Revelation. Is it true? Truth, as accordance with the Laws of being, having different meanings in relation to the different elements of Holy Scripture   297–299

II. The Historical element. The requirement of historic truth; the acceptance of the miraculous element. The stress mainly on the New Testament, secondarily on the Old as connected with it; the significance of modern criticism in its various types, and the issues involved   299–307

III. The Prophetic element. The requirement of moral truth: (*a*) In Law: its necessary limitations and imperfections, leading up to the Law of Christ; yet the need in its fundamental principles of moral truth. (*b*) In Prophecy: its higher character and preparation for Christ; its perfection in His word, spoken by Himself and His Apostles; the need of perfect moral insight and truth   307–314

IV. The 'Psalmic' element. The requirement of subjective moral truth, in conception of God and man; imperfections in all others, perfection in Christ Himself   314–316

V. The Theologic Revelation. The requirement of Divine Truth according with, and transcending, lower revelations of God. The Scriptural Revelation widening and deepening, up to perfection in the word of Christ; in all cases at once personal and universal; the need here of absolute truth, so far as it can be known to man   316–319

VI. The relation of Criticism to all these phases of truth; its inevitable enquiry, the gravity and the hopefulness of such enquiry   319–322

VII. Conclusion. Plea for comprehensiveness of view, and the cumulative force of various evidence. The results of the three-fold witness of Science, to the reality, the expansiveness, the simplicity of Christianity, as gathered up in Christ. The cry for light, and *Dominus illuminatio mea*   322–329

NOTES   331–348

LECTURE I.

LAW LEADING TO CHRIST.

The Law was our schoolmaster to bring us to Christ, that we might be justified by faith.—Gal. iii. 24.

In these famous words—wide in application, not only to the particular struggle against Judaism, which called them out, but to the issues of universal significance involved in it—St. Paul sets forth to us the right relation of Law, both objectively to the manifestation of God in Christ, and subjectively to the education of that faith in Him, which is the essence of all true religion. What is the form in which that relation presents itself to us now? What is the underlying meaning for us of the opposition between rest on Law, and rest on Christ by faith, which, as in St. Paul's days, so in all ages, has been found to be a matter of life and death to the spirituality, and therefore to the Catholicity, of the Gospel?

I. Law is clearly the manifestation and expression of a Supreme Power over the world, regarded as absolutely and infinitely above man; having no necessary connection of spiritual sympathy with the spirit within him; ignoring or coercing that personality of free-will, which is his surest and most intimate consciousness;

and accordingly ruling over men, almost as over things, with a despotic and undiscriminating authority. There were those in St. Paul's day, who were ready to idolize Law—represented especially in the strong and awful majesty of the Law of Sinai—as the supreme exponent of the Divine Righteousness. For they were fascinated, as men are apt to be fascinated, by its sweeping generality, its clear, stern simplicity, its infinite exaltation above human littleness and changeableness, through which it looks out over the turmoil and perplexity of life with the solemn impassiveness of a great Egyptian deity. Against that idolatry St. Paul protests with all possible vehemence,—in the name of God, as against an imperfect and unworthy exhibition of His Nature, who is not Law but Love—in the name of man, as against a childish, and even slavish, retrogression from maturer knowledge and higher consciousness.

But mere Iconoclasm is never the true remedy for idolatry; for thoughtful worship seldom attaches to what has no claim whatever to reverence. So he gives meaning and discrimination to his protest by marking out in the text the true function of Law in the education of the higher life. 'It was' (he says) 'the schoolmaster'—the παιδαγωγός—'to bring us to Christ.'

In this description there is a double-edged significance. On the one side, of necessary depreciation. For the παιδαγωγός (as we know), whatever might be his personal qualifications, was still a slave, useful to protect the free boy, and in some sense to restrain him from grosser evil by a delegated authority, but, from the nature of the case, unable so to educate, to teach, to inspire him, that he might grow up in his rightful freedom. That Divine function for all humanity belonged (says the Apostle) only to One, who was the living manifestation of the Supreme Righteousness, as a Righteousness in Love, recognising and cherishing the free human personality, having itself likeness to man, communion with man, incarnation in man. And it could be realized by man only through the faith, which in its full Christian sense is essentially consciousness of a personal relation, implying reliance of the whole personality of mind and conscience and will on some higher, and, if it is to be absolute, on some Divine Personality, having spiritual communion with it[1]. Law therefore was at best, even if it were 'holy and just and good,' a rough and imperfect manifestation of the true Righteousness; and such function as it had properly belonged to the cruder and more childish stages of human growth. It could regulate the outer life by fear; it could not so lay hold of the human spirit by love, as to give it, weak in itself and sinful, a power to attain to righteousness by release from the guilt and bondage of evil; nay, by ignoring the divine impulse of freedom, and substituting for the worse bondage of sin a bondage lighter and nobler, yet a bondage still, it might actually stir the spirit of rebellion, the misguided desire of a false independence to which the first Temptation appealed[2]. When it was exalted to the highest place, and justification by law substituted for justification in Christ through faith, it was necessary to speak out in stern

---

[1] See Note A, on the true character of Faith.
[2] See Rom. vii. 9–13.

indignant protest, to reject, even in comparison to despise, a slavish παιδαγωγός, because set on the seat of the true Teacher.

Yet, on the other hand, there is in the text a recognition that Law has, and in various degrees always will have, a real subordinate function in the education of true humanity. 'Added it was because of transgression,' to unmask and to scourge evil—'added' (we may venture to say) 'because of blindness,' to guide aright by its clear, stern warning those who had not yet grown 'to be a law to themselves'—and so telling, not on the few, who, at one extreme, are above law in spiritual freedom, not on those who, at the other, fall below law in hardened spiritual apostasy, but on the many, who stand between the two extremes, needing spiritual restraint and chastisement, and capable of profiting by both. So it could in its right place become a discipline, and (as the very word implies) enable men to be learners from a teaching higher than its own. At least it did reveal an eternal and sovereign Righteousness, of which, though heaven and earth should pass, no jot or tittle could cease to have obligation and enforcement. So it could by contrast create a consciousness of sin, and a 'hunger and thirst for' participation in that 'righteousness'; even if it could not show how to take away the one, and to satisfy the other. At least by its command of obedience, it implied that obedience was possible; nay, it taught that it was to issue from love of all the mind and heart and soul; although it could not show how that possibility was to be realized, and in itself tended to create a godly fear rather than a godly love. At least it taught that the righteousness to be loved and obeyed was the attribute of the Jehovah, the ultimate and absolute Being, who alone is in Himself, and is the Fount of all created life; and that by it the Eternal entered into moral relation with man—a 'covenant,' which implied man's freedom, and so preserved man's personality, even in this relation to God. Thus in every direction Law pointed out, and even advanced on, the various lines of approach to God; but it completed none; it 'made nothing perfect.' By that very advance, by that very imperfection, its right function was to lead to the Christ.

Now *mutatis mutandis*—and I grant that the *mutanda* are many—I cannot but think that in this conception is shadowed forth the relation, in which the systematized knowledge, which we call Science, ought to stand to the higher knowledge of God and Man in the Lord Jesus Christ.

For Science claims it, as its function and its glory, to enforce and continually to advance, both in clearness and in scope, the recognition of the 'reign of Law.' I press advisedly the literal meaning of both words. For, although the representatives of Science are never weary of reminding us that its so-called 'Laws,' so far as the discoveries of pure observation and experiment go, are nothing more than general expressions of universally recurring and connected facts, yet the persistent use of the word 'Laws,'—drawn by analogy from our own creations in the social and political sphere, where they certainly have behind them not only an enforcing power, but an original cause, in will guided by purpose—witnesses to the intellectual necessity of going beyond or below the mere record of facts, yielded by such observation and experiment, and implies the conviction that these recurrences are strictly 'Laws'—that is, expressions of some universal and supreme Power, which really, though invisibly, reigns. If the word Law is still to be used in scientific language, it is but right to fix it to its own proper sense; and in this respect it seems plainly our duty, if we would avoid delusion or ambiguity, to go further still, and contend that no man ought to use the word 'Laws,' with all the associations and inferences that it carries, unless he is prepared to complete the analogy, and acknowledge in the Supreme Power a Supreme Will, reigning with design and purpose, both over things and over persons [1].

I must hold, therefore, that Science really and properly declares, either by discovery or necessary inference from discovery, a 'reign of Law'; and that its ultimate conception is of a true First Cause, a supreme reigning Power. That conception is clearly so far like the conception to which St. Paul refers, that it views its expression through Law, as absolute and universal, having, or at least known to have, no spiritual relation

---

[1] See Note B. From the scientific side, as well as the theological, this truth appears to be increasingly recognised. I observe that the more thoughtful advocates of a 'mechanical view of Nature' nevertheless speak of 'the Laws of Nature as the permanent expressions of the Will'—implying self-consciousness and purpose 'of a Creative Principle,' 'a spiritual First Cause.' (Weissmann's *Studies in Descent*, English translation, pp. 713, 717.)

to individual man. Accordingly, in working out its conclusions, it ignores, if it does not practically deny, human personality; and it overbears by Determinism, which is a Fatalism veiled under worship of force of circumstances or a stream of tendency, the reality of human freedom of will. But it fails, even more than the law as understood by St. Paul, to account for our moral nature, or satisfy our moral needs; for it does not even assume, as that assumed, the supremacy in the Sovereign Power of a moral righteousness.

II. How stands then our position, as Christians, in face of that proclamation of a Supreme Power, expressing itself in Law, as the one sufficient solution of the great problem of Being? Like St. Paul's position in the text, it has a two-fold aspect, of protest and of recognition.

Against the scientific idolatry of law, our protest is, for the reason above referred to, even stronger than his. For, as it seems to us, its claim to our worship is still more untenable. It invites us, under the name of progress, to a worse form of what St. Paul holds to be retrogression; for it bids us give up what lies at the heart of our higher humanity—the belief in a spiritual communion with man of the Supreme Power as a Divine Spirit—and to accept the cruder conception of it as perhaps an impersonal Force, perhaps a Will, but in any case to us unknown and unknowable, to which we have simply to yield what by a self-delusion we hold to be our own freedom, and, in this, our own personality.

Against that invitation, even if—which is to me

more than doubtful—it satisfies our intellectual demand of a true and sufficient Cause, analogous to the only cause of action and production, which we can be said really to know, yet certainly our moral nature revolts, claiming that any conception of the ultimate Sovereignty over our world must satisfy its needs, at least as much as the cravings and reasonings of the intellect. It can hardly be doubted that the progress, which we call civilization, tends to bring out, to guard, to educate more and more, our free individual personality; and that accordingly it is a retrogression to accept any theory of the being and rule of the world, which has to ignore it or explain it away, instead of simply subordinating it, and that, moreover, not to an iron law, but to the moving of a Divine Spirit. Accordingly, it has been felt by some who have spoken from this place, to be their duty to vindicate, against the idolatry of Law, the reality of personal freedom and responsibility, and the province of that faith, which is essentially a free personal relation of the living soul to a living God.

But surely there is also for us a duty of recognition. Is it not to be expected that, in its right place, the scientific conception of Law will prove to be a παιδαγωγός to lead us to the Christ? Not, indeed, in the same way as the Law of which St. Paul spoke. For this, as setting forth a Divine Righteousness, looked and appealed primarily to man's moral consciousness—its fundamental defect being that, while it thus acknowledged moral needs and responsibilities, it failed to satisfy them. On the other hand, the Law, as science recognises it, is looked at simply from an intellectual point of view, implying a Supreme First Cause, infinite indeed in power, probably infinite as a Divine Mind, but ignoring the demand of our own moral nature for a Moral Being, at once a source and object of righteousness and love.

I do not mean that Science, properly so called, takes no cognisance of the existence of a moral element in the world and its government. For it is, of course, an usurpation, which Oxford, in virtue of its noblest and wisest traditions, is especially bound to repudiate, to claim for merely physical investigation any exclusive right to the great name of Science. The mind can study, and must study, not only the outer world of things, but the nearer world of personality, through which indeed it knows what underlies mere phenomena in that world of things. It studies that higher world, partly as known to us by our own inner consciousness, partly through the knowledge, aided by the light of that consciousness, of our fellow-men; and, when it enters on that study, it is clear to all, who look at facts in themselves, independently of any theories about them, that the phenomena of will, conscience, freedom, however they may have been developed, and however correlated to universal law, are, to say the least, as certain and as necessary to be accounted for, as the visible phenomena of which our senses inform us. But what I mean is that Science, as Science, tends to look even at these moral phenomena, and the Power from which they proceed, impassively through the understanding, and not sympathetically through a moral sense in ourselves. It regards them (so to speak) from without, to observe, to tabulate, to generalize, to theorize, under the 'dry light' of purely intellectual conception, without any sense of moral sympathy, allegiance, worship—without, indeed, any realization of our own personality in the matter—either ignoring these elements of consciousness altogether, or possibly relegating them to a sphere of their own, from which the scientific investigation of law is to be kept altogether distinct. How far this is really philosophical—how far it is reasonable to ignore that insight into nature and life which belongs to our moral consciousness, adding as it does the intuition of right to the intellectual intuition of causality—I do not here enquire. But that, in fact, this is the tendency of modern thought, increasing with the increasing specialization of scientific study, is (I think) beyond all reasonable doubt[1].

If then Law, as Science recognises it, is to be in any sense a παιδαγωγὸς εἰς Χριστόν, it will not be, as in the Law of which St. Paul speaks, through its moral acknowledgments, but through its intellectual discoveries or conceptions. It will lead up to Christian doctrine, rather than to Christian life; it will bear on the truth, rather than on the grace, of the Gospel; if it guides us to Christ, it will be to Him as 'the Word,' revealer at once of Godhead and Humanity, and of both as One in Himself, rather than to Him as the

---

[1] Dr. Martineau truly says, 'Science lays aside as obtrusive the moral consciousness, with its postulates and beliefs, and enters the field under pure guidance of the perceptive and comparing powers.' (See 'Nature and God' in *Essays, Reviews, and Addresses*.)

Redeemer from sin and death; if it leads on to the adhesion of faith in Him, it is that we may be (if I may so express it) 'justified,' not from the guilt and bondage and moral death of sin, but from the blankness of ignorance and the delusions of error.

Now the view which, in these Lectures, I desire to suggest, is that, while scientific idolatry of Law must supersede faith and virtually ignore the Christ, yet that the recognition of Law in its true sphere does really thus lead up to faith in the Gospel of Christ, as the true and all-sufficient satisfaction of the maturest thought. I venture to urge the truth of St. Paul's bold contention, that such faith really belongs to maturity of idea and character, and that the absolute rest on Law—so confidently set forth to us as an advance towards the firm, sad grasp of ultimate truth, at the sacrifice of bright childish delusions and hopes,—is really a going back instead of forward; because it ignores that consciousness of a spiritual self, which is the sign of growth out of childhood to manhood, and that recognition in faith of an ultimate spiritual sovereignty, ruling not by compulsion but through freedom, which alone can harmonize with that inner consciousness.

Rightly have those, who in these days bear witness for Christ, seen the need of vindicating the Province of Faith, as a great universal power in human life and progress, having its supreme and perfect culmination in the faith which the Gospel claims for Him [1]. And to those who discern this clearly it will, I think, be evident, that there are few greater fallacies than the

[1] See Dr. Wace's *Bampton Lectures* for 1879.

frequent assumption that the faith of a mature and scientific age, if it survives at all, must be content to be a smaller and weaker power, than it was in those simpler, earlier times of the world, to which the title of 'the Ages of Faith' is popularly given. It seems to me, on the contrary, to be like the faith of a thoughtful manhood in the individual, as contrasted with the faith of childhood. Narrower (so to speak) in scope 'of length and breadth': for it is, no doubt, true that many things, which in the earlier days we accepted on faith in God or man, we have come to know, if not perfectly, at least sufficiently, for ourselves. But yet, on the other hand, compensating for this diminution by a growth 'in depth and height'—more deeply based because, by its very difficulties and trials, it is forced to go down through secondary strata to its ultimate rest in mystery—rising to greater loftiness of idea, enthusiasm, aspiration, because through these same perplexities brought more closely face to face with the Divine. It is in no unreal 'pious imagination' that the Collect for S. Thomas' Day tells us of doubt—the doubt (be it always remembered) which does not rest in a complacent or despondent uncertainty, but which resolves to investigate, and to test what reveals itself as truth—as overruled to 'the more confirmation' of such faith as this. It is notable that when, in that great instance here referred to, sight was granted, the acceptance of mystery was faith still, and its utterance, far the highest and deepest of even Apostolic confessions, went in that faith infinitely beyond what could be seen.

Now this experience is typical, an exemplification of

the general position on which Christianity must take its stand. When it calls its summary of doctrine a Creed, it plainly avows that the ultimate truths on which it rests are, in the New Testament sense of the word, 'mysteries'—secrets (that is) of Being revealed to us in Christ, and accepted by our faith in His Word. It has been indeed shown again and again by Christian philosophy, how they are prepared for by the deepest human instincts, as wrought out by process of reason, both the speculative and moral reason—how they are verified in the soul and in the world by their spiritual power to solve our intellectual and moral problems. But all this is but subsidiary to faith in Him, as 'having the words of eternal life.' We have, of course, to know in whom we believe; but, when we do know Him, we can then sit at His feet, and by faith 'know' through the Divine Mind of Christ 'that which passes knowledge.'

III. But it is well to consider, somewhat more in detail, in what ways the scientific conception of Law is a schoolmaster to educate us to the Christian faith, which is at once a faith in a living God, and a faith in Him as revealed in the true Son of Man.

It seems to me to have an important bearing, first on the necessity of such faith, next upon its method, and thirdly upon the substance of that which it accepts. It is with the last of these points that these Lectures are properly concerned. But a brief reference to the other two will form the right introduction to its consideration.

(A) First, it will, I think, be seen that Science leads

up to the necessity of some faith in God, by its own continual approach to discovery or inference of unity in the Source of all Being. It is true that, along each line of scientific thought, we are brought ultimately to a mysterious reality, which we recognise, though we cannot comprehend. In the study of the Inorganic world, the process of gradual simplification of all the infinite variety of things which till it leads through molecules and atoms to the mystery of Matter and Force (if, indeed, they are distinct from each other), as a limit beyond which it cannot go. In the study of the Organic world the same process, pursued not so much theoretically as historically, leads to the recognition, not only, as before, of the matter which clothes it, but of the mystery of the origination in the simplest form of Life, having in it the potentiality of infinite differentiation and development. In the study of Humanity—closely connected with both these worlds, but yet having in it another and superior factor, which, however we may theorize as to its derivation from either, is in actual and historical experience absolutely distinct—we come finally to the mystery of a created Personality, implying, under whatever limits, will, thought, conscience, in the individual and in the race as a whole. But, while these ultimate realities present themselves to us as distinct, and all our experimental research fails to bridge over the gulf of distinction between them, yet (to use a well-known phrase) the 'scientific imagination' is driven by an instinctive and irresistible inference to believe that there is ultimate unity of all in some Eternal Being; and this not merely an Absolute

Being, unconnected with the created forms of existence which we know, and, in fact, little more to us than a necessary postulate of philosophic thought, but really (to use the old phrase) a 'First Cause,' from which, though we know not how, all these distinct orders of being proceed. One great scientific leader of thought[1] has gone so far as to speak of 'the confession of the universality of Order, and of the absolute validity in all times and under all circumstances of the law of Causation, as the one act of faith in the convert to science.' Faith, indeed, in our full sense of the word, it is not: for this implies a personal recognition of a Divine Personality, which cannot be accorded to an idea or a law. But, so far as it goes, there is an instructive significance to a Christian in the definition which follows—'It is an act of faith, because, by the nature of the case, the truth of such propositions is incapable of proof. But such faith is not blind but reasonable, because it is universally confirmed by experiment, and constitutes the sole trustworthy foundation of action.'

Nor, I think, will the scientific instinct be content simply with the recognition of this 'First Cause' as a something 'unknown and unknowable.' For this description of it, while, in respect of full comprehension, it is an obvious and barren truism, yet, in respect of partial knowledge, is contradictory to all our experience of causation in the lower sphere; where certainly the character of a cause is in degree known by study of the character of its effects. We must go

[1] Huxley, in *Life and Letters of Charls Darwin*, vol. ii. p. 200.

on to believe that, as it includes all these forms of being in its Creative power, while in its essence it transcends them all, such partial knowledge of its nature may be inferred from them, and best inferred not from that which is lowest and crudest, but from that which is highest and most comprehensive—therefore, not from mere force or life, but from the will, guided by wisdom and righteousness, which in ourselves we know to dominate both, and of which we cannot even form any conception, except as inherent in a true personality [1].

Now it seems to me clear, that in all this process, both of discovery and of inference beyond discovery, Science ought to be a παιδαγωγός to lead up to the realization of a God, a living God, by faith.

It has indeed been argued very forcibly, that in the earlier stages of human thought the belief in One God —either emerging in some distinctness, or vaguely underlying the worship of 'gods many and lords many'— has been in time anterior to this scientific inference of unity, and actually the parent of it. It may well be so: for this would only be the extension to the race of the mental process so familiarly known in the individual mind, in which the intuition of the moral sense anticipates and stimulates the discursive reasoning of the intellect. But no support can be derived from this for the artificial theory, which, as in the Comtist Law of the

---

[1] Dr. Abbott, in his *Through Nature to Christ*, truly says that, in the search after God, the forms of thought which we most use are necessarily either anthropomorphic, or zoomorphic, or azoomorphic, and that of these the first is surely the most rational, and the least likely to be unworthy or delusive.

'Three States of Knowledge'—Theological, Metaphysical, Positive—infers the reversal of the relation for which I contend, and would make the belief in God merely the preparation for a science, which shall supersede it. For clearly there can be no *a priori* ground for holding that these states are exclusive of one another, when it is clear that only the first is a theory of ultimate Cause, while the others seek merely to discern laws, through which obviously that Cause may work [1]. Nor can actual experience justify the notion that they are thus successive and mutually exclusive, for it is certain in fact that in various degrees they have always co-existed and interpenetrated one another. It may well be doubted whether the accumulation of positive knowledge ever really dispenses with the guidance of metaphysical idea; it is even more doubtful whether metaphysical investigation can fail, sooner or later, to enter upon that search after the ultimate Being, which leads to what is virtually theologic ground [2].

[1] According to Comte (says Mr. John Morley) 'in the Theological and Metaphysical states men seek a Cause or an Essence; in the Positive they are content with a Law.' But this is to use the word 'Law,' in what I contend to be an improper and delusive sense, of a mere systematized record of facts. Law in its true sense involves the Metaphysical, and implies the Theological idea. (Article COMTE in the *Encycl. Britannica*.)

[2] Dr. Martineau, in his *Study of Religion*, quotes the remark of an eminent English Positivist: 'You cannot make the slightest concession to Metaphysics without ending in a Theology'; which (as he truly says) amounts simply to the confession, 'If once you allow yourself to think of the origin and end of things, you will have to believe in a God.' (Preface, pp. 1, 2.) As he puts it elsewhere, 'Science discloses the Method of the world and not its Cause; Religion its Cause and not its Method.' (Essay on 'Science, Nescience, and Faith.')

Hence it must appear that for us, looking to the position of expectancy as to the First Cause, to which Science brings us, the real alternative is between an Agnosticism on this supreme question, disappointing that expectancy of the intellect, and failing to satisfy the moral sense of unity between our own personality and the Supreme Being, and the faith, accepting the revelation of a living Personal God, which at least answers the one and satisfies the other. And naturally that revelation presents itself to us in vitality and substantial power through a true Christian faith; for this not only accepts such revelation in a vague generality, but, taking up the scientific inference of which I have spoken as to the method of knowledge of the Supreme Being, teaches that this revelation, though shadowed out in some measure to human thought through the worlds of matter and life, yet is made clear to us through the world of human-kind, and perfected in a Humanity, at once ideal and real, of a Son of Man, who is also the Word of God.

For the other theories of a First Cause, claiming to meet this expectancy of Science, fail to satisfy any soul which strongly realizes its own personality, not only in abstract thought, but by experience of the needs and capacities of actual life, and which is thus forced to recognise in will—acting, of course, under conditions, but yet acting in consciousness of freedom and with purpose—the one originative cause of action, which we can be said really to know. Pure Materialism breaks down necessarily under this consciousness of a spiritual faculty of will and reason in man, which must imply in the Creative Force itself a corresponding spiritual nature, only infinite and eternal. There is, after all, an unanswerable argument implied in the old question, 'He that made the ear, shall He not hear? and He that made the eye, shall He not see?' The Pantheistic conception, again, of an indwelling Life in the universe, which clothes all matter with potentialities of mind, and of which individual being is but a fragment, breaks down before the further consciousness, that this spiritual life within us is a true, though mysterious, personality—having, we know not how, a real moral freedom and responsibility—claiming for itself a distinctiveness from a mere course of Nature, especially implied in the power to judge between good and evil in it—yet necessarily resting itself on some Supreme Personality, from which its own life is derived, and on which that life continually rests.

I have spoken here of the search of Science into the problem of Being, as it is conducted—according to that prevalent tendency to which I have alluded—under the sole guidance of the intuition of Causality, as the great 'Form of thought' for the pure intellect, without any consideration of the intuition of righteousness and a 'Power making for righteousness,' which is the guiding axiom of the moral sense. But I must in so doing again protest against that limitation of method as unphilosophical and unsound, a blinding of one of the two eyes of the soul in its search after the ultimate Being. The nature of man is one; not through one spiritual faculty, but through all, it must approach to the knowledge of the Creative Power. Now clearly the intuition of a supreme Righteousness, which must be a righteousness in love, is an intuition of a Supreme Personality: for the notion of an Impersonal Something, a 'stream of tendency making for righteousness,' is utterly unmeaning to any one who looks into his own soul, and knows that in himself righteousness is essentially an attribute of his personality. I do not see how that intuition can be rightly ignored, in considering what the nature of the First Cause is. It does not for a moment cross the inferences of the pure intellect; but it undoubtedly both confirms and supplements them. It claims a right to speak with power for a true Theism against both these answers of Materialism and Pantheism, which in different ways contradict its own witness, at once ignoring the human personality and denying the Divine; and, in order to do this, have also to deny the eternal distinction of good and evil in themselves—the conviction in the soul from the Creative and Sustaining Power not only 'of sin and righteousness,' but 'of judgment'—which is an integral and essential part of our higher humanity. The Study of Religion has for its true method (as Dr. Martineau has shown) the realization of the Supreme Power as Cause, the realization of that Power as Moral Perfection, and the union of these two realizations in One Being, the object alike of intellectual and moral search.

But, however this may be, still in any case those of us who strongly hold that a blank Agnosticism as to the ultimate problem of Being—vainly endeavouring to fill up the infinite void thus created with mere knowledge, however increased in scope, however ingeniously generalized and systematized, of things and men—is an attitude of the soul, in which the great mass of men will certainly never rest, and of which it may be doubted whether they ever really take it up—mainly because, however tolerable it may be to mere speculation, it can never satisfy their moral needs, or bear the wear and tear of the practical struggles of life—those of us, I say, who hold this conviction, and seem to themselves to see that it is verified by historical and actual experience of mankind, will conclude that in this respect Science must ultimately be a παιδαγωγός to bring men to Christ.

Not, we grant, without dangers of delusion, similar to those which St. Paul traced in the Judaizing conception of Law. It may arrest the right progress of the soul by that absorption in lower objects, which is idolatry. If it be science, untinctured by some larger philosophy, which teaches the correlation and right subordination of various forms of science, it may thus absorb the mind in the pursuit of some one partial study—of matter, of life, of humanity—when it should pass on to the unity beyond them all, which yet embraces them all. Even if it avoid this perversion—and I think that the whole tendency of thought in our own day is to break these narrow limits, and to seek wider and more ultimate conceptions—yet still it may so engross the whole energy of our nature in purely intellectual operation, as (according to the confession, so nobly candid yet so mournfully significant, of one of the great princes of science) to produce a moral atrophy, a 'colour-blindness' of incapacity for enthusiasm, admiration, worship, which denies to the imagination and to the heart their rightful insight into ultimate Being. But against both these delusions we believe that there is a safeguard in the sense of a larger humanity, with more than intellectual capacities, which is forced on the student, by the very fact that he is also a man, in the actual experience of his own individual and social life.

In its growing consciousness of difficulty and limitation in knowledge, Science may, indeed, dim the 'first thoughts' of universal human instinct of God by the 'second thoughts' of criticism and doubt. But since the mind cannot rest on these, we believe that it must pass on to the 'third thoughts,' in which the first emerge again, corrected, cleared, rationalized, and lay hold by faith of that real knowledge of God, in Christ, which 'is the life eternal.' Just as of old, seeing at once what it can and what it cannot give, we look seriously and yet hopefully on its growth, and doubt not that it must even so lead to Christ.

(B) But, again, looking upon Christian faith as not only a faith in God, but as faith in a perfect Son of Man, 'having the words of the eternal life,' and able in Himself to reveal God, I cannot but think that under another aspect, Science, by the analogy of its own processes, leads us up—less obviously, less unmistakeably but not less really—to this final consummation. It is often hastily assumed that the method of science and the method of Christian faith are irreconcileable, mutually exclusive of each other. But when we come to look closely into these methods, we shall rather be struck, I venture to think, by their mutual analogy—an analogy with difference, but a true analogy still.

I take it for granted that demonstrative knowledge we cannot have, except of the processes of our own mind and of its creations; that of all that is not ourselves—the world of things and persons and the Creative Cause of both, and even of our own nature, so far as by the power of reflection we study it, as if it were a distinct being—we can but have that science which we call Inductive, attaining in its results at most to what we call 'moral certainty.' Now looking at that science as a whole, both as it develops itself in the individual man, and, much more, as it is the treasure of the race, growing by inheritance from generation to generation, we know familiarly the processes by which it actually advances.

There is, first, the process of Observation, including in this the historical study of things or men in the past, carried on under the great axiomatic principles, of which we have spoken, as necessary 'forms of thought' —the idea of Causation in the intellectual, the intuition of Righteousness in the moral sphere—and so gradually classified and systematized, as to bring together, with continual balance and correction, the infinite number of single observations. Such in astronomy was the work of the earlier ages, perfected in the great generalizations of Kepler.

Then, perhaps at once, perhaps after many generations, comes the intuition of some universal Law, piercing to the inner meaning of all these results of observation, which discovers to us some one great force, material or spiritual, presenting itself as the Cause of them all; and which then accepts that discovery as true, and goes on to deduce from it necessarily other results, far beyond those originally observed, covering indeed in their generality the whole field with which the branch of science in question has to do. Such was the action of the genius of Newton, forming the greatest of all epochs in Astronomical science.

Then, lastly, perhaps through many hands and many generations, succeeds the process of Verification, testing the results, so deduced, by comparison with actual facts, and by their coincidence confirming, perhaps in detail correcting and modifying, the general law, and its disclosure of the Causative power. Such is the work, which for two centuries has gone on continually, and in which the wonderful discovery of the last planet of our system holds perhaps the highest place. Thus at last stands out complete the truth of Science, speculative or moral, to be the possession of the whole race.

Now in this, the actual process of advance of Science, there is undoubtedly throughout an element of faith. For it is clear that in all ages, even in our own age of increased diffusion of knowledge and education, all the forward steps are taken by the few; and the mass of men have to accept them in faith, at most testing them by the practical experience which follows from that acceptance. It is said, I know, that such faith is only provisional, retaining still the power, perhaps the duty, of understanding and verifying what is thus provisionally accepted. But there is little substance in this plea: for in actual fact, we know not only that men generally never dream of trying to repeat the observations or understand the law, but that in the vast majority of cases they are incapable, intellectually or morally, of even making the trial.

But it is in respect of the central portion of the process, the intuition of the Law and through it of the universal Cause, that the application of the Law of faith is most evident. For here it is on the very few—to be counted on the fingers in each generation—that the progress of humanity rests. Men of genius we call them, as distinct from the men of mere talent. They have before them only the same materials of knowledge, which at least in large degree, are inherited and open to all. But to them, meditating long and deeply upon these, the great general truth reveals itself (men say) and often reveals itself suddenly by a flash of intuition, and their reason, the speculative or moral reason, is somehow quickened to see and grasp what is dark to other men, and to declare it to the world. Such men the world calls in a vague sense 'inspired men'; conscious only that they are moved by some spiritual insight or enthusiasm, unknown to lesser minds. In that language there is a truth, which for one who believes profoundly in a living God, having a personal communion with man, passes beyond this vague consciousness into something far more definite and intelligible. In respect of all truth, he sees that here in another sphere the double experience of the prophet is reproduced. 'The word of the Lord came to me'; for all truth is the revelation of Him: 'the

Spirit of the Lord was upon me': for all quickening of the spirits of men to receive truth is by a Divine Inspiration. There are those who (like Newton) have felt this to the very depth of their souls, and for their high function of advance of the world's knowledge have thanked God. But, however that be, it is clear that on their exceptional impulse, not on the general action of human reason, the world depends. It sits more or less at their feet in faith. When the intuition is intellectual, it is mostly of the things without, and, if of God at all, it is of Him as the Supreme Ruler, above all, though pervading all; and to it there is a response of intelligence, fairly adequate from the comparatively few, very imperfect from the many, who (to use a common and significant phrase) take all these things 'on trust.' If the intuition be moral, or even imaginative, it looks more to the humanity within, individual and collective, and, where it witnesses of God, it is of God as spiritually present in that humanity; and accordingly the moral or emotional response is more widely diffused, but on the other hand, far more fully a response of faith and trustful loyalty. Of course, in either case, this faith in these masters of men's minds and hearts is both limited and provisional—imperfect (that is) both in scope and time. For they themselves are imperfect in wisdom and righteousness, and still more imperfect in prophetic foresight; and absolute trust in imperfection is idolatry. Hero-worship has at all times its right function; as a protest against the worship of the multitude, it may well have its special value in our days. But to make it absolute is necessarily impossible.

'See that thou do it not; I am thy fellow-servant,' is the cry of the true hero, as well as the true saint. Yet with all its limitations this faith in man is living and powerful; perhaps on the whole it errs in excess rather than defect; it has been forcibly argued that it has shown itself historically to be the greatest of all powers that move the world.

Now, in this undoubted and powerful element of scientific advance, is there not an analogy which makes it a $\pi\alpha\iota\delta\alpha\gamma\omega\gamma\acute{o}s$ to bring us to Christ?

For what is the Christian theory as to the growth of the knowledge of God, and of the world and man in Him? Is it not that which is expressed in the fullest sense of the famous words—that 'God of old times spoke to the fathers in divers portions' of the whole truth 'and in divers manners,' but 'at the end of these days hath spoken to us' once for all 'in His Son'—as 'the effulgence of His glory and the very image of His substance'? It declares, that, while there is for all humanity, feeling after God and in measure finding Him, an universal witness,—partly from the things without, partly by the consciousness within, through which these outer things are interpreted,—yet that it has pleased God to reveal Himself, in sundry forms and sundry measures, to those who were to be His prophets to all mankind. We hold, indeed, that this process of revelation has wrought itself out, especially and supernaturally, within the circle of a special covenant of knowledge and grace, given for the future blessing of all families of the earth. But yet not exclusively; the wisest Christian teachers have always acknowledged a lower natural exemplification of that appointed order in the great teachers of the world. Not without significance does Clement of Alexandria see a Greek Moses in Plato, and Dante make Virgil lead the soul into the lower spheres of the Divine working. Not without good ground have we in our own days been taught to recognise—what, indeed, Holy Scripture itself implies—that in the dimmer light, outside the brighter pale of the special covenant, men have not only been found of God themselves, but have declared Him to their fellow men. And to us all this culminates in the full revelation in the Lord Jesus Christ, as the Light of the world, the Light which lighteth every man and lighteth for all time. In that theory of Christian faith, the final and supreme element, indeed, is confessedly and absolutely supernatural. It is in respect of the perfection claimed for the revelation in Christ, and therefore the unlimited trust claimed as His due, that a real Christian faith stands out in essential distinction from the qualified belief and reverence, which all thoughtful and serious men accord to Jesus of Nazareth, as the greatest of merely human teachers in the moral and spiritual sphere; and that Christianity stands out unique among the religions of the world, and advances its claim to be an absolute and universal religion, accepting what is good and true in the other faiths of humanity, as broken lights from that Face of God, which is revealed in perfect radiance in Christ, but utterly refusing to be content with a place of equality with them, or superiority only in degree. As the actual manifestation of Christ Himself in word and power cannot be accounted for as a part of the purely natural order—as the Christ of the Gospel is infinitely greater than the Christ of expectation, and even the Christ of prophecy—so the faith claimed for Him is unique and supernatural. Advancing that supreme claim of authority for its Master, Christianity necessarily sets forth as the only justification of that claim, the mystery of the Incarnation of Godhead in Him : for how can there be absoluteness of trust, unless in Him the faith in man is identified with faith in God, who alone can claim fulness of worship from his creatures? Yet still this supernatural element, while it thus plainly transcends, does not contradict the natural; it is seen to be the crown and completion of that natural law of faith, as a guiding element in the growth of human knowledge, which else remains headless and imperfect : and, therefore, so far, the perception of that Law leads us up to Christ.

The analogy, moreover, thus suggested, applies also in this respect—that this Divine intuition and declaration of the whole Truth of God, has its subordinate stages, of preparation by observation on the one hand, and of development by verification on the other. Of preparation, in all which human thought and experience has discerned or surmised of the working of the Providence and the Spirit of God, and in all earlier revelations given to meet these searchings of humanity; for these supply (so to speak) the standing-point from which the new revelation starts. Of development, by the continual verification through the ages in the Church of Christ, under the promised gift of the Spirit, of all the declarations and all the promises which the Gospel contains. But these (to use our Lord's own distinction) can touch only 'the earthly things,' the visible manifestations (that is) of the heavenly realities: the knowledge of those 'heavenly things' themselves is unhesitatingly claimed for Him, and for Him alone. The true Teacher reveals what the mere παιδαγωγός can perhaps indicate as possible, and as earnestly to be longed for, but cannot know in fulness and in reality.

(C) But there is a third exercise of this function of Law, in respect of the substance of what we call 'the Faith,' that is the fundamental doctrines of the revelation to faith in the Lord Jesus Christ. What can the scientific discovery of Law, whether of nature or of humanity, do here?

Clearly we cannot, by the nature of the case, expect that Science will anticipate or prove the 'heavenly things' themselves—the ultimate mysteries of the Gospel, which profess to declare the counsels and the nature of God Himself; for, if they are true at all, they lie above the plane to which earthly science can reach. The 'Natural Theology' of man, through mind, conscience, imagination, heart—and all these not in separation, but in combination—does, we profoundly believe, rise up towards God. But it is to us a fundamental acknowledgment, that its approach needs to be met, and is met, by the revelation of God in Christ. Otherwise the very reason for such revelation is gone. To apply in a different sense St. Paul's words, 'If they who are of the Law'—content with the reign of Law, as Science discloses or surmises it—'are heirs' of the perfect Truth, 'then faith is made void' and needless, and 'Christ Himself' is revealed ' in vain.'

Clearly for the same reason it cannot disprove or ignore them. It cannot disprove them: for so to do would be to arrogate to Science a perfect and demonstrative knowledge of all the mysteries of Being, and to claim that the truth, which it discovers, is not only the real truth, but the whole truth. It has no right to ignore them, as unreal, as fantastic, as lying beyond the possibility of real knowledge. As well might the student of the inorganic world deny the reality of life, because he cannot bring it under the laws or refer it to the causes, which he finds to be working them. As well might the student of organic life deny the reality of mind and conscience, because he can discern neither by his knowledge of the organisation through which it works.

No! it is with 'the earthly things,' through which the heavenly things are manifested, that Science has to do. The revelation of Christ presupposes great laws of God in the world and in humanity; it comes to us through the witness of men—under the inspiration of God, but men still—and is practically embodied in institutions, which can be seen as telling on human society; it appealed to men at its first coming by signs physical and spiritual, which they could test and understand; it has for times past and present its signs in its historical power over this world, and by these its fruits it offers to be judged; it claims to be able to give to those who will receive it a new spiritual life, which can actually subdue the flesh and overcome the world. In these respects it enters on the region of human thought and human experience, with which Science, as the systematization of both, can deal, and from its own lower point of view, is bound to deal. In respect of these it is impossible to keep apart from each other the revelation accepted in faith, and the witness of Science as understood by reason; for the truth of God, however known to us, is one, and the humanity which it concerns is one also. It is vain to attempt a separation here between our intellectual and our moral and spiritual nature, to assign knowledge to the one, and religion to the other, as though the intellect had no function in religious belief, and moral intuition no place in the pursuit of knowledge. 'If a man' (it has been truly said)[1] 'be at once savant and theologian, how is he to manage this partition of his creed—one side of him denying all knowledge but of necessity and of nature, and the other believing in freedom and in God? No earnest mind can endure a life of double consciousness.' Meeting-points there must be. We know, indeed, even in science itself, that it is often difficult to discern these clearly, when they are reached by two different methods—now starting from fundamental principles, accepted as true, and deducing from them what ought to be—now starting from observation of actual facts, and ascending from these to what actually is. It is but according to our actual experience, that for a time this may seem to involve us in contradiction and perplexity, making men, according to their mental character, doubt the truth of the first principles accepted on the

[1] Martineau's *Nature and God.*

one hand, or the accuracy of the inductions made on the other. But yet these meeting-points must really be, and in the end they must, more or less distinctly, be seen to be, meeting-points not of discord, but of harmony.

It is here that we may expect—and we shall find (as I believe) grounds for justifying this expectation—that Science will be, through its discovery of law, a παιδαγωγός to lead us to Christ. To use the words of a distinguished predecessor in this lectureship, it has 'its office in making perpetually clearer the true and full meaning of revelation itself.' 'It is intended, that as men advance in knowledge of God's works, they should find themselves better able to interpret the message, which they have received from their Father in heaven[1].'

That office may not always be rightly discharged. Just as in St. Paul's time there were those who idolized the Law, and neglected or despised the Gospel of the Spirit, and there were also those, who, in their zeal for the freedom of the Spirit, depreciated or denounced the Law, instead of 'using it lawfully'; so there is now a tendency, on the one side, to insist that the truth of Science is all in all, and that beyond it there can be nothing but the 'unknown and unknowable,' and on the other, in those to whom faith in Christ is the very life of life, to undervalue scientific discovery, perhaps even to fear or hate the advance of scientific research and knowledge. But neither of these tendencies can hold or ought to hold. It is often the highest wisdom of this imperfect life to 'wait and hope'—'to wait' in the

[1] Temple's *Bampton Lectures for* 1884, p. 245.

possession of two truths or principles, each of which we have reason to accept, although as yet reconcilement may be to us impossible—'to hope,' in a faith which already in human experience has found some justification and reward, that in due time the whole truth will emerge out of apparent contradictions, and what seemed to be discords will subserve a subtler and richer harmony —'one music as before, but vaster.'

Now it is only with this last relation of Science to faith, of Law to Christ, that these lectures will attempt to deal; and even of this it is obvious that an exhaustive treatment would, within their necessary limits, be impossible. All that can be attempted is to give what appear to be specimens of this relation of the advance of scientific conception to the unchanged essence of our Christianity—of the manifestation (that is) of Supreme Power through Law to the manifestation of God in Christ, bringing with it that personal unity of the spirit of man with the Godhead, to which the very form of Christian baptism bears continual witness.

It appears to me that this effect shows itself in various forms.

Sometimes it is directly confirmatory, as showing that the great laws of humanity, which the manifestation of God in Christ assumes, and through which it works with a force supernatural and divine, are true laws, more and more fully realized by our modern scientific thought. In that light I would ask you to consider the significance of the great principle of Heredity, as showing the solidarity of all humankind, and of Evolution in its largest sense, as illustrating the progress in all creation to a higher perfection. The one will appear (I think) to bear on the fundamental Christian doctrine of Mediation; the other on the doctrine of the Incarnation, as the germ of a new life engrafted in humanity, destined to perfect itself under the providence and grace of God till the end of this dispensation. Both are incapable, of course, of anticipating the great Christian mysteries, and yet both prepare for them, by showing their harmony with God's natural laws, and so lead up to the true Revealer of the mystery of God, the Lord Jesus Christ Himself.

Sometimes, again, the same witness shows itself, rather as elucidating, and bringing out in their right significance, certain elements of the Gospel message, which, till that witness was borne, were comparatively in abeyance, acknowledged, but hardly realized, by the faith of Christendom. Eternal verities, in their essence incapable of change or decay, yet manifest themselves in different aspects to the conditions, intellectual and spiritual, of various ages of man—just as the same eternal Creative Power manifests itself to different cycles of time in different orders of being. What is at one period only the background of faith is brought into prominence, as 'knowledge grows from more to more.' So it seems to me that the infinite enlargement of our scientific conception of the universe, as one great whole, in which the earth with all its inhabitants is but a speck, forces us to consider the significance of those revelations (as in the Epistles to the Ephesians and Colossians) which speak of the Headship of Christ, not only over His Church, not only over humanity, but over all created being gathered up in Himself, and refuse to conceive of His relation to it as limited either by space or time. To the knowledge of creation in the early age, it was but natural that this grander conception of the faith should be held (so to speak) only implicitly, as the worthy completion of the Christian doxology to the Incarnate Son of God. Now it seems to be brought into explicit prominence, and to show His kingdom and salvation, expanding to the full expansion of all the regions of His creation. So, again, in a wholly different sphere, I cannot but feel that the growth of the social side of the Science of Humanity—bidding us consider how the inalienable individual freedom is tempered and subordinated, without being destroyed, by the common life of human society—forces us, as Christians, to enquire into the doctrine of the unity of all humanity in Christ, alike in the supernatural society, coextensive in idea with the world itself, which we call the Catholic Church, and in the various bonds of natural society, which He is pleased to regenerate to a new life. Just as the new birth of individual thought and freedom in the sixteenth century brought out, with new force and vitality, the truth of Christian Individualism, face to face with God in Christ, and seeking from Him alone the saving gift both of pardon and of grace, so—now that this Individualism has been established, and, taken alone, has been found insufficient to solve the problems of civilisation,—the truth of a Christian unity, which shall not deny or crush, but temper and rule it, is called forth by the pressing needs of our own nineteenth century, into a prominence which as yet modern thought has but imperfectly realized.

Sometimes, once more, this same teaching of Science assumes towards the faith of the Gospel, an attitude which we may call corrective and critical, coming closest to that view of it, which I have already quoted, as 'making' and forcing us to make, 'perpetually clearer the true meaning of the revelation itself.' It is corrective, as testing, and often rejecting or modifying, interpretations of the eternal verities, or deductions from them, which are really but the work of science as theologic, and which yet we are apt to make as sacred as the verities themselves. It is critical, as distinguishing in the Revelation itself what is Divine from what is human, what is primary and essential from what is secondary and subsidiary. As such, it leads the mind, in theology as in other forms of thought, from absolute scholastic systems, which claim to embrace all truth, and form it into a vast and symmetrical but artificial coherence, to the simpler grasp of great fundamental principles, fulfilling themselves to us in many ways: while we recognise in them irregularities, which we cannot square into rule, and mysteries which defy accurate definition. Clearly this effect of Science has shown, and is showing, itself, in regard to the very conception of what we call the Supernatural in the Revelation—the element of Miracle in the largest sense, whether in the realm of matter or the realm of mind. It bids us ask what is its proper meaning and significance—what is its relation to those natural forces and laws, which it is the very object of science to discover—a relation which must be one not of discord, not of unison, but of harmony. Nor less clear, and hardly less important, is the bearing of criticism on Holy Scripture, in which the essence of that Revelation is concentrated for us—to distinguish, though we cannot separate, the Divine from the human element in it—to compare its declarations with the truths discovered, with more or less of certainty, by science, physical, historical, linguistic, —to examine how far its main purpose, clearly spiritual, is indissolubly connected with the forms, historical, legal, didactic, in which it has clothed itself. It is plain that this critical relation of Science to Revelation is more apt to be, or to seem to be, antagonistic, and in some of its phases it undoubtedly deserves its common appellation of 'destructive.' But yet it is one which must be faced quietly and resolutely. Our duty is not to denounce or ignore it, but (if I may so say) to submit it in its turn to criticism from the other side, which may distinguish in it what is really proved from what is mere assumption, probable or improbable, and so refuse what in it is false, while we welcome what is true, and use it to clear our own conception of the higher truth, which we hold in faith. The experience of the last half-century may, I must think, read to us here lessons of encouragement. I have myself seen methods of such criticism come and go, sometimes destroying each other. I have seen results of criticism, once accepted as final and imperishable, now rejected on all hands, and doctrines of revelation, once scouted as unphilosophical and impossible, now allowed to be accordant with the truest and deepest philosophy. But all this restless and sometimes bewildering activity has not been in vain. In a very literal sense it has, I think, tended to fulfil the idea of the text, because it has taught us to pass from simply accepting Christianity, as a system of doctrine and institution, to resting in all our being on the living Christ Himself.

IV. Under these three aspects, I shall ask you to consider with me whether Science ought not to tend, and has not in great degree tended, to be the schoolmaster to bring us to a higher teaching. We cannot, of course, be unaware that this is not the whole truth of the case; that the advance of Science, encroaching (as we believe) on domains not its own, and claiming to do what it cannot do for the full satisfaction of human needs, has too often come to bar the progress towards God in Christ, which it ought to further, and to unsettle the old childlike faith of days, less knowing than our own, yet perhaps not less wise; that accordingly the Christian teacher has, like St. Paul, to resist such usurpation, to expose the vanity of such claims, to protest against 'the science, falsely so called,' which simply despoils us of our spiritual inheritance and gives us nothing in its room [1]. But yet it seems to me that the brighter side of the truth, which I have indicated, is one which needs to be dwelt upon more frequently and more hopefully, and moreover that it is one which our age most urgently demands, and is

---

[1] The title, I observe, of the Boyle Lectures for 1890, by Professor Bonney, is the 'Conflict of Science and Faith.'

ready to receive. The age is weary of mere doubts and negations. It will not, because by spiritual necessity it cannot, be contented with an Agnostic despair of advance to ultimate truth, even if there be offered accumulation of what calls itself 'positive knowledge' of lower and secondary truths, which declines (as has been bitterly said) even to think of 'the kernel of nature, and goes on sifting its husks'—'vacant husks' (we may add), 'well meant for grain.' It honours, and rightly honours, the advance of Science towards the discovery of the reign of Law, for its own sake as well as for the fruits of usefulness which it has brought; but it asks, 'What is there behind Law, and yet in that Law truly though imperfectly expressed?' Nor will it accept as sufficient the answer, 'A something not ourselves, which creates being and makes for righteousness.' It is not enough to describe it by mere negation, and so to make our confession of faith (as has been sarcastically said by Charles Kingsley[1]), a declaration that 'the Something our Nothing is one Something.' We must find some better answer, which can satisfy the needs of our own inner personality in all its faculties —the instincts of truth, of righteousness, of love, of faith. Such an answer we believe to have been given, capable of being understood by the simplest, and verified by the maturest thought. We believe that the Living God, who is Power, Wisdom, Righteousness, Love, has revealed Himself to His creatures, and that this Revelation is perfected in the Lord Jesus Christ. Therefore we believe that all lower discoveries of His work must

[1] In *Phaethon, or Loose Thoughts for Loose Thinkers.*

eventually lead to Christ, and in that confidence we look not only calmly but gladly and thankfully on their continual growth.

In Tennyson's 'Sea Dreams' there is the weird vision of a vast flood, swelling up again and again out of a far off 'belt of luminous vapour,' not without strange low sounds of Nature's music, breaking 'mixt with awful light' against the heights, which are seen as 'huge cathedral fronts of every age,' and sweeping away, one by one, the images of sacred beauty from the niches of time-honoured reverence; and at last rising to—

> 'two fair images
> Both crowned with stars and high among the stars,
> The Virgin-Mother standing with her child;
> Till she began to totter, and the child
> Clung to the mother, and sent forth a cry.'

The allegory is plain and ominous. Were the heights of our Christianity indeed only a grand and venerable fabric built up by man, it might be true. But what if they be, as we believe them to be, the 'stone made without hands,' going right down to the Eternal Rock of truth, and growing, by an inner force of life, to fill the whole earth? What if upon them there stands, not the mere ideal image of a holy child, but the living personality of Him, who can say to the wildest storm, 'Peace, be still'? Then we may put the desponding suggestions of the allegory aside, and take up the old confidence, which cries out that 'we will not fear, though the waters rage and swell'; for out of that swelling rage those heights will still rise unshaken, only brighter in purity, more visibly majestic in strength; and the very waters which threatened to shake His sovereign royalty shall be subdued to His will, even to 'make glad the city of God, the holy place of the Tabernacle of the Most Highest.'

LECTURE II.

HEREDITY AND MEDIATION.

As in Adam all die, even so in Christ shall all be made alive.—1 Cor. xv. 22.

IN working out the general idea already indicated, and considering how far the witness of Science to the reign of Law is 'a schoolmaster' to lead us to the higher knowledge of God in Christ, we enter first on its directly confirmatory relation to that higher knowledge; and our consideration of this relation may well begin by examining the bearing of scientific research into the unity of the human race, both in the present and in the past, upon the great doctrine of Mediation. That doctrine lies at the root of distinctive Christianity; for Christianity is at once a religion of God and a religion of Humanity, and the link between the two is the Mediation, by which God and man are made one.

(I) In the famous words of the text the whole truth of Mediation, as a Redemption from evil, is expressed with a graphic and comprehensive brevity. It assumes, first, that there is a real and effective unity in our nature, in virtue of which all humanity is viewed and treated as a whole; it asserts, next, an inheritance of sin and death from a primeval origin of evil, as actually affecting all that collective humanity; and, lastly, it

declares a Divine Mediation in Christ, taking away
that alienation of our humanity from God, which is its
spiritual death, and renewing in it the communion
with Him, which is spiritual life. That Mediation is
set forth as doubly a Redemption and a Re-creation
of humanity; primarily as restoring the higher unity,
through which 'it lives and moves and has its being'
in God, and, secondarily, through this Divine principle,
as regenerating and strengthening the bonds of the
human unity itself, which, through all ages and in all
nations and languages, should make it one. All are
one with God in Christ, and all are therefore members
one of another. The text appeals to actual experience
of this unity of all mankind in the inheritance and continual intensification of a moral corruption, a germ of
evil at the beginning of human history, now inborn and
engrained in all the individual souls who make up
humanity, and sowing in all the seeds of a common
death. It declares it, as in the same experience manifested for a Diviner good, far more than overcoming
the evil, in the similar development of a new germ of
higher life, implanted by the Incarnation in humanity
of the Son of God, and worked out through all the
ages, gradually pervading that humanity and overcoming all opposing influences, till at His Coming again
it shall be perfected in the fulness of Eternal Life.

It must, indeed, be remembered that this view of
the Mediation, as a salvation from the sin brought in
by the Fall—glorious as it is, and perhaps closest to
the needs and aspirations of our sinful world—is yet
far from exhausting the whole fulness of its Divine

meaning. The Mediation of the Son of God and Man is set forth to us as the crown of the Divine purpose in the very creation of humanity. 'If man' (it has been truly said) 'had fulfilled the law of his being, he would still, so far as we can see, have stood in need of a Mediator, through whom the relation of fellowship with God might have been sustained, and deepened, and perfected. Nor is it easy to suppose that this fellowship could have been made stable and permanent in any other way, than by the union in due time of man with God, accomplished by the union of man with Him, who was the Mediator between man and God, and in whose image man was made.' 'The Incarnation was,' we believe, 'independent of the Fall,' although everything of suffering and shame 'connected with the Incarnation was due to the Fall[1].' This larger sense seems, we may remark, clearly implied in the celebrated Creed of the Manifestation of the Son of God in the Epistle to the Philippians[2], in which the first part of the 'great humility'—'being in the form of God .. He emptied Himself, taking the form of a servant'—is distinguished from the second part—'being found in fashion as a man, He humbled Himself, and became obedient even unto death, yea, the death of the Cross.'

[1] See Bishop Westcott on *The Gospel of Creation* in *The Epistles of St. John*, pp. 273–315; with its singularly interesting catena of authorities from the twelfth to the sixteenth centuries. With his conclusion most theologians will agree. 'The thought that the Incarnation, the union of man with God and of creation in man, was part of the Divine purpose in creation, opens to us, I believe, wider views of the wisdom of God than we commonly embrace, which must react upon life.'

[2] Phil. ii. 6–8.

That distinction the practice of the Church embodies, when it celebrates the first in the unclouded joy of Christmas, and the second with the mingled sorrow and thankfulness of Good Friday. But it is sufficient for the present purpose to consider the Mediation as it actually is, not to man in his original righteousness, but to man as sinful.

Now in relation to the acceptance of this great Christian doctrine of Mediation a twofold difficulty has been created by the deep sense of Individuality in the human soul—conscious (as has been said) in its supreme moments of but two existences, God and itself. We find a speculative difficulty, in the doubt whether there is such a thing as real and effective unity in human nature, and whether, after all, humanity is anything more than a convenient term for an infinite number of individual beings, having certain points of natural likeness—the old contention of Nominalism against Realism in days gone by[1]. We find a graver moral difficulty, in the question how, if this unity be real—so real as to affect our nature, even in its spiritual relations to God—this reality of power over us can be compatible with our own personal responsibility to God, of which conscience bears so unhesitating a witness, and, as correspondent to this, with His perfect

---

[1] Nominalism, as represented by Roscelin, 'the authoritative interpreter' to the Middle Ages, 'if not the author of the system,' 'peremptorily denied the real existence of universals; nothing actually *is* but the individual. ... Universals were mere conventional phrases. Each animal subsists; the animal race is but an aggregate of thought. Man lives; humankind is a creation of the mind.'—*Milman's Latin Christianity*, Book viii. c. 5.

righteousness of dealing with each human personality. Like all moral difficulties, it presses more hardly upon the soul than any question of mere speculation. It is a perplexity well known to all students of the theology of the past, especially in the days of St. Augustine, and of the revival of Augustinian influence in the sixteenth century; and, if now less prominent in doctrinal controversy than in days of a more pronounced individualism of thought, yet it constantly recurs to the spiritual experience of the soul itself in its personal relation to God.

(II) Now it seems clear that, in respect of this twofold difficulty, barring the way against acceptance in faith of the great Christian doctrine of Mediation, the whole course of modern thought exemplifies that character of Science, as 'the schoolmaster to lead us to Christ,' of which in these Lectures I desire to speak.

For, in the first place, we see that its progress is always towards an ever-increasing recognition of a true and effective solidarity in humanity at large, through a network of ties, binding individuals and generations together—ties which are indeed cemented by mutual needs, and quickened by mutual affections, yet which obviously depend neither on need nor on affection, but are rooted deep in that nature itself. The recognition of this truth has indeed grown to be so strong, that there is even some tendency to overbear by it all belief in individuality, to study humanity only in the mass, and to trace all growth of mind and character to the spiritual and material environment of the personal life —in respect of idea to refer all in the 'spirit of the age'—in respect of action and interest, to sink the individual in Society. The day, therefore, may come, when, as of old, Christianity shall have to assert, against such exaggeration, the reality and sacredness of individual right and freedom. But in its place the recognition of unity is true. In practice it is of the essence of the advance of modern civilisation, whether in its material, or its intellectual, or its moral aspect. In theory it is one of the latest words of our modern science.

But, beyond this, we are being taught in the same school to refer this solidarity in the present greatly, perhaps mainly, to the principle of Heredity; and so to see in it an inheritance from the parentage of the past. Not to speak as yet of theories of common descent, not only of humanity, but of the whole realm of organic creation, from some original germ or germs of life—that principle of Heredity in our race itself is being deeply studied, both in fact and in theory, and is certainly brought out more and more as an undoubted reality; through which what we may call the raw material of character, both physical and spiritual, is seen to be transmitted to all descendants from a common stock. This transmitted character is discerned, moreover, as indissolubly one in all its parts. For certainly modern thought brings out more and more clearly the truth that all the elements of our complex nature, distinct yet never separate, are full of mutual actions and reactions—that (as St. Paul indeed expressly teaches[1]) the body with its appetites, the soul with its passions

[1] 1 Thess. v. 23.

and affections, the spirit with its reason and moral sense, are all integral parts of one true self, and accordingly so tell upon one another, that no one can be affected without influence upon the rest. Whatever may be the force of the Law of Heredity, it is clearly exercised on man's nature as a whole.

This force cannot, indeed, by any but mere theorists, be conceived as absolute in determining the character of any individual. It is modified from without in each generation by changes in the physical and spiritual environment of life; and it is one chief object of civilisation so to determine these conditions, that they may mitigate or eradicate all that in those inherited tendencies is evil, and may stimulate all that is good. But the combined effect of both these forces from without is still more powerfully modified in each personal being by a real and energetic individuality, originated, we know not how, by the creative Power—so that in the multitude of human characters, as of human faces, we find at once likeness and unlikeness, an underlying element which is common, and an individual stamp of peculiarity.

What are the proportions and relations of these various forces in producing the complex result of human character, we can hardly estimate in any single case, and can probably never hope to define generally by an universal rule. As yet our whole knowledge of the subject is crude and vague; although the collection of careful observations now going on may, we hope, do something in the direction of greater definiteness, and help to some rough estimate of the true conditions of the problem. But, if it be difficult to balance inheritance from the past and environment of the present, how infinitely more difficult it is to estimate and account for this undoubted, though mysterious, element of individuality! How it is originated, and to what extent it is in each case a new force, engrafting itself as a fresh and fruitful germ on the parent stock, we cannot even pretend to guess. Witness the hopeless controversy of Traducianism and Creationism as to the human soul in days gone by—as far from solution now as in the time of St. Augustine. It is but one form of the ever-recurring mystery, of the relation of the *Ego* to the *Non Ego*, of the reconcilement of our own conscious personality with the reign of universal Law, and the existence of a corporate humanity. It is but the highest phase of that introduction of individual variations, which is one main element in the development of species in organic life. But that in every child of man there is a balance, and that there must be a harmony, of all these forces from within and from without, is to us perfectly clear.

On the one hand, the reality of this continuous life through Heredity is unquestionable. In rough generality it has been observed and acknowledged in all ages; in our own day that reality, and some of the laws which regulate it, have been most carefully studied, with some results of all but moral certainty. On its physical side we are told, in relation to the whole organic world, that, while the evidence of the transmission of artificially induced peculiarities and acquired habits of an individual is still precarious, yet 'no structural modification is so slight, and no functional peculiarity so insignificant in either parent, that it may not make its appearance in their offspring'; and that 'peculiarities which have arisen naturally, and have been hereditary through many antecedent generations, tend to appear in their progeny with great force[1]'. On the spiritual side it is at least equally certain, though naturally the proof of it is less obvious, that traits of mental and moral character, and through these proclivities to good or evil, are similarly transmitted, in varying degrees of power—and that power, moreover, more or less intermittent—from generation to generation. In both cases an element of complication is introduced by the fact of double parentage, from individuals previously unconnected with each other, and the consequent balance or conflict of the inheritance of distinctive characteristics from the father's and the mother's side. But this complication does not touch the general truth of Heredity, nor diminish the power of the combined influence, whatever may be the still unknown laws of its combination, on the individuality of the descendant. There it is, visible at all times in different degrees as a great universal Law, and exceptionally

[1] See Professor Huxley's Article on BIOLOGY in the *Encyclopædia Britannica*, vol. iii. p. 687. In relation to the physical transmission of acquired habits, Professor Weismann goes somewhat further. His conclusion is that 'it has never been proved, either by direct observation or by experiment, that acquired characters are transmitted, and it has never been demonstrated that, without the aid of such transmission, the evolution of the organic world becomes unintelligible.' (*Essays on Heredity and kindred Biological Problems*. English Translation. Oxford, Clarendon Press, 1889.)

illustrated to us from time to time by startling instances of the occurrence of a likeness, which is almost reproduction, of some near or remote ancestor, both in body and (perhaps in less degree) in character. We trace it, moreover, with greater distinctness, in proportion to the closeness of relation to some common parentage—strong in family likeness, and strongest, in all but identity of resemblance, in children twin-born—weaker in local or national types—yet in all real, till we come at last to the touch of nature, which makes the whole world kin. Alike in history and in fiction [1] we see how strangely the effect for good or evil of the strain of race works, in combination or in conflict with individual character, and with the education and associations of present life. It is, indeed, the sense of this continuity, which gives occasion and justification to the historical method of the study of all that concerns humanity, in respect of knowledge, thought, character, as well as in respect of physical structure and conditions of life.

But, on the other hand, real as this power is, and great as is in some cases its apparently preponderating strength, still that it is not absolute—that it does not extinguish or overwhelm individuality—is equally obvious.

That individuality comes out plainly enough on the physical side. In fact its appearance in such variations from the inherited type, as are favourable to victory in the struggle for existence, is noted in the whole organic world as one chief element in the process of Evolution.

[1] As in George Eliot's *Spanish Gypsy*.

In humanity it is to be traced clearly and unmistakeably, sometimes in striking physical contrast between the progeny of the same parents, growing up under the same circumstances, more often in the subtler individual differences, coexisting with the ordinary family likeness. But it is with the reality of this individuality in the moral and spiritual sphere that we are especially concerned. Here we have, indeed, a witness, anterior to all observation from without, more direct and more impressive in its power. It comes from within. For the personal freedom and responsibility which belong to a true individuality, there are both the unquestionable and irresistible testimony of each man's moral consciousness—the most certain, as certain, as it seems to me, of all the forms of consciousness of which we are capable—and the testimony of collective humanity in all the laws, institutions, languages of the world. To any contrary assertion of Determinism through Heredity Butler's grave irony applies, that, whatever be the abstract truth of the matter, certainly in the order of the world 'we are treated as if we were free.' But, even scientific observation tends, in proportion to the thoroughness and determination of its study, to confirm this witness. If inherited genius and inherited character are clearly traced, yet they are almost invariably modified in transmission; and that with a modification, for which neither change of circumstance, nor combination of parental peculiarities can adequately account, and which in each individual, if it seems in its beginning to be due to some natural proclivity, yet grows to maturity by the actual effect through habit of his own conscious energy, or his own conscious assimilation of external influences[1]. This seems to be established beyond all doubt as a constant law, and from time to time this general law is illustrated by startling exceptional instances of the emergence of a dominant and overmastering individuality. As we study the world's history, especially in the great critical epochs of progress, the effect both of Heredity and of the environment of life is not indeed effaced, but altogether thrown into the shade again and again, by the brilliant and original force of some commanding personality, to which we find nothing like either before or after, and on which the subsequent history of generations is seen to turn. No doubt it has its 'epoch of preparation' —sometimes its individual precursors. 'The hour,' as we say, ' has come '; a wave of general influence passes over the whole face of human society, or moves it as an undercurrent from below. But 'the man' must come also in his exceptional power and mission; else the hour will pass fruitless away. Even the advance of civilisation, and the growth of democracy—over which men sometimes groan, as tending to restrain free originality, and reduce humanity to a dead mediocrity—yet will be, I think, seen rather to alter the form and method, than impair the force, of this influence of strong individuality in mind or will. It rules perhaps more by consent, but it rules with unabated power.

The result, to which we are led by study of the actual facts, without squaring them artificially to preconceived

---

[1] This fact is strikingly illustrated in Mr. Galton's interesting work on *Hereditary Genius*.

theory, is to give frank recognition to this force of Heredity as real and strong, but to refuse to accept, in respect of it, the rigid Determinism, which requires us to hold that the deep inner consciousness of freedom is a simple delusion, and that the individual is but the product of inherited forces, developed by the environment of life. It manifests itself plainly as what we may call a Predisposition; under which that conscious individuality works with varying degrees of power, and which may perhaps be held to determine practically for the mass of men the limits of its exercise; but which does not take away its freedom and responsibility, either in action for itself, or in reaction upon that general condition of humanity, which it has inherited. The degree of this individual power may vary, from an almost complete mastery over inheritance and circumstance in the strong, to what seems to approach to a mere slavery under them in the weak. In the unhappy conditions of inheritance and environment, with which we are but too familiar in our densely crowded cities, that slavery often appears to us as a hopeless slavery, under which we fail to trace any personal freedom, or to understand any personal responsibility. The limits of its exercise may similarly vary from a wide enlargement to a narrow circumscription of scope. But, while these exceptional extremes strikingly illustrate the reality of the two distinct forces, it is in the average case that we see most clearly their mutual action and reaction upon each other. Perhaps the advance of science tends at this moment to bring out more clearly the reality of the general influence over that individuality, which is witnessed to without science by vivid internal consciousness and by simpler observation of experience. But the acceptance of both truths is demanded by those actual conditions of our humanity, which we take for granted in the shaping of our own personal life, and in the framing and working of our several institutions; and I may add in passing that it seems well to harmonize with the essentially religious conception of life—the belief that its controlling Power is not an iron indiscriminating Law, irreconcileable with individual variety and freedom, but the rule of a Supreme Personality in an elastic and discriminating equity, allowing for and yet directing freedom, sanctioning variety, and yet blending it in a comprehensive unity, to work out one transcendent purpose.

Now if this be, as I think it is, a true sketch of the conclusions on this subject, to which scientific investigation is now leading us[1], it is surely clear that they are in striking harmony with the Scriptural doctrine brought out in the great antithesis of the text.

(III) In the words, 'As in Adam all die,' we find taken for granted the truth of an inheritance from

[1] Its present position may be studied in the various works of Mr. F. Galton, from his *Hereditary Genius* in 1869, to his *Natural Inheritance* in 1889; in Weismann's *Studies in the Theory of Descent* (1880–1882) and his *Essays upon Heredity and kindred Biological Problems* (Oxford, 1889); and in the various articles, by many able hands, which will be found referred to under the title HEREDITY in the Index to the *Encyclopædia Britannica* (9th Edition). The chief questions at present under discussion are said to be the following, (a) The transmission of acquired habits; (b) The relation between germ and sperm elements; (c) The real meaning of types, and the bearing of Natural Selection upon them.

the beginning of a corruption of our moral nature, not accidental, but intrinsic and universal, having in it, if left to work itself out, the seeds of spiritual death.

Now of this truth we may note, that its enunciation in the New Testament, while it is perfectly clear, is yet both simple and exceptional, bearing no proportion to the space which it occupies, and the elaboration of definition and treatment given to it, in some systems of Christian Theology. It is hardly too much to say that it belongs all but exclusively to one stage in the Apostolic teaching, illustrated to us in the four great Epistles of St. Paul to the Corinthians, the Galatians, and the Romans, which mark the crisis of the Judaistic controversy; that, even here, it is wrought out with any degree of fulness only in one passage of the great argument of Justification in the Epistle to the Romans[1]; and that solely in connection with the truth of the Mediation of Christ, on which that argument depends, is it treated at all.

As a rule, it is the fact of what has been called 'Original Sin,' but would better be called an inborn tendency to sin in our human nature itself,—'a fault and corruption of the nature of every man, that naturally

---

[1] Rom. v. 12–19. Note the repeated emphasis on the truth that 'where sin abounded'—overflowed in its moral consequences to all humanity—'grace did much more abound.' It is only in the glad conviction of this abounding grace, flowing from the Atonement, that St. Paul will even contemplate the natural inheritance of evil. So in the same Epistle the brightness of the eighth chapter swallows up the gloom of the seventh: the 'law of sin' brings out 'the glorious liberty of the children of God.'

is engendered of the offspring of Adam [1]'—that Holy Scripture bears continual witness. It is this, which is manifested in a terrible practical reality through the history; which is exposed, menaced, coerced, in the stern righteousness of Law; which is dealt with by spiritual teaching and exhortation, and by promise of spiritual power to overcome it, in the Prophecy; which is confessed with repentance and prayer for forgiveness and regeneration in the Psalm; which is set forth with terrible and unsparing power in St. Paul's Epistles, especially the opening chapters of the great Epistle to the Romans. In all these aspects it is, of course, no new or peculiar doctrine of revelation. I do not see how its truth can be altogether ignored by any man, who goes about the world with his eyes open, and sees it writ large in history, past and present, or who looks with any truthful introspection into the workings of his own soul. It may be extenuated at one time by the Optimism, which feels that it is unnatural, and so hopes that it is unreal; it may be, as now, exaggerated by a gloomy Pessimism into a dominant Law in human nature. But recognised in some way it must be, and it has been, by all thoughtful study of the world and the soul, not as we wish them to be, but as they are. Its terrible reality grows upon us continually, as we ourselves advance with advancing years in our knowledge of the world, and as humanity itself grows older and more self-conscious. When, therefore, Holy Scripture speaks on this matter, it does but set its seal of sanction on this recognition; and declare with certainty

---

[1] See the Ninth Article of the Church of England.

—what otherwise might be but a probable inference,—that in its essence it is not merely Vice, as against our own individual nature, not merely Crime, as against collective humanity, but sin against God—rebellion against His righteous Will, outrage against His Love.

The true and characteristic revelation, indeed,—which places Christianity as a religion of hope in bright contrast with Buddhism as the religion of despair, and with the Pessimistic philosophies or mysticisms which seem to borrow from it—is what perhaps only a revelation can proclaim with certainty. It is the doctrine, not of Original Sin, but of Original Righteousness—the declaration that sin, strong and engrained as it is, is no part of man's true nature, that as it was not in the beginning, so it shall not be in the end—the promise that the Divine image in man, if only he will, shall conquer sin, not indeed, in an inherent strength of its own, but by the salvation and the grace of God. For this conviction it is, which alone makes life worth living, and which yet is continually dimmed and overclouded by sad experience, from without and from within. Hence, in the strife of the Two Voices, we need some Word of God to strike in with authority; some Gospel of victory and salvation is of urgent spiritual necessity, to meet and to satisfy the consciousness of weakness and of strength—the sense of sore need and high aspiration in every soul. It is only under the higher light of this Gospel that Christianity dares to contemplate the dark reality of a sin engrained in humanity [1].

[1] See Note C.

But when, from the confession, sad though not hopeless, of the terrible fact the enquiry,—the inevitable enquiry,—arises, 'How comes this fact to be?' then certainly the answer of Christianity points us to the great Law of Heredity. It tells us of an entrance of Evil into the world, in the infancy of the human race, by impulse from another sphere of created being —as a germ (so to speak) of evil, fructifying and intensifying itself by inheritance through all man's history, and bringing with it death [1]. In strict accordance, moreover, with that internal unity of each man's individual nature, of which we have spoken, this evil, in its origin spiritual, is represented as in its results telling upon man's physical, as well as his spiritual nature,—bringing upon it the burden of labour and of suffering, and the consummation of these in decay and death. But, more and more clearly as the revelation advances, it is on the spiritual evil that the stress is laid; it is the corruption of the image of God in man, having in it the seeds of spiritual death, which is seen as passing by inheritance to all men. Not, be it always noted, that this is the whole of his natural inheritance. As in the body, so in the spirit, the image of God, the original righteousness, marred yet not destroyed by sin, remains, although in discrowned majesty, and its effect must necessarily work through the same Law of Heredity; it must perpetuate and intensify itself in a better inheritance. The goodness, as well as the sin, of the fathers is visited upon the children. But we are in the text concerned simply with the

[1] See Note D.

Heredity of Evil. 'In Adam all die'; 'death passed upon all; for that all sinned.'

Now, when we look carefully at the Christian doctrine, we must see that it points us to one form of that inherited Predisposition in the individual, which the study of Heredity discloses to our science of humanity.

We commonly and rightly speak of it as a fall from righteousness. It is manifested, first, as an enfeebling and impairing of the power of the spirit within us, a weakening of the moral sense, which commands indeed with unquestionable authority, but ought also to rule with unresisted power; it is shown again as intensifying the power of 'the flesh,' that is, of the turbulent strength of the appetites and passions, till it rebels against that authority, and disputes or usurps that power; it is, beyond all this, a perversion and corruption even of the higher nature itself, into what may become the reprobate mind, loving evil simply as evil, which is a living blasphemy against humanity and against God. Under all these aspects it seems not only to correspond with a terrible accuracy to the facts of our ordinary experience and consciousness, but to bring out, in what St. Paul calls a 'Law of sin' in us, just the Law of Predisposition which the doctrine of Heredity is seen to imply. It has been curiously like that doctrine, as elsewhere taught, even in its perversions.

There has been the exaggeration of it, as if it included the whole Law of Heredity—as if (to use old theological words) man was not only 'far gone from original righteousness, but wholly destitute of it'—as if, therefore, there could be no natural inheritance except of evil and of condemnation—as if it were only on the individual side of our nature, that we could realize, through God's personal gift of grace, the preservation of His image within us. Against that exaggeration there has risen protest, not only from the practical experience of every day, but from the thoughtful study of human nature in its complex unity of good and evil. How the doctrine of Mediation bears upon it, we shall see hereafter. Meanwhile it is against the exaggeration, not against the true Scriptural doctrine, that the protest is rightly and even religiously made.

It has been exaggerated, again, just as some modern thought exaggerates Heredity in general, into a Determinism to Evil, against which it is vain for man to strive, under which, indeed, individual freedom, and with freedom responsibility, go out. The darkest hours of spiritual experience of bondage, such as St. Paul unveils in the seventh chapter of his Roman Epistle, are taken as expressing the whole of man's moral life, if life, indeed, it can be called. A ruthless logic, determined to reduce all to one comprehensible system, at the expense both of actual observation and of moral protest, goes so far as to insist on a predestination and reprobation through it to spiritual death, except within the narrow circle of the elect. Like all other phases of Determinism, it is simply an idolatry of Law, an iron Law of Predestination, contradicting our ineradicable consciousness of a freedom, guided by the Providence and moulded by the Spirit of God. But it is a phase of that idolatry which most directly revolts our whole moral being, and which most flagrantly sins against any worthy conception of the Divine Righteousness.

But in support of this exaggeration, which attaches equally to non-religious forms of Determinism, there has come one worst perversion, which belongs to it in virtue of its religious character. As religious, it must realize intensely the Being of a living and all-righteous God, with whom the soul stands face to face, and before whom, therefore, its consciousness of sin brings with it that, which belongs emphatically to Individuality— the sense of personal guilt, with the acknowledgment of the bitter fruits of sin, not only as an inevitable consequence, but as a righteous retribution.

How does this consciousness bear upon the conception of an inherited Determinism to Evil? The answer is that strange, almost monstrous, assertion not only of the inheritance of a corruption of nature, but of the imputation from the past of that guilt, which is inalienably personal. It is, as it would seem, the very same perversion of the truth of the visitation of the sins of the fathers upon the children, which Ezekiel so authoritatively rebuked [1]—mistaking, as it does, an inheritance of consequence for an inheritance of guilt. Yet it has been renewed again and again; isolated passages of Holy Scripture, against the whole tenour of Revelation, have been pressed into its service. For it, I need hardly say, neither history nor experience bears preparatory witness; against it the moral instinct of each soul, the moral common-sense of humanity, in-

[1] Ezek. xviii.

dignantly protest. But it is no part of true Christian doctrine; many Christian thinkers, and some great thinkers, of ancient and modern times, in that longing for complete logical system, which has been said to be 'the last infirmity of noble minds,' have been misguided into accepting it; but the Church of Christ has never made it a part of the Creed of Christendom. Our own Church once had it earnestly pressed upon her; but happily she deliberately refused to admit it into her confession of the sin of human-kind [1].

No! in Christian doctrine, as in scientific study of fact, Predisposition to evil is not properly Determinism. Under it the individuality of each man still remains. It has still its moral insight, clearly discerning the law of the eternal righteousness 'as holy and just and good.' It gives still its moral adhesion to that Law, in 'the hunger and thirst after righteousness,' and the 'delight in it after the inner man.' It still has 'the power to will present' with the soul; and in that power it struggles against the enslaving law of sin [2]. Its original righteousness is weakened and marred, but not lost. Even under its worst sense of bondage it treasures an ineradicable conviction, that in some way the un-

---

[1] It was proposed by the 'Assembly of Divines' in 1643 to insert in the Ninth Article the words 'together with Adam's first sin imputed,' and to change 'very far gone from original righteousness' into 'wholly deprived of original righteousness.' That proposition was never accepted. Against it there is on the main principles of the doctrine a virtual *consensus* between the Augsburg Confession, the Canons of the Council of Trent, and the Articles of the Church of England.

[2] Rom. vii. 12, 18, 22.

natural bondage of evil can be broken; and this inextinguishable hope of a salvation from sin it bases on the belief not only in the Love, but even in the Righteousness, of God [1].

(IV) That hope, like all ineradicable instincts of humanity, is not in vain. To the cry out of the darkness, 'O wretched man that I am! who shall deliver me from the body of this death?' there has come for eighteen centuries an answer, in which countless human souls have found the dawn of a new day, 'I thank God through Jesus Christ our Lord.' That answer leads up to the great doctrine of Mediation, 'Even so in Christ shall all be made alive.' Necessarily this truth needs a Word of the Lord to reveal it in certainty. Of deliverance from the inherited bondage of sin, as of deliverance from death, the message of the Gospel is 'Behold! I show you a mystery.' It cannot, like the other truth, be assumed on appeal to man's natural consciousness and experience. In relation to these—whatever natural hope may shine through them—it is a mystery, a truth supernatural, to be accepted, if accepted at all, through faith in the Self-revelation of the Lord Jesus Christ.

Yet the Supernatural has here the clearest analogy to the Natural. The very application of the title of 'the Second Adam,' the 'Second Man,' to 'the Lord from heaven,' and the comparison, more fully drawn out in the Epistle to the Romans, between 'the sin which abounded or overflowed' from the first Adam and

---

[1] 'If we confess our sins, He is *faithful and just* to forgive us our sins, and to cleanse us from all unrighteousness' (1 John i. 9.)

the grace 'which did overflow more exceedingly' from the second, clearly show that there is still suggestion of an analogy here, between that which is in nature and that which is above nature. The Manifestation in the flesh of the Son of God, always taken as a whole, indissoluble in all its parts—in the Incarnation and the Atonement, the Resurrection and the Ascension, the royalty in heaven and the judgment which is to crown it at the Great Day—is clearly set forth as involving a new creation, a regeneration of humanity, into the inheritance of which each individual soul enters, as into the old Creation, by a birth, but a new birth, not of the flesh but 'of water and the Spirit.' That which avails for salvation in Christ Jesus (says St. Paul) is 'new creation.' Whoever 'is in Him, is a new creature'; 'putting on the new man, which after God is created in righteousness and true holiness [1].'

In respect of that new creation, again, as of the old, and of the corruption, which passed upon the old, the truth of the internal unity of man's nature is distinctly brought out. Mainly, of course, viewed as a renewed spiritual life 'hid with Christ in God,' it is yet always

---

[1] Gal. vi. 15; 2 Cor. v. 17; Eph. iv. 24. This truth is strikingly illustrated in the ancient treatment of the idea of the Lord's Day,—(not, of course, confounded, but contrasted, with the Sabbath) as at once 'the first day and the eighth'—the beginning of the new creation after the completion of the old, in the resurrection of humanity to a new life by the Resurrection of the Lord Himself. Again and again that is implied, which is expressly brought out in the *De Sabbato et Circumcisione*, ascribed to S. Athanasius, that the Lord's Day, as the day of Creation of the Spiritual Light, is μνήμη ἀρχῆς δευτέρας ἀνακτίσεως (vol. iii. p. 44, Bened. Ed.).

recognised as telling also upon man's bodily nature, and for it also destined in its final perfection to 'swallow up death in victory.' By it even the body is consecrated anew as a temple of God, and through communion with the Saviour 'preserved unto everlasting life.' In the Church of Christ the Sacramental system itself is a continual witness to this regeneration in Him of man's nature as a whole. In Christian morality, in spite of Gnostic fallacies and false Asceticisms, the body is held to be sacred through this regeneration; bodily purity accordingly, ignored or lost in the Pagan civilisations of the early days of Christianity, is rescued and exalted to its right dignity: the body, instead of being looked upon as a clog or prison-house, from which death is a joyful deliverance of the spirit for ever, is reverenced, as here, and in the better life of the Resurrection, destined to be a part of our true humanity.

So touching our whole nature, the new creation is seen as working on humanity at large (so to speak) under a law of a spiritual Heredity in the regenerate, for the continuous renewal of the successive generations of men, till the consummation of all things shall come. In the individual soul, born again into the inheritance of the Christian covenant, it works from the beginning on the unfolding life, with the twofold grace of justification in the one great Atonement, and of sanctification in the indwelling of Christ in the soul—the one complete in God's infinite love, without any work of ours—the other begun in that same love, but gradually perfecting itself, and demanding the fellow-working of man. For all, for each, it is thus a Mediation, which breaks down all barriers raised by sin, and unites God and man for ever in Him, who is both in one.

That new creation (be it always remembered) is set forth to us as foreordained in the Divine counsels before the foundation of the world[1], and ordained for the whole of mankind. But to be ordained in the eternal counsels is to have efficacy. So it is in its grace effective in some sense from the beginning, for the spiritual life of all humanity as such, and for the redemption of humanity as sinful; so that man was never left to the unchecked predisposition to evil, of which we have spoken, and the image of God, in which he was created after the likeness of the Son of God Himself, was never allowed to be blotted out[2]. But in the Incarnation of the Son of God, in the Divine life of voluntary humiliation closed in the 'It is finished' of completed atonement, in the drawing of all in Himself to the new life of the Resurrection, in the new birth of humanity at Pentecost, it is brought into the course of this visible world, to act upon humanity through the laws of God's dispensation to it, as a new supernatural reality; and from the Day of Pentecost onwards, it has

---

[1] 'Ye were redeemed ... by the precious blood of Christ ... who verily was ordained before the foundation of the world' (1 Pet. i. 18-20.) So in Rev. xiii. 8, He is 'the Lamb slain from the foundation of the world.' The reference is especially to the Atonement, but all the acts of the Divine Manifestation in Him are indissolubly one.

[2] There is no limitation to the great declaration (John i. 4) 'In Him was life: and the life was the light of men.' 'It embraces' (says Bishop Westcott) 'the experience of Judaism and Heathendom, of pre-Christian and post-Christian times.'

been working directly on the souls of men up to the future perfection of the Great Day [1].

All this is unquestionably a doctrine of faith. We may see, as Christian thinkers have seen, that the personal manifestation of God in our nature, through an ideal yet actual humanity, is the appropriate crown and completion of His lower manifestations of Himself, in the world of Matter, in the world of Life, in the world of humankind; and that, in its redemptive aspect, it is that, which all the moral philosophies and religions of the world have been feeling after, and in some sense finding by anticipation and hope. We may know, as eighteen Christian centuries have known, by experience, that, when accepted and realized by faith, it has wrought out these effects, both in the secret history of the individual soul, and the visible history 'writ large' of human society. But yet in itself it rests on the word of the Lord Jesus Christ as the 'word of eternal life'; it is a 'mystery' in the New Testament sense of the word, that is, a secret of God, before unknown or dimly seen, but now plainly revealed in Him, even to babes. The science of humanity, as the 'schoolmaster,' may thus lead us to the true Teacher, and even show us by their results the truth of the lessons, which He imparts. But the truth so taught lies in itself above the sphere with which Science has

---

[1] The comparison, and the contrast, between the anticipations of the Divine action on the souls of men through the Eternal Word of God, and the perfection of that action in the Manifestation of Him in the flesh, is wrought out fully in the Prologue of the Gospel according to St. John (John i. 1-14).

to do. St. Paul argues in this very Epistle that, as it is spiritually revealed, so it is spiritually discerned, 'Eye hath not seen, nor ear heard it'; for who through these 'hath known the mind of the Lord[1]'? Unknown it must be and unknowable; unless we are content to know it by faith through 'the Mind of Christ.'

But yet while this is true of the 'heavenly thing,' the mysterious reality itself, which only He can know, yet, as to the earthly manifestation of it, we can see that this new and Diviner spiritual force, introduced into humanity as a whole, works there in striking analogy to that force of Heredity, which Science indicates to us, and which the Revelation itself assumes as known. The analogy, of course, is not perfect; for, as usual, the supernatural reality transcends it. This relation to the Mediation of the Lord is not merely to a germ of blessing sown in the past; it is the perpetual communion with a present source of life. As St. Paul expresses it[2], 'the first Adam' was but 'a living soul,' which gave its impulse to the race, and on earth ceased to be; 'the second Adam' is 'a quickening Spirit,' ever radiating life, working by an indwelling Presence in humanity, even to the end of the world; while yet, by virtue of His Divine Majesty, He transcends humanity in 'the glory which He had with the Father before the world was.'

Nor, even so, is this the whole truth. As in the old creation there is a mysterious individuality—which 'lives and moves and has its being in the God,' who breathes into each soul the breath of life—coexisting in

[1] 1 Cor. ii. 9, 16.   [2] See 1 Cor. xv. 45.

harmony with the solidarity of human nature, so in the new creation there is a still more living and sacred individuality, of which the secret is the Presence of Christ in each soul by the Spirit—a 'personal Christianity,' as we rightly term it, which dares to say with St. Paul, 'I live, yet not I, but Christ liveth in me.' But there is at the same time an indwelling Presence in the whole body of redeemed humanity; the same Christ, who is the Head of each man, is the Head of the whole Church. It is the Law of Christian life, as He Himself ordained it, that into this corporate life every individual nature should be engrafted and in it sustained. The existence of a Church Catholic in all space and time is not accidental, but of the essence of that Law; otherwise it could not correspond to and lay hold of the human nature, which is at once individual and social. The very ordinance by Him of the Sacraments both declares that Law and fulfils it; for, as has been truly said, 'that saving grace which Christ originally is or hath for the general good of His whole Church, by Sacraments He severally deriveth into every member thereof'[1]. As in nature, so in grace, unity, embracing and cherishing individuality, is the true life of humanity.

It is in this corporate life in Christ that the analogy to the force of Heredity is manifest. Inherited by the individual by a new birth into sonship to God, and sustained in him by grace of Communion—inherited by the whole race by the regeneration of humanity in a Church, which is Holy as centred on God in Christ, is

[1] Hooker's *Eccl. Polity*, Book V. c. lvii. sect. 5.

Catholic in its continual expansion over the whole area of human society—the Mediatorial gift manifests itself to our actual observation as a Divine predisposition to good, striving against and mastering the predisposition to evil, taking up and inspiring with a higher life whatever in our nature resists that deadly inheritance from ancestral sin.

A 'Predisposition to good'—the phrase, although indeed in its ultimate sense it means a conforming to the likeness of God, yet may well sound feeble and inadequate and prosaic to one who by faith knows in his own soul the Divine reality. For that reality, so the Gospel teaches, is the implanting and the development of the 'Christ in us'—a likeness of God Himself, in the power to know, the power to will, the power to love—in which we are constantly said to be 'heirs through Him' of a Kingdom of Heaven, and (in the unique and daring phrase of the Second Epistle of St. Peter) 'partakers of the Divine Nature[1].' Faith knows it thus in its essence. To use the words of the maturest Apostolic utterance, at once philosophically complete in thought, and glowing with prophetic inspiration[2], it acknowledges this 'indwelling of Christ in the heart'; it traces its spiritual development, first in 'the love,' which is the free enthusiastic recognition of unity with God in Christ, 'rooting and grounding' our whole soul in Him; next, in the 'being strong' not, indeed, to comprehend, but 'to apprehend'—in all 'the length and breadth' of visible expansion, and in

[1] 2 Cor. iv. 4; Col. i. 15, 27; Rom. viii. 17; 2 Pet. i. 4.
[2] Eph. iii. 17-19.

all 'the depth and height' which lose themselves in the invisible—that manifestation of 'the love of Christ,' the very soul of His Mediation, 'which passeth knowledge'; and so, lastly, in the gradual 'filling up' of our nature, to the utmost limit of its finite capacity, with all that is Divine of knowledge, of strength, of glory, of goodness, 'unto all the fulness of God Himself.' But when, leaving out of view this knowledge through faith, we come down to the lower knowledge of observation, both of the soul and of the world, it is just this predisposition to good which manifests itself. For such observation can only claim to test it in its signs and fruits; and that test does not fail, whether in the exaltation and renewal of individual lives, or in the moral and spiritual regeneration of humanity in the Church of Christ, or even in the *Gesta Christi* of the civilisation of the post-Christian world. The secret of life in the little mustard-seed our observation cannot see; but it can see, and it must see, how it has taken root and overshadowed the whole earth. The secret of pervasive influence in the leaven it understands not; but it does show us how it has actually leavened, and is leavening still, the three measures of the body, the soul, and the spirit of every child of man, who has received it.

But even here Predisposition is not Determinism. Even to salvation 'God enforceth not the will[1].' Naturally the tendency to Determinism, so universally felt by all who contemplate the reign of Supreme Law, and who, being unable to reconcile with it the reality of free will, maintain logical completeness by the sacrifice

[1] See the Article 'Of Grace' in the Forty-two Articles of 1552.

of unmanageable truth, is strongest and most serious in
religious thought. For such thought brings us face to
face with Supreme Sovereignty, not as veiled in an
impersonal Law, but unveiled in the Infinite Personality
of a living God: who, as the Source and Sustainer of all
finite being, must in some way foresee and fore-ordain
all things. Before Him he, who would find himself,
must first lose himself, in the Will of Eternal Righteousness and the grace of Eternal Love. Naturally, therefore, from the days of St. Augustine downwards, those,
who feeling intensely their own littleness and sinfulness
before Him, are inclined, and even eager, to sink consciousness of self in the overwhelming and adoring consciousness of God, have been unable to conceive how a
grace of salvation and renewal, which is Divine, should
not also be irresistible. Therefore they have come at last
to hold (with the framers of the Lambeth Articles of 1595)
that in those who have once been partakers of it [1], it is
not 'extinguished, nor fails, nor fades away, either totally
or finally'; and have accordingly been forced to explain
the unquestionable fact of failure in those who have been
admitted into membership of Christ, and believe that
they have lived in it, by denial that they who fail have
ever received that grace at all. Therefore they have been
led finally to declare that 'such grace is not assigned, is
not communicated, is not granted to all, that by it they
may be saved, if they will,' and to set forth the awful
doctrine of an absolute and irreversible election, out of
the sole will and pleasure of God, by which He from all

---

[1] So the words stood in the original draft, afterwards altered by the Bishops into 'in the elect.'

eternity 'predestinated some to life and reprobated others'—whether positively or negatively it matters not—'to Death[1].' How singular the contrast of that doctrine, in the ruthless logical dogmatism, which it thus by degrees assumed, with the reserved and modest treatment of the subject by St. Paul himself, even in the ninth chapter of the Roman Epistle—where he deals with it only as forced upon him by questions, which should not have been asked, and even then in the last resort by the 'What if' of reverent speculation, rather than by absolute assertion[2]! Like the *Kismet* of Islam, it has an awful and majestic simplicity; in the absolute submission to it of a soul, willing, or believing itself to be willing, to suffer even eternal loss for the glory of God, there is a misguided heroism, greater than the greatest heroism of martyrdom. But its simplicity is no evidence of truth. It marks, as usual in all that deals with the complex problem of humanity, the half-truth, which is proverbially more delusive than sheer falsehood. It is, no doubt, clear that logically it is impossible to reconcile man's freedom with God's Sovereignty. Milton spoke, it may be, out of his own spiritual experience, when, as the type of the fruitless labour of lost spirits, he chose, not the weaving of ropes of sand, but the reasoning high

> Of Providence, foreknowledge, will and fate,
> Fix'd fate, free-will, foreknowledge absolute,
> Which found no end, in wand'ring mazes lost.

[1] The quotations are from the Lambeth Articles of 1595, for which the leaders of the Puritan party at the Hampton Court Conference in 1604 demanded that they should be added to our XXXIX Articles. See Note E. [2] Rom. ix. 14, 19, 22, 23.

But our wisdom is to accept truths which commend themselves as truths, even though to our knowledge they seem irreconcileable. And this absolute Predestination, extinguishing freedom, is emphatically contradicted by the most direct religious consciousness; it is incompatible, even after the subtlest attempts of reasoning, with the confidence in the eternal righteousness, which asks 'Shall not the Judge of all the earth do right?' by discriminating equity to every child of man; even though isolated passages of Holy Scripture be wrested to its service, it is equally at variance with the whole tenour of God's Word, alike in what it says and in what it implies.

No! This Predisposition to good, this prevenient grace, this antagonistic and victorious force against Predisposition to evil, is not absolute. Under it the free Individuality of man has still its scope—its power to accept and use it, and so pass from mere capacity of spiritual life into energy—its power to reject, to misuse, to quench it.

But, though it be not absolute, it is profoundly and universally real. From the effect of the Divine Mediation there is but one class of men absolutely excluded; and that is the class of those who deliberately exercise that mysterious and terrible power of rejection, 'treading under foot' the Divine Mediator Himself, and 'putting Him to an open shame[1].' For all others that Mediation has its beneficent and saving force. Even the world of those who, before or after He came on earth, have not known Him by faith, is

[1] Heb. vi. 6, ix. 29.

known of Him, because for them He came down from
Heaven to be incarnate and to die. 'He gave His
Flesh' (so He Himself said) 'for the life of the world.'
By His Blood (says one Apostle) 'He is the propitiation
for the sins of the whole world.' 'He is' (says another)
'the Saviour of all men,' though 'especially of those
who believe'; for 'God was in Him, reconciling the
world to Himself[1].' Even on that world (so He
Himself teaches) the grace of the Holy Spirit, given
through His Mediation, impresses with effective power
the three great moral realities of 'sin and righteousness
and judgment,' in order through these to lead all to
Him, and to God in Him[2]. Whatever is true and
good in humanity has drawn unconsciously its strength
from that unknown Mediation; whatever there has been
of feeling after God in all the religions, which cover
the whole field of humanity, is being led through it,
as an ignorant worship, to the God unknown, but not
unfelt.

But from the actual Manifestation of the Son of God
in our nature begins the new era of the complete and
living realization of that Mediatorial power by faith,
as a supreme force visibly acting upon humanity—
'drawing all men to Him' as 'lifted up' for all in the
Cross and in the Ascension—'forming Christ' as the
image of God in every redeemed soul, and through
that unity making all one in God. It is into this that,
from the Day of Pentecost onwards, Baptism has been
the entrance; for it is through this that it is a Baptism

---

[1] John vi. 51; 1 John ii. 2; 1 Tim. iv. 10; 2 Cor. v. 19.
[2] John xvi. 8-11.

'into the Name of the Father and of the Son and of the Holy Ghost,' and in that Divine Communion into a 'newness of life.' It is notable that in the early days of Christianity, when such Baptism was mainly Adult Baptism, the conscious assimilation of that new life is spoken of commonly in the New Testament as a 'Resurrection'—a passing (that is) at once from death to life in all its fulness. But when, by a natural and universal inference from what was 'most agreeable with the Institution of Christ,' Baptism became in its regular and normal type a Baptism of Infants, then it was rather recognised (in accordance with that teaching of our Lord Himself, which only the Gospel of St. John records) as a 'regeneration'—an entrance, as in the old birth, not on the fulness, but on the germ and capacity of the new life, and, like that old birth, brought to bear in each nature upon the unfolding consciousness from its very beginning, to inspire and mould for good the whole development of thought, of conscience, of love, of will [1]. In the individual soul this spiritual growth must be, of course, known in itself to God alone, and by human observation inferred but vaguely from its fruits. But in relation to human society as a whole, where the breadth of the scope of observation gives it certainty and solidity, it has plainly shown

---

[1] Comp. Rom. vi. 3-11 and Col. ii. 12, where the whole idea is of a spiritual Resurrection, with the 'laver of Regeneration,' in Tit. iii. 5, and the teaching of our Lord, recorded by St. John at the close of the Apostolic age (John iii. 3-13), with unquestionable reference to the Baptism, which was then as much an established ordinance in the Church as it is at this day.

itself as a regeneration of that whole to a higher moral, intellectual, spiritual life. By no accident the races, on which it laid strong hold, have become the conquering, the ruling, the teaching, races of the world. Imperfect as its power still is, working slowly, as the Divine forces in humanity always do work—resisted, under God's mysterious permission, by sin in the world without, and by sin from within the Church and the individual Christian soul—yet it is unquestionably the one great advancing spiritual power already, and to that advance the promise of a full Catholicity in the future is a strength and an inspiration. And the analogy to the power of Heredity in nature is perfect in this, that each generation, each individual soul, while receiving from that power, is able, by the development of its own fellow-working with it, to contribute in some degree, however slight, to its future strength, or to weaken it by every influence of perversion or failure. To spread the kingdom of Christ is (we say) to 'propagate the Gospel'—to help (that is) to communicate it as a continuous life, from generation to generation, from soul to soul.

True, indeed, it is that this Divine influence, being spiritual, must be spiritually received, and in its reception, therefore, there is brought out with exceptional clearness and vividness, the necessity for the free action of that personal individuality, which has its central stronghold in the spirit. The relation on which it depends, being a living relation of the spirit to a Divine Personality, is felt as having an elasticity and variety of life, which cannot attach to a mere law of development.

So the personal adhesion of faith, promised even for the unconscious infant soul, when entering upon its spiritual inheritance, is in various degrees of growth essential at all times to its realisation; and, when, through lack of this essential condition, there have been spiritual torpor and apparent spiritual death, it is a familiar experience that, with sudden birth or revival of that faith, there come epochs of spiritual resurrection or refreshment; in which it seems as if for the first time the light and grace of the great Mediation were given to the conscious soul; although perhaps it is only in the power to receive and transmit to others that ever-present influence—to absorb and to reflect the rays of the unfailing Sun of Righteousness—that there is real newness. But yet even for this there is some natural analogy. In respect of the law of natural Heredity, the influences, which affect the body, grow upon the individual inevitably and insensibly, except so far as he may indirectly strengthen or weaken them by conscious bodily discipline. But in those, which touch either the mind or the moral being, the individual will to receive or refuse is always more or less plainly energetic, consciously assimilating what seems to it good, modifying or rejecting what seems to it evil; and that energy comes out with a new and exceptional force at great critical periods of the mental and moral history. Even in this, therefore, the law of spiritual inheritance in the Mediatorial kingdom is seen as a supernatural and transcendent exaltation of the natural Law of Heredity. And it is significant that to the Apostolic insight it reveals itself as in its present form coextensive with it in scope, both of space and time. For in space it touches the whole of our humanity; in time it is to endure under its present laws, till the end of this dispensation shall come, when the Mediatorial kingdom, having completed its victorious work in the abolition of sin and death, shall be 'delivered up to God, even the Father, that God may be all in all.' Nay, even beyond that great day, since the seed of newness in Christ is the seed of an eternal life—since the union of Godhead and humanity in Him is an eternal union—we cannot doubt that in some higher and diviner form, the Mediation shall remain, the same and yet not the same, to be the glory of the new heavens and the new earth, to conform the redeemed humanity more and more perfectly to the likeness of Christ, and so in Him to be the life-giving power of that perfect communion with God, which we call heaven. In the Apocalyptic visions of heaven Christ is still all in all, manifested under various aspects as the true Mediator; and the plain unmetaphorical description of what 'we know' of our own mysterious future is that 'we shall see Him as He is,' and by the very sight 'be made like Him' in the perfect image of God.

(V) So it is that our latest Science by its study of human nature and human history should prepare the way for faith in the Divine Revelation and be the schoolmaster to lead us to the Christ. The striking analogy, which it brings out now between the natural and supernatural, goes deeper than that which Bishop Butler so unanswerably showed, as suggested by the

Science of his age, in his great chapter on Mediation [1]. The analogy there drawn out, in reference mainly to the Redemptive aspect of the Divine Mediation, has only to do with the visible working in actual life of the laws of God's moral government of the world. But it is the special lesson of the Science of our day to go back from the present to the germ in the past, of which the present is the development; and, in accordance with this conception, the Mediation of the Lord can now be contemplated, as having relation to the whole growth of our human nature from the beginning, and especially as striving against and overcoming the inherited tendency to sin from the infancy of our race. In that view we trace an analogy both deeper and closer. For those human mediations in action, which Butler brings out as working in the visible world, can only change a man's circumstances absolutely, and cannot touch, except by consent of his own will, his inner nature. But in both the clauses of the text the influence is seen as acting antecedently on the humanity itself, into which each is born, or born again, and determining the conditions, natural or supernatural, under which the individual will is to work together with God. The more searchingly we look into the matter, the more ready are we to accept the analogy suggested in the text, only including in it the present as well as the future. 'As in Adam all die, even so in Christ all' are made alive in conflict with evil now, and 'shall be made alive' in the victory over evil of the hereafter.

[1] Analogy, Part ii. c. 5.

Yes! an analogy deep and close, but not identity, between what we ordinarily know as the Natural and Supernatural. Both, as has been often shown—working out that pregnant hint of the Analogy in which Butler was so infinitely in advance of his age—doubtless form part of one great order, to which the word 'Natural' may be applied, if we accept it (to use his words) in 'its only distinct meaning' of what is 'stated, fixed, settled' under God's Law Eternal, 'our notion' of which 'will be enlarged, in proportion to our greater knowledge of the works of God and the dispensations of His Providence[1].' But such larger unity does not preclude or obliterate distinction between what we usually call the Supernatural in the Mediation of the Lord Jesus Christ, and the Natural Law, exemplified in Natural Heredity. That fundamental distinction is of the essence of true Christianity, as contrasted with theories, which, like the old Gnosticism, take up its language, and strive to weave it into their own systems. Of these theories, even if they deal with Christianity tenderly and reverently, we have still to beware. We look them plainly in the face, and see that, instead of leading to the true Christ, as the Son of God, they seek to include Him in the merely natural order, and refer the spiritual progress of humanity to the working out of that order, to which He holds but a high place, side by side, if on a somewhat higher pedestal, with other great

---

[1] See *Anal.*, Part i, c. i. We may note also the splendid comprehensiveness of Hooker's view of the 'Law eternal,' as in all its parts, natural and supernatural forming but one manifestation of Him who is One. (See *Eccl. Polity*, Book i. cc. ii, iii.)

leaders and teachers of men. Out of that Science we have seen issue an attempt, not unpathetic, to frame a worship of collective humanity, as the true Christ—as the true revelation of God, if not the Godhead itself—in that sense reading even the *Imitatio Christi*, and venturing in its service on adaptation, or rather travesty, of Christian theology, Christian devotion, and even Christian ritual[1].

But that conclusion we cannot accept as scientific, even if the moral witness of faith be put for the moment aside, simply because it is, as has been shown again and again, utterly incapable of accounting for the facts, either of ideal or of actual Christianity; and because the qualified reverence, which it accords to Him, is at once too much and too little—too much when it makes Him, as a mere man, the universal teacher, in respect of humanity and of God, of all races and all ages of the world—too little, when it is compared with what He, so regarded, unquestionably claims for Himself. That worship of Humanity we cannot offer; for, except in the true Son of Man, Humanity is either a mere

[1] 'The basis of Religion is to be found in Humanity, past, present, and to come, conceived as the great Being'; who is (to use Comte's own words) 'the ruling power within the great universal order,' 'the undeniable Providence,' 'the supreme dispenser of our destinies,' 'the common centre of all our affections, our thoughts, and our actions.' 'The singularity of Comte's construction ... is the transfer of the worship and discipline of Catholicism to a system, in which the conception of God is superseded by the abstract idea of Humanity, conceived as a kind of Personality. ... Hitherto Comte's Utopia has pleased the followers of the Catholic, just as little as those of the scientific spirit.' Mr. John Morley on COMTE in *Encycl. Britannica*, vol. vi. p. 237.

abstraction, or in the concrete a many-headed idol, compact of iron and miry clay, of the strength of human goodness, and the weakness and pollution of human evil; and, moreover, is itself but a part of a far greater creation, in the vastness of which it is lost, and before the forces of which its strength is but impotence.

Even for ourselves, I think we can see that the Advent of the Lord Jesus Christ on earth is actually a new departure, absolutely unique in the dispensation of God; that it is the entrance on a higher spiritual order, the introduction into the world of a spiritual power, as yet unapproached and unapproachable. To learn what this supernatural reality is we claim to be led to Christ Himself. We convince ourselves by study of His self-manifestation in deed, in word, in character, that we can have a perfect and absolute faith in Him. We ask Him what His Mediation means. He answers, in words, which never mere man spoke, 'I, if I be lifted up, will draw all men unto Me'; that 'As Thou, Father, art in Me, and I in Thee, they also may be one in Us.' Lifted up He has been, as once on the Cross of Atonement, so now in the ascended Royalty of Heaven. On His promise therefore we now rest. Already we see it fulfilled in true, though imperfect, earnest. If we know too well the fatal power of a spiritual gravitation downwards to evil, yet we see already a great drawing upwards of all humanity—strangely marred and resisted still, but yet through all and in spite of all, proving itself a victorious power, against the dull weight of passive resistance and the struggling antagonism of positive sin. So we can, even through reason, be brought to look on in faith to the perfect fulfilment; and for it, even if, for ourselves and for humanity, we groan under the pain of conscious imperfection and of hope deferred, we can yet be content to wait.

LECTURE III.

EVOLUTION—NATURAL AND SUPERNATURAL.

When the fulness of the time was come, God sent forth His Son . . . that we might receive the adoption of sons.—Gal. iv. 4, 5.

THE Coming of the Son of God is here set forth to us, as fore-ordained indeed in the eternal counsels of the Father, but yet in itself the consummation, up to which all things had been working through the ages, till the fulness of an ordained time had come, and till the human race had been prepared by a Divine education to receive the full sonship of God. Elsewhere that same Coming is viewed, on the other hand, as the beginning of a new Dispensation, having also its time appointed in the counsels of God, through which all things are again to work up to a final consummation at the Second Coming of the Son of God, which shall be for humanity the entrance on a higher perfection of sonship, 'the glorious liberty of the children of God.' Have we for this conception, as for the doctrine of Mediation, any analogy in the reign of Law as discovered by Science, through which the knowledge of that Law becomes 'a schoolmaster to bring us to Christ'?

(I) The very conception itself obviously suggests to us the consideration under this aspect of that great Law of Evolution in its largest sense, which seems to be plainly traced in different forms through all the provinces of being. The phrase, of doubtful accuracy perhaps, in relation both to its history and to its etymology [1], has yet won its way to almost universal acceptance, as expressing the truth that the order of the world is one continuous growth, in which 'the higher and more complex forms of existence follow and depend upon the lower and simpler forms,' and which is 'a gradual transition from the indeterminate to the determinate, from the uniform to the varied,' from 'the homogeneous to the heterogeneous [2].' The process is traced with some distinctness through each distinct province—the world of Inorganic Matter, the world of Life, the world of Humanity; and it is partly seen, partly surmised, that the developments in all are correlated to one another, successively or contemporaneously. The growth of the whole world is thus

[1] 'It was introduced' (says Professor Huxley) 'into biological writing in the former half of the eighteenth century, to denote the mode, in which some of the most eminent physiologists' (Malpighi, Bonnet, Haller) 'conceived that generation of living things took place, in opposition to the hypothesis' (of *Epigenesis*) 'advocated in the previous century by Harvey, which alone would give him a claim to rank among the founders of biological Science.' 'The conclusions,' he adds, 'originally denoted by "Evolution" and "development" were shown to be untenable.' Article EVOLUTION in *Encycl. Brit.* vol. viii. p. 744 (ninth ed.).

[2] See the latter section of the same Article by Mr. James Sully; and Herbert Spencer's Essay on 'The Factors of Organic Evolution' in his collected *Essays* (London, 1891).

embraced in one great universal theory, not indeed attempting to solve the problem of the origin of being, or to ascertain all the causes of variation and development, but contenting itself with bringing out the methods, under which the great whole, in its marvellous variety and complexity, has come to be what it is.

This, neither more nor less, is the Law of Evolution in itself. Before we proceed to examine its bearing upon our subject, there are two considerations which must be kept constantly in view.

(A) The first is this—that the Law, as properly understood, and as in great measure established, does not imply what the name Evolution by its etymology might seem to suggest, and what originally it was in all probability intended to suggest—viz. that all the properties of the higher forms of being were contained implicitly or potentially in the simpler forms which preceded them; as, for example, life and consciousness in inorganic matter, or (as it was once put rhetorically) human genius, and moral aspiration in a 'ring of cosmical vapour.' Under these circumstances it is perhaps unfortunate that the word should still be used. For, as Coleridge remarked long ago, errors in nomenclature are apt to avenge themselves by generating errors of idea; and both the advocates and opponents of Evolution, while rejecting the idea etymologically suggested, seem not unfrequently to glide into lines of argument, which are properly applicable to it. But it is now so firmly established, that we must be content to accept it, only guarding ourselves against the theory, which it was first intended to imply; of which it may be doubted whether it has now any real acceptance, and of which it is certain that we can produce no evidence of certainty or even probability. Nor does it carry with it, as is often assumed, the conviction —closely connected with this, if not substantially identical with it—that the cause, the sole cause, of this process is immanent in the world thus transformed. If it did, it would be, of course, essentially Pantheistic, if not Materialistic; and, as such, absolutely incompatible with any belief in an original Creative Mind, at once immanent and transcendent, guiding and determining throughout the process of development. But this is again a pure assumption, not only without possibility of evidence, but clearly at variance with much of which we are conscious in our own experience of origination and direction, within limits, of growth under natural laws. That assumption has, indeed, been loosely made by some adherents of the theory of Evolution, who seem, strangely enough, to be unable to conceive the reality of a Supreme Will and Purpose, acting through a fixed Order. It is often vaguely acquiesced in by the world at large, because, in their minds, the effect of the idea of a long process of Evolution, with many destructions and many survivals, is to put further away from us the working of Creative Will and Design, and thus, naturally though of course unreasonably, to obscure its reality. It was against this assumption, as virtually materialistic or Pantheistic, that the very soul, not only of Theology, but of Religion, rose up in rightful and indignant antagonism. Unfortunately, though perhaps naturally, it accepted too hastily the confident declaration that it was implied in, or indissolubly connected with, the law of Evolution itself[1].

But the truth of the matter is now emerging plainly enough. 'The doctrine of Evolution' (says Professor Huxley) 'is neither Theistic nor Anti-Theistic[2].' In relation to the idea of Original Creation, he says, 'It seemed to me then,' at the first reading of the Vestiges of Creation' '(as it does now), that Creation in the ordinary sense of the word is perfectly conceivable.' '.... The *a priori* arguments against Theism, and, given a Deity, against the possibility of Creative acts,

---

[1] It is easy to reflect in this matter on the blindness or prejudice of theologians. But we cannot but remember with what flourish of trumpets the Darwinian theory of Evolution was hailed in the Anti-Theistic camp, and pushed rashly to conclusions, which its great author never sanctioned. Even now I read with some surprise in Mr. Sully's part of the Article on Evolution to which reference has been made, the following passage, 'It is clear that the doctrine of Evolution is directly antagonistic to that of Creation'; while yet a few lines below the author declines to dwell on the question, whether 'the doctrine of Evolution, in its most extended and elaborate form, absolutely excludes the idea of Creative activity' (*Encycl. Brit.* vol. viii. p. 752.

[2] 'It has' (he adds) 'no more to do with Theism than the First Book of Euclid has.' ... 'The doctrine of Evolution does not even come in contact with Theism, considered as a scientific doctrine. That with which it does collide, and with which it is irreconcileable, is the conception of Creation, which theological speculators have based on the history narrated in the opening of the book of Genesis.' He goes on to note that 'the Evolution of a chicken from a microscopic cellular germ to its full size and complication of structure undoubtedly goes on every day. Therefore' (he adds) 'to borrow an argument from Butler, this must be consistent with the Attributes of the Deity, if such a Being exists; and if so, the Evolution of the Universe, which is neither more nor less explicable than that of a chicken, must also be consistent with these Attributes.'

appeared to me devoid of reasonable foundation.' His conclusion is that in 'Theological Science, as a matter of fact, physical Science has created no religious difficulties.' In relation to the process of development (he adds) 'the theological equivalent of the scientific conception of Order is Providence'; and Theology can accept the statement, so far as it acknowledges that its belief in a Divine Providence presupposes and accounts for Laws of Order, and that by further discoveries of them it is untouched in its essence, although it may be modified in its conception of method. But it must be added that it is more than an equivalent; for it implies the conviction that the Order itself is in the true sense of the word a 'Law'—an expression (that is) of a Supreme Will acting with foresight and moral purpose—and that through this ordained Order the Will that framed it is still unceasingly an energetic and unfettered cause. This conviction is one, which satisfies not only the intellect but the conscience and the heart; and the true conception of it must prevent our accepting the conclusion that 'the doctrine of Determinism follows' from it, 'as surely as from the universality of natural causation, assumed by the men of Science [1].'

But even this declaration of neutrality in the great conflict is not the whole truth. It was long ago noticed [2] that the language of the *Origin of Species*, being always plain and straightforward, is constantly Teleological and often virtually Theistic. And now

[1] See *Life of Darwin*, vol. ii. pp. 187, 203.
[2] By the Duke of Argyle in the *Problems of Faith*, p. 41.

many of the most thoughtful and philosophical exponents of the doctrine of Evolution declare with one voice that it places on a wider and therefore firmer basis the doctrine of Teleology—the belief (that is) in a Design and Purpose, which the whole order of the universe subserves, and is intended to subserve. It has been said by the same acute and outspoken critic, that while 'the doctrine of Evolution is the most formidable opponent of the commoner and cruder forms of Teleology, yet perhaps the most remarkable service to the philosophy of Biology rendered by Mr. Darwin is the reconciliation of Teleology with Morphology'—the idea of Design (that is) with the discovery of fixed Laws of Order—'and the explanation of the facts of both.' 'The wider Teleology is ... actually based on the fundamental proposition of Evolution [1].' Darwin himself, although the sense of the mystery of the beginning of things, and the great stumbling block of the existence of evil in suffering and sin, made his mind gravitate, or perhaps oscillate, in the direction of Agnosticism, felt (as he says) ' the immense difficulty or rather impossibility of

---

[1] See *Darwin's Life*, vol. ii. p. 201. Professor Huxley adds, ' The Teleological and Mechanical conceptions of Nature are not, necessarily, mutually exclusive. On the contrary, the more purely a mechanist the speculator is, the more firmly must he assume a primordial molecular arrangement, of which all the phenomena of the universe are the consequence, and the more completely is he at the mercy of the Teleologist, who can always defy him to disprove that this primordial arrangement was not intended to evolve the phenomena of the Universe.' The statement is obviously true so far as it goes; although Christian faith could not accept it as an adequate statement of the whole truth, which must include sustaining and directing Providence, as well as original Creation.

conceiving this great and wonderful universe, including man with his capacity of looking far backwards, and forwards into futurity, as the result of blind chance or necessity. When thus reflecting I feel compelled to look to a First Cause having an intelligent mind in some degree analogous to that of man; and I deserve to be called a Theist[1].' Not only, as we have said, is his language, in respect to that phase of the theory of Evolution, which he has made his own, plainly Teleological, but the very phrase 'Natural Selection'—suggested, of course, by the experiments made by himself with deliberate purpose, for selection under natural law—in itself (as Mr. Herbert Spencer notes[2]) 'personalizes the cause' of Evolution.

Professor Weismann, who now occupies a foremost place among the students and teachers of Evolution, speaks of 'the immanent Teleology of a Universe as of a machine[3],' because, as he clearly sees, 'the assumption

[1] *Darwin's Life*, vol. i. pp. 312, 313.
[2] See his 'Essay on the Factors of Organic Evolution.' It is customary to regard the phrase as unfortunate; and Darwin himself points out defects in the Analogy between 'Natural' and 'artificial selection,' apologizing for 'speaking of Natural Selection as an intelligent power' and 'personifying Nature.' But the fact remains that it was his own artificial selection, which suggested to him the variability of species, and that, moreover, human language is such that it is hardly possible to avoid using terms which suggest a directing mind. In the Essay above referred to the author laments that even his own favourite phrase 'the survival of the fittest' 'calls up an anthropocentric idea.'
[3] The comparison shows that the word 'immanent' must be taken to mean inherent or essential. For the maker is distinct from the machine. Certainly Teleology must imply transcendence, as well as immanence, in the First Cause.

III.] *Change of View in Science and Theology.*

of an eternal matter with its eternal laws by no means satisfies our intellectual need for causality'—or (as he elsewhere calls it) 'the craving of the human mind for a spiritual First Cause.' 'We require beyond everything an explanation of the fact, that relationships everywhere exist between the parts of the Universe'; and, to account for this, he declares that 'behind the co-operating forces of Nature, which aim at a purpose, we must admit a Cause ... inconceivable in its nature, of which we can say only one thing with certainty, viz. that it must be Teleological.' 'By the side of mere mechanism, it is impossible not to acknowledge a Teleological principle.' The one question is, How does it act? 'Does it interfere with the mechanism, or is it behind as the Final Cause of the Mechanism?' 'If we conceive a Divine Universal Power exercising volition, as the ultimate basis of matter and of the natural laws resident therein, we reconcile the apparent contradiction between the mechanical conception' (of the Universe) 'and Teleology [1].'

This course of thought on the Scientific side of the question has naturally been met by a like approximation towards reconciliation from the side of Theology. It may, in view of some well-known utterances on the subject, be doubted whether declaration of war was not made first from the camp of Evolution. Now, however, theologians have come to see that, raised only by a noisy minority, it had been rashly accepted as coming from the true leaders, and from the whole body of

---

[1] Weismann's *Studies in the Theory of Descent* (English translation, 1882), vol. ii. pp. 710–713.

their followers. Naturally they had at first come to the consideration of the theory not without prejudice; for if prejudice really implies (as the word should imply) the result of a previous rational judgment, it may well exist in different degrees in all thoughtful minds, when an entirely new theory is presented to them. If they have on other grounds strongly convinced themselves of a fundamental principle, with which the new theory seems to be inconsistent, they cannot but subject to a keen and even suspicious scrutiny the arguments, by which that theory is supported. Thus the Theologian, who, from a wholly different point of view, mainly moral and spiritual, had grasped, as a part of his very being, the faith in a living God, Creator of heaven and earth and Father of man, could not possibly regard without suspicion a line of thought, which through many of its prominent advocates claimed to set that faith aside. Now that this claim is seen to be plainly untenable, and, as such, is disavowed in the name of Science, Theology naturally lays aside this rightful prejudice; it is able to consider dispassionately all which the theory of Evolution teaches, either with certainty or by probable inference; it is not surprised to find that it harmonizes marvellously with the great fundamental truth, to which it was once set in deliberate antagonism.

But this course of thought on the whole subject is singularly interesting and instructive. We cannot (be it remarked in passing) fail to trace in it the natural progress of human speculation, as it was shown long ago in the old Greek philosophy, when from the primordial material elements of the Ionic School, it passed, through the belief in Number—that is, proportion and combination—of the Pythagoreans, to the recognition by Anaxagoras of the 'Mind which came and set all things in order.' For, after all ingenious attempts to wed the belief in Teleology with Pantheism—the belief in an order, designed to an appointed end, with the conception, whatever this may mean, of 'a Soul of the Universe, becoming in humanity conscious of itself,'—the fact remains, and the broad common-sense of humanity will recognise it, that the discovery in the world of a Design, whether of usefulness or of beauty, clearly indicates the existence of the Laws of Nature in idea before their embodiment in fact, and so connects itself with Theism and Theism alone. 'Even in the view of Science' (says Sir James Paget) 'the first Essence may have been a Being, willing and knowing, the prime Source of all the forces whose operation we see.' But in view of the wonders of Design (he adds) : 'I cannot imagine anything before natural force except Supernatural Will ; and a belief of this kind is held by untutored minds as if it were instinctive knowledge [1].'

If, therefore, it be true that the Law of Evolution strengthens, because it widens, the idea of Teleology, it is so far a witness to a Living God—not like the God of the older Deism, who simply sets the machine of the Universe in motion and leaves it to work by

---

[1] See the *Hunterian Oration* of 1877. The distinguished author's conclusion is, 'Time—or, if not time, Eternity—will prove that Science and Christian Theology are but two sides of truth, and that both sides are as yet known only in part.'

itself, but One, who in the language of Holy Scripture is not only 'above all,' but 'through all and in all.'

It will not be the first time in the history of human thought that discoveries of Law, which at first sight appeared to shake or dim our faith in God, have been found only to enlarge our conceptions of the wonder of His Creative and Sustaining Work. Perhaps, as when, without increase of the object-glass and so of the entering light, we increase the magnifying power of a telescope, the effect is to diminish the brilliance at each point in the larger field, and for a time the clearness of our vision in it; but the mental eye soon accustoms itself to the changed conditions, so as under these to see deeper into the heart of things, and discover more of their wondrous order. The Teleology of Paley—a masterpiece in itself, even anticipating (as has been pointed out by Professor Huxley[1]) some conception of Evolution—may have been made partly obsolete by that increase of our knowledge of the unity and development of the whole, which forbids us to consider any one thing alone, and to examine it merely as it is, without thought of how it came to be what it is. But the Teleology, to which Evolution bears witness, if less luminously direct and obvious in its vision of the Hand of God—if troubled by the sense of apparent waste in Nature, and the still more painful

---

[1] 'The acute champion, Paley, saw no difficulty in admitting that the production of things may be the result of mechanical arrangements made beforehand, and kept in action by a power in the centre; that is to say, he proleptically accepted the modern doctrine of Evolution.' (See *Darwin's Life*, vol. ii. p. 202.)

sense of suffering and death—is clearly grander, subtler, deeper, and so far a worthier thought of the Infinite Wisdom and Power, as far above the designing and manufacturing art of man, as the heavens are higher than the earth.

(B) The second point to be observed—of considerable, although perhaps inferior, importance—is that the Law of Evolution is not to be identified, as in common usage it often seems to be identified, with the Darwinian theory; which properly touches it only in the field of Organic Life, and which, by the testimony of its great author and his wisest followers, does not claim to give even in that field an exhaustive description of the whole cause of Variation and Development. It is true, indeed, that the 'Origin of Species' first gave basis and reality to theories of Evolution, which had previously been floating and shadowy, and so was, as really as Newton's *Principia*, an Epoch-making book in the history of human thought [1]. Few men, I suppose,

---

[1] The effect of its appearance is described most graphically in the chapter (vol. ii. pp. 179-204) contributed to the *Life of Darwin* by Professor Huxley, from which several quotations have been made. 'The publication of the Darwin and Wallace papers in 1858, and still more that of the "Origin" in 1859, had the effect of the flash of light, which to a man, who has lost himself on a dark night, suddenly reveals a road, which, whether it takes him straight home or not, certainly goes his way.' Of course, he cannot quite refrain from some sarcastic reflections on the opposition of theologians to a theory, which, it must be remembered, was hailed, although not by its author, as anti-Theistic; but he candidly acknowledges that 'if a General Council of the Church Scientific had been held at the time, we, as adherents of Darwinism, should have been condemned by an overwhelming majority'; and speaks of 'that complete *volte-face* of the whole

now doubt that the mutability of allied species, once considered as fixed and unchangeable, has been substantially proved; that the idea of the derivation of the whole Organic World from some few simple germs of life has gained at least considerable probability; that a real analogy has been established between the actual growth of the individual being from the embryonic cell or cells, and the supposed growth of the whole sum of Organic beings from these original germs. No one, again, seriously doubts that in this development the process, which Darwin termed 'Natural Selection,' is one potent factor. The struggle for existence, and the survival of those who are fittest from various causes to meet that struggle, are (I suppose) accepted as facts, established by patient and laborious induction, and shown to exercise an actual and very considerable influence over the differentiation of species. But whether they are to be regarded as constituting the sole influence, because in themselves sufficient to account for all the facts of the case—whether the analogy already referred to does not suggest some inherent power of differentiation, or what Darwin himself called 'a mysterious innate tendency to perfectibility,' correlative to and co-operating with that Darwinian process, which lays chief stress on the effect of the environment of circumstance and contact with other existences—is another question [1].

Scientific world, which must seem so surprising to the present generation.' See also Mr. Herbert Spencer's *Essays*, vol. i. pp. 393–396.

[1] 'How far "Natural Selection" suffices for the production of species remains to be seen. Few can doubt that if not the whole cause, it is an important factor in that operation. . . . But the causes and con-

Clearly the Darwinian theory taken alone is professedly imperfect; for it does not profess to account, first, for the origin of Organic Life, next, for the 'variations,' which gave the start of advantage in the great struggle, or lastly, for the adaptation of the outward forces and circumstances to the capacities of the inner life, which produces the 'fitness' designated as the cause of survival. Its imperfection in these respects was acknowledged with his usual candour by its thoughtful originator; and (so far as any one not an expert may venture to pronounce an opinion) it appears to be now more and more distinctly recognised by philosophical thinkers, as the natural enthusiasm, excited by the enunciation and victorious establishment of the theory, gives way to a more thoughtful estimate of its true significance. It is seen clearly that the causes of the differentiation of species may be a 'tendency to vary' in an organism 'in virtue of its molecular structure, indefinite or limited to certain directions by intrinsic conditions,' or 'a variation brought about by the influence of conditions external to it, either indefinite or defined by intrinsic

ditions of variation have yet to be explored; and the importance of Natural Selection will not be impaired, even if further enquiries should prove that variability is definite, and is determined in certain directions rather than others by conditions inherent in that which varies.' (Huxley on EVOLUTION, *Encycl. Brit.*, vol. viii. p. 751.) So Mr. Herbert Spencer says (*Essays*, vol. i. p. 397): 'Recognising in full this process brought into clear view by Mr. Darwin, and traced out by him with so much care and skill, can we conclude that, taken alone, it accounts for Organic Evolution? Has the natural selection of favourable variations been the sole factor? On critically examining the evidence, we shall find reason to think that it by no means explains all that has to be explained.'

limitation'; or a 'combination of both extrinsic and intrinsic conditions.' It is, indeed, held that 'evidence to justify the positive adoption of any one of these views can hardly be said to exist.' Yet the present tendency of opinion appears to incline towards the co-existence of some internal and external influences [1]; and it may be remarked that this view harmonizes best with the belief in one Supreme Purpose, ruling over and combining both. But on this matter we wait calmly for further thought and investigation. It is with the doctrine of Evolution in general that we are concerned, and the decision of the place occupied in it by Darwinism, properly so called, is not to us of a primary concern.

(II) Let us then see, somewhat more in detail, how this general process of Evolution presents itself, partly to the observation, partly to the speculation, of Science in relation to our own world.

We may, indeed, not unreasonably believe that in the vaster Universe itself, it works under the same general Laws—in developments, however, of which we have indeed some indications, but which are in general unknown to us, and cannot without rashness be assumed to be absolutely identical with those of our own world. But it will be enough to consider that world alone, of

---

[1] See Professor Huxley's article on BIOLOGY in the *Encycl. Britannica*, vol. iii. p. 690; and compare Mr. Herbert Spencer ' On the Factors of Organic Evolution ' in his *Essays*, vol. i. pp. 389-465, ed. of 1891; criticised from a Darwinian point of view in Wallace's *Darwinism*, c. xiv. See also Mr. Aubrey Moore's most interesting Essays on ' Darwinism and the Christian Faith,' in his *Science and the Faith*, especially pp. 162-165.

which we do know much, and can safely infer more, in its three great provinces of being—the world of Inorganic Matter, the world of Life, the world of Humanity.

Let me here say at once that I speak of those Provinces of Being as distinct, simply because to our present knowledge they show themselves as distinct. Whatever speculation, more or less imaginative, may do to bridge over in idea the divisions between them, yet the whole evidence is on all hands allowed to be distinctly against the derivation of Organic Life from Inorganic Force; and I cannot but contend that it is at least equally strong against the derivation of Humanity from the merely animal being. But I must add that, should these breaks ever be filled up to human knowledge, so that we may trace—what now to us is a complete mystery—the process of transition from one to another, I fail to see how it ought to shake our faith in the dependence of this unbroken Evolution on the Will and Purpose of God, although it might possibly make some evidences of it less striking to the ordinary mind. If a current of Electricity be passed through a wire, having in it breaks, at each of which a pinch of gunpowder is placed, then the ignition of that gunpowder at each break is a simple and visible evidence of the passage of the current. If those breaks are made up, so that the wire becomes continuous, the passage of the current through it will lose these visible manifestations of its presence; but it will not be the less real in itself, and its reality can be ascertained by less obvious, but perhaps more instructive, tests. So it may be true that those breaks in our conception of the Order of Creation serve to bring home vividly to the mind the irresistible inference of the action of a Supreme Creative Will, and the fulfilment of a Supreme Purpose; but the real fundamental grounds of belief in that truth are independent of their existence, and would be absolutely unshaken, if they ceased to exist for us.

Now in respect of the Inorganic world of Matter and Force, we may, I suppose, consider some form of the Nebular hypothesis as describing what is now generally supposed to be the process of Evolution. Out of a homogeneous indeterminate form of what we call nebulous matter—such as that which our Astronomy plainly discerns as existing now in the field of the heavens, and even within the limits of our Solar System—endowed, we know not how, with the simplest form of rotatory motion, and acted upon by the forces of light and heat—it bids us conceive that by gradual differentiation into heterogeneous conditions, the air, the earth with its plains and mountains and rivers, the sea with its fixed currents and its intermittent tides, grew out into the marvellous variety and beauty of inanimate Nature, and into fitness to sustain Organic Life [1]. We can see and turn over in our geological strata the successive leaves of this history of Evolution; we can trace there the action of fire, of water, of ice, of atmospheric influences, of chemical and electrical agencies; we can with much probability construct

[1] See Mr. Herbert Spencer's Essay on 'The Nebular Hypothesis' (*Essays*, vol. i. pp. 108-181).

a record of the past ages, if we are allowed to assume—by an assumption, of course, strictly unproved[1]—that the existing physical forces, and they alone, wrought through those ages with much the same power which they manifest now.

But the inner meaning of this historic record Physical Science unaided cannot read; the moulding and directing Force under which all grew from a Chaos into a Kosmos, it cannot adequately discern or account for. To the inevitable enquiry, 'How under these purely physical influences did all grow, as clearly it has grown, into a great whole of Order and Beauty?' there is no real and substantial answer in vague suggestions of mysterious 'potentialities of matter,' 'essential laws of polarity of molecules and molecular structure,' 'operations of immanent properties,' and the like, which are hardly susceptible of any definite meaning in themselves, and which utterly fail to explain the visible unity of order, and the irresistible inference of Design. It would surely be as reasonable to account for the existence and working of a steam engine, simply by the properties of iron and the expansive force of steam, ignoring the directing mind, which through these worked out its preconceived end, and the superintendence, which continually guides and controls it. Without Design all would be (as has been

[1] At the recent meeting of the British Association at Edinburgh, much interesting reference was made, in the President's Address and elsewhere, to the conflict as to the duration which must be assigned to the prehistoric ages, between the Geologists, making this assumption, on the one hand, and the Physicists, bringing in the correction of other considerations, on the other.

said by Von Hartmann) 'only a weak chaos of obstinate and capricious forces.' To refer all to 'Laws of Nature' gives a rational account of Causation, only if we take them in the true sense of the word to be really 'laws'— the expressions (that is) of a Supreme Will and Purpose, belonging to an Eternal Mind. Otherwise the study of them reveals nothing but a great order of relation and instrumentality; it yields no satisfaction whatever to the enquiry into the Cause underlying them, although perhaps it suggests that, as created mind discerns this Order, and within limits uses it for its own purposes, it is but reasonable to infer that it must be Supreme Mind, which ordains it and works out Purpose through it. After all we must come back to discern behind these Laws a 'Cause of which' (to use the words quoted above) 'we know but one thing with certainty that it is Teleological'; and to me such a Teleological Cause as this simply means a Supreme Mind.

But at some stage of this growth, there comes in the first germ of Organic Life, when the physical condition of the Inorganic world is such as to give it scope and opportunity. It is an established fact, that now, neither by natural process, nor by art of man, is it producible out of inanimate Matter and the Forces which pervade it. What has been called, somewhat strangely, *Biogenesis*[1] —the invariable production of life out of life alone— is accepted as an incontrovertible law, even by those whose inclination would lead them to desire and to expect an opposite opinion. If the past is, as usual,

---

[1] The name is now too generally established to admit of alteration; but surely it ought to be *Zoogenesis*.

to be judged of by the present, the inference must be, that the force of Life is different in kind from the purely physical forces, and that, when it came into this world, it appeared as a new power—adapting itself to the stage already reached in the growth of the Inorganic World, able to use its forces, and to assimilate its substance, but not derived from them, or capable of resolution into them. It is possible, of course, to suppose that what we discern as an universal law now, did not hold then; but to assume this without a shred of evidence is to contradict the invariable postulate of scientific investigation. Is it reasonable through a supposed 'intellectual necessity' to 'cross the boundary of experimental evidence, and discern in matter the promise and potency of life[1]?' The introduction of life into the great Order of the World may be reasonably referred to 'natural forces'—forces (that is) belonging to the system of Nature as a whole,—but this does not imply that they were the forces previously existing on the earth. It is clearly a part of the general process of Evolution, but we must remember the caution against concluding that what is found in its later conditions was necessarily existent implicitly in the earlier. However it came into our world—and Science through the mouth of its greatest leaders can only form suppositions on this matter, of which it confesses that they 'may seem wild and visionary[2]'—it is the germ of a new order

---

[1] Professor Tyndall's Belfast Address.

[2] See Sir W. Thomson's (Lord Kelvin's) Presidential Address at Edinburgh in 1871; where he speculates as to the possibility of 'seed-bearing meteoric stones' careering through space from other worlds,

of things—a new start (as it appears to us) in the process of development.

But from this point the Evolution theory seems to unfold to us with high probability a process of gradual growth and differentiation into many forms. Looking first to fact, in the actual growth of the individual Organic being, it starts from the germ, defined as 'matter potentially alive and having within itself the tendency to assume a definite living form.' What is that germ? Analysis of it only shows us, in all known instances, the material elements of 'Carbon, hydrogen, oxygen, and nitrogen, united in the ill-defined compound called *protein*.' But there is in it something beyond the test of this analysis, which makes it living matter. By that living force, in all animals and plants above the lowest, the original cell is divided, and becomes an aggregate of cells; in sexual propagation the sperm and germ cells are fused together. Gradually out of what seems in all cases the same original protein, there is a mysterious differentiation into an all but infinite diversity of beings, although all seem to pass through the same process, and to assimilate from without the same food.

<small>and of ' one such falling on the earth,' which ' might, by what we blindly call natural causes, lead to its becoming covered with vegetation.' ' The hypothesis' (he adds) 'may seem wild and visionary : all I maintain is, that it is not unscientific.' Whatever be the value of the hypothesis, which seems incapable either of proof or disproof, its distinguished author rightly sees that it is consistent with the 'overwhelmingly strong proofs of intelligent and benevolent Design all around us . . . showing to us through Nature the influence of a free will, and teaching us that all living beings depend on one everlasting Creator and Ruler.'</small>

Starting from this observation of actual fact in the development of the individual being, the Evolution Theory forms the idea of a substantial analogy in the development of the sum of all living beings from some original germ or germs of Organic Life. The most direct suggestion of the idea is probably due to 'the observation of the existence of an analogy between the series of gradations presented by the species, which compose any great group of animals and plants, and the series of embryonic conditions of the highest,' that is the most complex, 'members of each group.' But, as we are told on the best authority, 'the modern scientific form of the doctrine can be traced historically to the influence of several converging lines of philosophical speculation and of physical observation'—including the observation of a general unity of structure in each group, which shows many gradations of complexity, and of organs rudimentary and apparently useless in our species of the group, which are fully developed and have definite functions in another, and also of the effects of varying external conditions in modifying living organisms, and of the facts of geographical distribution and geological succession of life [1]. The great impulse, which gave fresh life and reality to the conclusions thus gradually forming themselves—the electric spark, which brought all these elements into combination—was the discovery by Darwin, and all but simultaneously by Wallace, of the power of 'Natural Selection' in the origination of

[1] In the article on Evolution, from which I quote, Professor Huxley enumerates eight of these converging lines of speculation. (*Encycl. Brit.* vol. viii. p. 747.)

species. From this new start the Evolution Theory has taken firm hold of the whole mind of Physiological Speculation: in many forms and by many hands—after some modifications already, with more showing themselves at no distant future [1]—it is being wrought out.

From the primordial germ of Organic Life, the first differentiation is of vegetable and animal life, almost undistinguishable in their simplest and crudest forms, gradually becoming widely distinguished—mainly perhaps by the development in the animal life of what we call Instinct, which is a foreshadowing of personality, from the most rudimentary impulses of conscious life up to some resemblance to our own intellectual and moral qualities. Then in each section a continual differentiation into genera, species, varieties, individuals—these in their later developments becoming less susceptible of change, and within the range of historical investigation all but absolutely fixed, and incapable of blending with one another. The comparison suggested is of a great tree of Organic Life, having 'a common root, whence two main trunks, one representing the vegetable and one the animal world, spring; and, each dividing into a few main branches, these subdivide into multitudes of branchlets, and these into smaller groups of twigs.'

The idea is clearly one of grandeur and beauty, and

---

[1] I observe, for instance, that Professor Weismann has doubts as to the single homogeneous root of Organic Life, and inclines to think that 'numerous Organisms first arose' simultaneously, and 'spontaneously' —that is, of course, without derivation from one another.

it at least accounts with probability for large numbers of facts otherwise unaccountable. The evidence for it is, and must be, infinitely less clear and certain, than that of the Evolution of the individual being. There are gaps in it not yet filled up; 'missing links' not yet forged in the chain; contradictions not yet removed. From these may probably result modifications of some portions of the theory. But it has advanced and is advancing to completeness. Whatever corrections or enlargements it may receive, it is universally accepted as containing substantial truth.

But here even more clearly than in the Inorganic World, we see that it is a Theory of Method and Order, not of Cause. Of the origin of Life it professes not to have the slightest knowledge; of the character of the indwelling force, which out of the one original cell developes the marvellous diversity of structure in the individual beings, and of the variations, which gave a start to the process of Natural Selection in the differentiation of species, it can tell us nothing; of the marvellous adaptation of the external conditions of the Inorganic World to the growth and differentiation of Organic Life it gives no account; the unity of all this infinite variety of development in one great Order having a continual progress towards a higher perfection, it sees clearly, but it cannot find its Cause. No wonder that, as we have seen, those who study it most deeply and philosophically are driven to go behind it in the search after the true Cause, and that it sends them to that search with an irresistible Teleological conviction of an overruling Design and Purpose. Is there, after all, a fundamental incompatibility between it and that older theory, which Sir Richard Owen worked out with so much skill and force, of a general archetypal idea of structure pervading each great family of organic being, and varied in each species and variety in minute and subtle gradations, so that each can discharge its special function [1]? For clearly the development under fixed laws and gradual process of the Organic World, no more prevents the original Creative and directive Idea from being the true Cause of all, than the passing of the individual being through all the stages of embryonic existence from the simple cell makes it less the creature of the Supreme Hand. That the Archetypal Idea of the Creative Mind may fulfil itself equally, whether it act directly or through intermediate gradations, we can see clearly, not only by abstract theory, but by experience of our own 'creations.'

This province of Being has been from old time the chosen field of Natural Theology; partly, because it manifests overruling Design in a subtler and more striking perfection, under the form of what, using human analogy, men call instinctively contrivance [2],

[1] Owen on the 'Nature of Limbs' (1849).

[2] It is strange that even John Stuart Mill should fall into the popular fallacy of assuming that this idea of Contrivance is unworthily anthropomorphic, because Contrivance argues defect of power in the Contriver. 'What is meant' (he says) 'by Design? Contrivance; the adaptation of means to an end. But the necessity of contrivance is a consequence of the limitation of power.' ('Essay on Theism,' part ii.) A necessity imposed from without would, of course, be so. But we are familiar every day in our own experience of necessity imposed from within, by resolution to work for a special purpose and through special instrumentality. There is sounder philosophy in

which is simply the action of Mind working under fixed laws for a foreseen purpose; partly because, when we enter upon the region of sentient life, we at once infer from our own higher humanity, and believe that we have strong confirmation of that inference in the observation of Nature as a whole, that this Design is pervaded by a care for these sentient creatures, and such care is an inseparable attribute of Personality. On both sides it is true, that the conclusions of universal human instinct are troubled under the light of fuller knowledge by thoughts of hesitation and perplexity—in the apparent waste of Nature, and the presence in it of mutual conflict and of pain. But out of these emerges the final thought, correcting and extending and yet establishing the first—in part discovering, especially through the great conception of Evolution, that what seemed to us defects and offences really subserve a transcendent Purpose—in part, while we recognise speculative and moral difficulties, yet seeing that they are insufficient to set aside the original conception—in part, if on other grounds we have a strong faith in God, inclining to refer them to the imperfection of our knowledge and so, in the strict sense of the phrase, to accept them as 'trials of faith.' If some of the simpler and cruder arguments of the old Natural Theology are obsolete, yet in the study of the Organic sphere of life this 'Science of God' lives in grander, subtler, and therefore nobler form.

Hooker's conception of 'the Law Eternal which God has set Himself to work all things by'—without which, indeed, no fellow-working of His creatures would be possible.

Lastly, from this sphere of Organic Life, we pass into the higher sphere of Humanity. I make no apology (as I have already said) for treating it as distinct; for historically and actually it is distinct. We know, of course, that in respect of man's bodily organisation, Science has taught us to trace, not indeed identity, but through wonderful gradations an intimate connection, with lower orders of animal being[1]. We have learnt, even beyond this, to see in what we roughly call 'animal instinct' similarities, more or less strong, within the sphere of sensation, to human reason and affection, and even to the moral sense of relation and resulting duty; we are now discovering not indistinct traces of some kind of language, audible or otherwise, as a means of communication of these developments of instinct; we see some dawning in rudimentary form even of that willing self-sacrifice for the weak, fighting against the selfish struggle for existence, which we emphatically call 'humanity.' But, interesting as these similarities are—showing, indeed, that the properly human faculties follow those (so to speak) naturally, in the gradual progress towards perfection,—yet there is an unmistakeable line of

---

[1] See Wallace's *Darwinism*, c. xv. pp. 450-459, and its reference to St. George Mivart's *Man and Apes*. He quotes an instructive remark of Professor Huxley: 'In conclusion, I may say, that the fossil remains of man hitherto discovered do not seem to me to take us appreciably nearer to that lower pithecoid form, by the modification of which he has probably become what he is'; and adds significantly, 'that it is an unsolved problem why no traces of the long line of man's ancestors, back to the remote period when he first branched off from the pithecoid type, have been discovered.'

demarcation still between them and the highest instinct; which can be no more really identified with them than the internal power of structure in crystallisation with the power of true growth in Organic Life[1]. 'Beasts' (said our first great Anglican theologian more than three hundred years ago) 'are in sensible capacity as ripe as men themselves, perhaps more ripe. But the soul of man hath a further ability, whereof is in them no show at all, an ability of reaching higher than to sensible things[2].' That old witness is true. Man has the power of 'seeing the invisible'—in understanding and imagination, of conceiving abstract ideas; in moral sense, of recognising abstract principles of right, and hearing an inner voice which ear never heard; in will, of curbing, in accordance with these, the physical forces of appetite and passion, and the motives of hope and fear; in heart, of rising above sensual or even personal affection to the universal and spiritual principle of love; in spirit, as all history past and present testifies, of feeling after and finding an Invisible God, unknown perhaps, yet known to be. With this higher capacity are bound up the wonderful faculty of true language, which is its outward expression, and the capacity of education of the individual and in the race that unlimited progress, which we call Civilisation—

[1] It is not, I trust, presumptuous to note in relation to Darwin's speculations on this subject, that his Psychology is hardly so strong as his Physiology. So far as I can see, the great fundamental distinction is ignored, between the power in man of abstract idea, moral and intellectual, and the lower power of perception and deduction within the realm of sense.

[2] Hooker's *Eccl. Pol.* i. c. vi. sections 2, 3.

in mastery over Nature, rule over the lower orders of animal being, discovery of the Laws of the Universe, realization of the social, political, moral ties which bind humanity together, advance through thought and faith to a spiritual knowledge of God.

There this characteristic human capacity is, obviously, a new and distinct capacity; even the semblances of it in brute instinct are largely developed by its reflex influence through what we call domestication. The history of the world proves its absolute distinctness. Whatever may be guessed or inferred as to physical and psychical ancestry, the spiritual faculty can find no progenitor, and all efforts to trace it back are rejected by the common-sense of human consciousness. Between the highest order of the brute creation and the lowest race of man—like those savages of Tierra del Fuego, whom Darwin at one time placed hopelessly low in the scale, and yet recognised frankly, not without astonishment, as capable of being civilized by spiritual influence[1],—there is clearly a great gulf fixed. Its reality has been acknowledged by profound believers in Evolution ; by one at least of the very

[1] 'Mr. Darwin' (says Admiral Sir James Sulivan) 'had often expressed to me his conviction that it was utterly useless to send missionaries to such a set of savages as the Fuegians, probably the very lowest of the human race. I had always replied that I did not believe any human beings existed too low to comprehend the simple message of the Gospel of Christ. After many years he wrote to me that the recent account of the mission showed that he had been wrong and I right... and he requested me to forward to the Society an enclosed cheque for £5, as a testimony of his interest in their good work.' This subscription he seems to have continued annually till his death. (*Darwin's Life*, vol. iii. pp. 127, 128.)

highest authorities in the Evolutionist School, who rejoices in it as a 'relief from a crushing mental burden' —a 'hopeless and soul-deadening belief[1].' To ordinary minds it seems as real, if not as wide, a gulf as that which separates the living from the lifeless realm. We may refer it to what origin we will; talk vaguely of 'higher potentialities' in matter and animal life, draw analogies (as, for example, between the Social Instincts of Animals and the commanding moral Sense in Man) which indicate likeness, and vainly attempt from them to prove essential identity; or leave it alone as a matter to us mysterious, in hope that some day it may cease to be 'unknown and unknowable.' Or we may, on the other hand, accept the doctrine, in which the simplest Christianity, even the simplest Theism, finds at least a simple and intelligible account for it in Divine Will and Purpose, which, though man's frame be allied to the very 'dust of the earth,' yet gave him 'the image of God,' and with it the lordship over creation, and made all lower things work together for his progress to perfection. But in any case it seems clear that the distinction is a great unmistakeable reality, and that,

[1] See Wallace's *Darwinism*, c. xv. (Macmillan, 1890). The whole chapter is worthy of the most careful study. His conclusion is this: 'We thus find that the Darwinian theory, even when carried out to its extreme logical conclusion, not only does not oppose, but lends a decided support to, a belief in the spiritual nature of man. It shows us how man's body may have been developed from that of a lower animal form under the Law of Natural Selection; but it also teaches us that we possess intellectual and moral faculties, which could not have been so developed, but must have had another origin: and for this origin we can only find an adequate cause in the unseen Universe of Spirit.'

when we enter the sphere of humanity, we enter an altogether distinct and higher province of being.

But, within that province, we cannot refuse to trace once more the great Law of Evolution, a continual progress towards what we call civilisation, including both the development of the individual, and the harmonious development of the whole race as one. In this phase of Evolution, as in others, the development of the individual is in great degree an instructive type of the development of the race. We look to this individual development from the rudimentary condition of infancy, full of capacities as yet dormant, to the conscious maturity of full manhood; we can trace the actual process, by which it is wrought out, in the harmonious combination of these capacities within, and of influences, material and spiritual, from without. By no mere metaphor, but by a real analogy—which, however, like other analogies, may have its imperfections—we apply what we here learn distinctly to the larger and more complex growth from the childhood to the manhood of the whole race, or of the lesser national divisions which make up the whole. The germ of this higher life has, like the germ of the Organic life, an order of gradual development, of which it has been truly said that it bears a likeness to that process of differentiation from the simple to the complex, which is characteristic of the lower Evolution[1].

Yes! a likeness, which consciously or unconsciously

---

[1] See Herbert Spencer on 'Progress; its Law and Cause' (*Essays*, vol. i. pp. 8–62), the ideas and illustrations of which are incorporated in his 'First Principles.'

we continually discern and imply. But yet a likeness with difference. This higher Evolution shows itself as one less simple, less equable, less continuous, because in the forces working it out, there is included the real though mysterious power of free human will, which the sense of its mystery can not justify us in explaining away, and which has the power to accept and further, and power to ignore and resist, the Laws of humanity. Ruled, of course, that power must be by the Supreme Power; but, after another and a freer fashion, not by compulsion, but by some action, whether of direct spiritual influence or of the indirect power of circumstance, which conserves and works through freedom. Such action of spirit on spirit within limits we know by our own experience; and so can conceive it without limitation and imperfection, as a part of the Supreme rule of God over His creatures. Thus in this Evolution of humanity the equability and continuity of progress vary, in proportion as it requires more or less strictly the co-operation of human will. It is greatest in the material progress of conquest over the forces of Nature; it is less complete in the intellectual; it is less unbroken still in the moral and spiritual sphere, where it has to meet and combat the disturbing forces of moral evil, subtler perhaps, yet not less intense, as the world grows older. In all, though in different degrees, it has apparently its places and its periods of stagnation, conflict, retrogression. To our eyes it is not a calm unbroken stream, but a restless sea, yet having a tide, moved by an attraction from above, which makes it set towards an appointed shore. In the lesser unities, as of national life, it seems to complete the likeness to the individual life, by showing the phenomena of sudden extinction or senile decay; and speculation sometimes asks in its gloomier moods, whether these phenomena may not at some future day manifest themselves in relation to the whole race.

Nor is this human Evolution worked out wholly by the same forces. It has its relation to the Environment of things, and so to the physical laws of material development, which, according to the old saying, we must rule by obeying. It has the element corresponding to the struggle for existence—the will to live and work—the supersession of the weak, physically, intellectually, morally weak, whether races or individuals, which Darwinism shows us in the Organic World. But it has, rising above and tempering this, the nobler element, which we call essentially 'humanity'—the will to love, the self-sacrifice of the strong, and the sense of a duty laid upon them, to 'bear the infirmities of the weak,' and to labour to strengthen and to improve them, as working out on their behalf the beneficent purpose of the Supreme Power.

Yet, unlike in these and other respects, the Evolution in humanity is not less real. We can actually discern its working; because in history, past and present, we see the human race in various stages, and watch its passage from one to another, not merely by internal capacity and the aid of physical circumstance, but also by the conscious action on those in the lower stages of those who have reached the higher. In spite of the hindrances and antagonisms of which we have spoken, under which, indeed, men groan till they are tempted in sheer despair to exalt them into co-ordinate or dominant Laws of life, there is, we believe, out of the germ of the higher humanity an Evolution towards a higher perfection.

But behind this Evolution, even more distinctly than the others, it is impossible for deeper human thought not to see a Supreme Power originative, directive, immanent, but with a Design and Purpose, here felt to be distinctly moral—'making' (to use the modern phrase) 'for Truth and Righteousness'—showing (to use Butler's more intelligible phrase) 'the Moral Government' of a Divine Person. The universal witness to the existence of such a Power, in all the religious and in the noblest philosophies of the world—expressing itself in all human languages and literatures—cannot lightly be set aside. There that Power is—telling both on the individual soul and on the collective humanity—telling both by the Laws of the orderly Environment of life (including in this for each man the influence of his fellow-men) and by some guidance and inspiration of that spiritual life within of thought and conscience and will, which is the distinctive human faculty. This development in each person cannot be considered in isolation; for there are great Laws, which in respect of it bind all in one; and yet the indestructible consciousness of personality, which expresses itself in all language and literature, refuses to be absorbed and lost in human society as a whole. As in the lower Evolutions, there must be some Supreme

Power, on which rest each and all for life and growth—some central source of attraction, round which all move, each with its own tendency to free motion, all with the lesser mutual attractions to one another. For my own part, if I realize my own moral personality, I can form no intelligible conception of that Supreme Power, which is not distinctly personal; nor will human language suffer me to speak of it without using terms which imply personality. If all Teleology—all recognition of Design and Purpose—inevitably implies this, the implication is doubly strong when that Purpose is recognised as moral; for moral idea and being are of the very essence of personality. The soul of man can bow down, and always has bowed down, to a Divine Personality; the reserve of unbounded reverence, felt in all natures and most felt in the noblest, finds its right employment in such worship. But to a Force, a diffused Life, an impersonal Law, it can no more pay spiritual homage, than the Three Children could fall down and worship the golden image in the plains of Dura. In the Evolution of the inanimate world, our immediate inference may be of Supreme Force, and in that of the Organic World of a Supreme Life, while the further inference of Will and so of Personality lies behind these; but, in respect of the world of conscious personal being, that which there lay in the background comes out as the most primary inference. There the Supreme Power must be a Supreme Moral Will; and what is this but a Supreme Personality?

(III) Now if this be a true, however imperfect, sketch

of what we can trace by Science, physical and metaphysical, of Evolution in the three great provinces of being, how stands Christian doctrine in relation to it? We must answer, here as elsewhere, that, on the one hand, it accepts and confirms what we discover naturally of the Law; it extends it on the other beyond the reach of our discovery into the realm of the Supernatural.

(A) Consider in broad outline, without discussion of details—however interesting and important—passing through the letter addressed to the ancient simplicity to the spirit of the underlying truth, which is for all time—the Revelation of the growth of the world, as a whole, to be what it is, not only as expressly declared in the records of Creation, but as implied everywhere in the Holy Scripture, which is the charter of our Christian faith.

In the first place, it is certainly in the largest sense the story of a development out of the nebulous Chaos, 'without form and void,' first of Inorganic Nature, then of the world of vegetable and animal life, lastly of the world of humanity. All these steps in Creation, however they may be related in time, are recorded in one continuous history, because all are parts of one great system, steps in one great natural process. 'Successive Creation' in one sense undoubtedly there is; for every one of these steps is, of course, referred to the Creative Will and Purpose, which must underlie them all, and this reference is made in language, which the simplest minds and the simplest ages could understand. But 'Successive Creation,' in the sense which has been assigned to that word, implying a series of progressions *per saltum*, and in each the bringing forth in perfection from the beginning of all the infinite variety, now filling each province of created being, is nowhere expressed, nowhere necessarily implied. It is not in the narrative itself, but in the interpretations of the narrative—not least, as has been noted, that of Milton in the *Paradise Lost*—that this theory is found. In the original,—'God spake,' 'and it was so'—the great fundamental truth of all vital Religion, is set forth to us in a sublime simplicity. How it was so—this is one of the secrets of God, which, in measure but in measure only, it was left to the human mind to learn by study through all ages. But in the revelation of the growth of the great world—always regarded in its relation to man—by these successive stages at once of Creation and of development, Holy Scripture certainly anticipated to men of old the essence of much which we are now discovering to be in main outline the order of fact.

It is hard to exaggerate the extraordinary significance of this anticipation. Yet in our unceasing discussions on each side of the great controversy over minute difficulties of detail in relation to this recorded order, or etymological shades of meaning in the words used, or the right interpretation of the 'days' of Creation, and the like, we are apt to lose sight of the marvel of the essential accordance of this simple record, coming to us through thousands of years from the earliest childhood of man in history, with all that the maturest Science has slowly and painfully discovered as to the laws and processes of the great realm of Nature. On the Christian's view of what Holy Scripture is, that accordance is easily explicable. The Word of God naturally accords with the Works of God. On any other who can explain what stands out as a phenomenon strikingly unique in itself, still more striking in its contrast with all other cosmogonies, religious or philosophical, of days gone by?

In the next place, the Scripture brings out explicitly what mere speculation can but suggest as an inference of reasoning, in regard to the nature of the unseen Cause, which lies behind this process of Evolution. In speaking of the origin of all things, it strikes in (so to speak) decisively upon the battle of Theism and Pantheism, by its revelation of the First Cause as an Eternal Will, expressed in a Creative Word, working by a Creative Spirit. But beyond this, it goes on to bring out with equal explicitness, as ruling over each stage of development, that which Teleology implies, and to which, as that which we have seen, our maturest Science bears witness—the Design of an ever-present Wisdom, ordering it because for the Divine purpose it was to be, and it was, 'very good.' All the lower developments it crowns by the creation of man as having lordship over Creation, in virtue of a spiritual nature which is 'the Image of God,' beyond which no development is traced in Nature, and on which accordingly the Creative Power is said to 'rest'; although, indeed, the fuller teaching of our Lord hereafter declares in distinct reference to this 'rest' of God 'My Father worketh up to this moment, and so work I.'

For these truths, again, belong to the essence of spiritual religion—the faith in the unceasing Providence, and the communion with man, of a Living God.

As to the process of Evolution which Science traces in each of the three provinces of being, there is in the Revelation significant difference. The purpose of that Revelation is to bring out God's dispensation to man; with other stages of His dealing with the world there is concern, only so far as they bear on this. So to the growth of the world of Inorganic Nature and Organic Life, there is but brief reference. They come from the Creative Wisdom; they show forth God's glory: how this may be, it matters not, if only it is. Yet we cannot but see that, even here, the obedience to the Creative Word of Design is set forth (so to speak) as a natural process under natural laws. 'God spake' and 'it was so'; 'the earth and the waters brought forth'; and we have been recently reminded [1] how some of the most thoughtful of ancient authorities held that it was *causaliter*, not *actualiter*, by reception of the power to produce. We cannot but be reminded by analogy of the Psalmist's reference to that embryonic growth, in which we see now a type of the growth of Organic Life itself, 'Thine eyes did see my substance, yet imperfect, and in thy Book were all my members written, which in continuance were fashioned, when as yet there were none of them.' The preconceived idea and purpose in the Divine Mind, working itself through a gradual development, here implied for

---

[1] By Mr. Aubrey Moore (*Science and the Faith*, p. 176). See Note F.

the individual being, may well be extended to that Evolution of the whole, of which the individual Evolution is the type.

But in the realm of humanity it has always seemed to me that there is most plainly in the Revelation the story of a growth from the first germ of true humanity to its perfection. Never was there a stranger perversion of the original, than in that artificial picture, with which Milton's genius has unhappily familiarized us, of what is virtually a full-grown manhood masquerading under the conditions of childhood. Nothing can be more really unscriptural than the idea so commonly and so loosely taken up on the one side, that the primeval state of man was a state of perfection, to which all subsequent history is a vain effort to return; except perhaps the random assertion on the other, that what we call the Fall was the first step in human progress out of what seems in this view 'a fool's Paradise.' In the Scriptural vision of primeval humanity, we trace indeed the germs of all civilization to come—in simple work the germ of material civilization, in the origin of language of the intellectual, in marriage of the social and moral, in the hearing of the voice of the Lord God of the religious. But it is in germ only; in a simplicity not brutish indeed, or savage, as we now see degraded savagery, but childlike, 'naked and not ashamed'; clearly the beginning of a development in all the elements of human nature—which the entrance of evil into the world disturbed and perverted by a morbid development of itself, but destroyed not—up to the perfection of manhood in the dispensation on earth, and the earnest of a higher perfection still in the world to come. The Scriptural history of man is so far like the scientific, that it is clearly a story of Progress. But that progress it refers, not to an immanent power in man, or to the action of a vague stream of tendency, but to the purpose and the direction of the living God. What indeed is the whole Scripture, but the story of such education of humanity under His Providence and by His Spirit—a Providence which orders all things for the salvation from evil and perfection in good, through history and through Law—a Spirit which always 'strives with man,' and inspires his intellectual and moral, as well as his spiritual life, guiding the lawgiver, the king, even the artificer, as well as the Prophet and the Apostle? In this development there is recognised, as we have seen, the unnatural element of an engrained power of evil, struggling under the Law of Heredity against good, to which all observation of the world, as it is, bears but too plain a witness. But there by distinct promise is sealed the hope, inherent in humanity itself, that this unnatural power shall be at last both conquered and overruled to the highest good. Only the scope of this Evolution is enlarged—for the individual beyond the limits of his life here—for humanity itself beyond the limits of this world's appointed time.

So far, as it seems to me, the Christian doctrine simply takes up, extends, illuminates, the great natural Law of Evolution.

(B) But, as yet we have not viewed it as distinctively Christian: we have not asked what is the bearing in this aspect of the Manifestation in the fulness of the time of the Son of God, as Son of Man?

The truth itself of that Manifestation—let us again put this clearly before ourselves, and proclaim it to the world—is the Divine mystery of mysteries, a secret of the Will and Nature of God, revealed only to faith in the word of Him who said, 'I came forth from the Father and am come into the world; again I leave the world and go unto the Father.' We should hardly dare to bring it into analogy with the lower manifestations of God to man, if we did not remember that in all analogy the higher reality necessarily transcends the lower, and that Our Lord Himself in His Parables taught us to shadow out by comparison with earthly things His Kingdom of Heaven. From these lower manifestations, who could have conceived beforehand—who can even now comprehend—the Personal Incarnation of Godhead in humanity? If it may perhaps be foreshadowed by the recognition of the power of God, as immanent in all creation, and more visibly immanent (so to speak) in humanity, yet how dim this foreshadowing, compared with the brightness of the reality!

But in what way is its actual working in the world represented to us? It is, as we have already seen, described as a 'new Creation'—the beginning of a new spiritual Order—which yet does not break continuity with the past, but, while it brings in a Divine spiritual force before unknown, takes up and subordinates to its higher purpose all the forces of the old Creation. Clearly in this representation there is a striking analogy to all that has gone before. By what is actually in

K

effect a new Creation[1]—whether it be connected or disconnected with the old—we have seen at each step the introduction into the world of a new power, as we pass from the Inorganic realm of lifeless Nature to the realm of Organic Life, from the realm of Organic Life to the realm of Humanity. Now that natural progress is shown to us as carried on to a Supernatural perfection by the bringing in of a new Divine Life—at once the Light and the Life of men—entering into the humanity which is the crown and culmination of the old development, in order to raise it to unity with the Divine Nature itself. This new Creation is set forth to us as an integral element, as the highest element, of the whole Divine Order—fore-ordained before the foundation of the world—in some way coexisting with the lower elements in anticipatory power before its actual Manifestation—prepared for under God's Providence through all 'the fulness of time.' The Manifestation, being in a Personality at once Divine and human, is necessarily complete in itself, unique, unapproachable, begun in the visible life of Christ on earth, continued still in its completeness in the invisible life of heaven. From the nature of the case, its relation to the human personality, as a living power, is a thing Supernatural, transcending the analogy on which we are now dwelling. But yet in its effect both on the individual and on

---

[1] It is notable that in the record of Creation in Gen. i., the word (בָּרָא) which, so far as human language can express a superhuman idea, denotes an actual creation of substance out of nothingness, is used only in vv. 1, 21, 27, first of the creation of the Inorganic world, next, of the creation of animal life, and lastly, of the creation of Man.

the collective life of all mankind, it is clearly (to use our Lord's own comparison) a seed sown in the spiritual soil of humanity—a leaven infused into its threefold nature—a germ to be developed through the ages of a new dispensation, which is to last till its work shall come to the full possible perfection, and then to give place to a higher dispensation still, 'that God may be all in all.'

Entering thus into the humanity, which has already in it, as we have seen, the two developments of original good and of an infused evil, its working necessarily shows itself under two aspects, as having relation to both. In respect of the one it is through the Incarnation simply the regeneration to a new glory of the image of God in humanity, taking up into the higher life all its energies, bodily, mental, spiritual, and bidding them grow in Christ towards the perfection which we call heaven, and on which the Ascension was the entrance of our human nature in Him. So far it harmonizes itself without struggle or difficulty with the higher humanity. But in respect to the other, it enters necessarily into a conflict with evil, involving pain and even agony, but, by victory in that conflict, it becomes a salvation from sin and death through the mystery of Atonement, made in the Passion, and shown as accepted in the Resurrection—at once (to use the Scriptural language) a Justification from sin's guilt, and a Sanctification delivering from sin's bondage. The two aspects of its life-giving power are distinct; ancient speculation dwelt on the one, as that which was destined for humanity simply as finite, on the second, as that which was needed by humanity as sinful [1]; and, without entering on these deeper speculations, the course of Christian thought in different ages has tended, as we have seen, to emphasize predominantly the one or the other, according to its predominant sense of righteousness or of sin in actual humanity. But, though they be distinct, they are absolutely inseparable. As in the body, so in the spirit, the same influence at once strengthens health and throws off disease. As the Christian Creed rests four-square on the Incarnation, the Atonement, the Resurrection, and the Ascension, so the actual Christian life realizes in one all the influences, which these represent and which flow from them to us.

Again, the new dispensation of the kingdom, once inaugurated, presents itself in relation to all humanity, as working by a Supernatural Law of Evolution. It begins from the germ of the new life, which is 'Christ in us, the hope of glory'; it gradually extends itself, 'propagated' (to use our significant phrase) from soul to soul, till it shall be coextensive with humanity itself; it works itself out slowly, as all Evolution must work, through the appointed ages, and as it works, it brings out, that it may dominate, the antagonistic power of evil. It is promised that it shall come to its appointed close hereafter in a new Manifestation of the Son of God, which shall destroy that antagonism for ever, and open, again in the fulness of time, the higher dispensation in heaven of rest, peace, communion with God,

---

[1] I would here refer once more to Bishop Westcott's most interesting Essay on 'The Gospel of Creation' in his *Epistles of St. John* (pp. 275–304).

given by the full likeness of Christ. If it be asked whether we can yet see the actual working of this new life in humanity, we may answer, 'In its beginning and imperfect growth, surely yes.' Not without significance do we reckon the years of our history from the birth of the Lord. The advent of Christianity into the world has shown itself plainly to be a new birth and growth in humanity, by the very contrast of the new with the older civilisations of the world—taking up all that was spiritual in them, and exalting it by the infusion of a Diviner life, which has preserved it from their decay—asserting itself victoriously against all antagonistic influences—revived again and again with fresh power out of periods of slumber and corruption—evidently the one great advancing and aggressive force in the spiritual battle of the world. It is part of the great analogy, at which we have glanced, that it works slowly, with a slownes of which human earnestness is impatient, eager to anticipate it by forcible and rapid artificial creations of its own; that it has to overcome opposing forces of evil, which from the beginning have been a grief and a perplexity to godly souls. But He, whose it is, foresaw, and bade us foresee, the slowness of advance, and the offences which must needs come. We are content, if each soul and each age has its little part in the progress, which needs for its accomplishment the fulness of time.

That germ of the new life, being a spiritual life, must work not by compulsion of Law, but through the power of the Spirit, freely received by the individual spirit of man.

For humanity, therefore, at large it is realized in its fulness—in its direct, as distinct from the indirect and reflected light, which from it is diffused over the whole world,—only in the Church of Christ, which represents that humanity as in faith and love accepting the Divine gift in Him, and in spite of frailty and sin, working with God for its development. The ideal of that development is a continuous unbroken growth through the ages, not only in expansion, but in purity and intensity of power, up to its perfection in the glorious Church, thronged with the 'multitude which no man could number,' and in itself not 'having spot or wrinkle or any such thing.' In practice, having to struggle against the antagonistic power of sin from without and from within, its progress, strangely as it seems to us, is often checked and broken by periods of spiritual decay, disintegration, corruption. Yet out of these—by an experience so familiar that we take it for granted in the Church, and forget how it contradicts human analogies in the lower experiences of the world —it emerges again and again in great epochs of spiritual revival; and thus, on the whole, advances continually in 'a progress by antagonism' towards the perfection, which, if we believe the Scriptural revelations of the future, is to be attained at last by a new Manifestation of the Son of God Himself.

As in the race, so in the individual soul, the same Law seems to rule. For in the individual the right normal order is still that of an Evolution from the germ of the new life implanted from the beginning, guiding and ruling the unfolding of all the faculties of human nature, subduing it gradually through the continual supply of the Divine grace, with more or less of struggle against the evil in it, till, when the fulness of its time has come, it shall pass through death into a higher stage, yet still of growth, in the unseen world beyond the grave. But that order is too often broken by the resistance, passive or active, of the will to this Divine power of good, by its yielding itself ignorantly or consciously to the power of evil; and, when it is so broken, either the soul is left spiritually dead, like dead matter thrown off from natural growth, or, the inner life, checked but not quenched, reasserts itself suddenly (as we deem of suddenness), on the new and fervent adhesion of the mature will in faith, by what is a 'resurrection' rather than a regeneration—in an abnormal progression *per saltum*, rather than a gradual growth.

So every way there comes out to us the conception of the development of the Life of Christ in humanity, as the supernatural crown of the great Order of Evolution; and, if this be so, Science, which has traced this order in its lower forms, thus becomes, or should become, the παιδαγωγός to lead us to the highest in Christ Himself. It is a part of this analogy, that in this highest sphere of the great Order there should be manifested a Law and a Power peculiarly its own. For in the various provinces of being, which show themselves to us as distinct, the one 'God fulfils Himself in many ways.' In one sphere Evolution is ordered through Matter and the physical forces which pervade it; in another there is added in combination with these the new force of Life, with its inner capacity of assimilation and growth; in a third there comes with both and above both the infused life of human personality, with reason, conscience, love, and freedom of will to use them. Closer and closer in each successive phase there is revealed to us, in relation to created being, the Personality of God—not His attributes, but Himself. So in this the supernatural sphere of the great Order, the new and dominant Force should by analogy be, as indeed it is, distinctly Supernatural, in harmony with the lower forces, but distinct from all. For it is the completion of that relation of true personality—all the number numberless of human souls being drawn to the Personality, at once Divine and human, of the Eternal Son, in a communion wrought out by the Eternal Spirit of God, and restoring us to the sonship of the Eternal Father. As He Himself upon earth, transcending in His Divine Nature all created being, yet entered into all phases of that being—swayed the forces of the material world, gave or restored the power of life, healed and ruled by a Divine sympathy the souls of men—so there is a similar power in the new life, which, by His presence in the soul, He implants and sustains in humanity. Supernatural in itself, yet it embraces, just because it transcends, all the lower forces, which tell upon the complex nature of man.

It belongs, again, to this analogy, that even that Kingdom of God, which the Incarnation inaugurated on earth, should have its appointed period of development, and then pass, by a closer relation still to God, into a new and higher Kingdom, when the fulness of its time has been accomplished. That for the individual man there should be a future perfection, of body and spirit—that the struggle of the Church militant should pass into the peace of the Church triumphant—that both these forms of perfection should come from perfected communion with God—is surely so far from being a strange thing, that it is accordant with the natural order—nay a part of that order in the larger sense of the word 'Natural,' at which we have already glanced.

As of the Christ in Himself, so is it also of the 'Christ of us.' In His Divine Person there were the material elements of His human body, akin to the lifeless material world; there was the physical life, a part of the great Organic Creation; there was the true humanity of the spiritual nature, in which He was in all points like His brethren; but crowning all, and yet interpenetrating all, there was the essence of the Divine Nature.

So the redeemed humanity, which He has made a part of Himself, is the crown of the continuous Evolution from the material to the psychical, from the psychical to the spiritual; but yet beyond that natural progress it rises even now into the Supernatural sphere of regeneration and salvation, by the indwelling in it of the Son of God; and shall rise hereafter, when He manifests Himself by a yet higher manifestation, into a higher perfection, because a yet closer communion with Him. The 'Christ in us' is at once 'our life' in the present, and 'the hope of glory' for the future.

LECTURE IV.

CHRIST AND ALL CREATION.

In the dispensation of the fulness of the times to gather up all things in Christ, both which are in heaven and which are in earth, even in Him, in whom we also have obtained inheritance.—Eph. i. 10, 11.

'ALL things in Christ'—the scope of this phrase, as in the New Testament, so in all Christian thought derived from it, grows by a continual expansion of meaning. As our knowledge itself expands, we pass from the sphere of our own individual being to the larger sphere of humanity, and the earth which subserves humanity, and then, beyond even this, to what seems to us the infinite greatness of the Universe itself. While we thus pass on, the light about us becomes dimmer, and yet larger and grander in its revelations, as our spiritual eye adapts itself to its new conditions. We 'lose ourselves,' on the one hand, in the increasing sense of our own material insignificance: we 'find ourselves,' on the other, in the wondering consciousness of the spiritual greatness of the mind, which thus advances continually towards the discovery of the great laws of all being. Such advance is inevitable; for, according to the profound teaching of Holy Scripture, the wisdom of man—the knowledge (that is) of the end and object of his individual life—is impossible without some glimpse of the 'Wisdom of God' in the great laws which rule all Creation. How shall this glimpse be ours? If we take with us the unchanged and unchangeable revelation of God in Christ, the two elements of this antithesis are brought together in one. In Him we see summed up all the infinite greatness of 'things in Heaven and things in Earth': and yet we know that in Him our own souls have 'received an inheritance'—the inheritance of a true sonship of God.

(I) In the course of thought as to the relation of scientific knowledge of Law to Christ, which we are seeking to trace out, we have hitherto considered leading examples of its effect of confirmation—by the establishment of the truth of the natural Laws of humanity, which the Christian revelation of the Supernatural assumes, that it may at once fill and transcend them. We go on now to the effect of what we may call elucidation, bringing out elements in the Revelation given to that faith, which in earlier days, being less correspondent with man's knowledge, were less explicitly realized, and being less needed for strong consciousness of God, were less practically regarded. Still, following the rapid advance of Physical discovery, we may consider, as thus brought out and illustrated by modern thought, the grand declaration—briefly enuntiated in the text, and worked out more fully in many of the later Books of the New Testament—of the Headship of Christ over the whole of created being, as 'gathered up' in Him.

Naturally enough that declaration, though unhesitatingly accepted, remained in comparative abeyance to the faith of earlier days. To the Psalmist or Prophet of old, meditating on the works of God, the earth, with all its store of wonder and beauty ministering to the welfare of man, occupied prominently, almost exclusively, the field of thought. It cannot, indeed, be supposed that in any age a thoughtful mind, gazing on the starlit sky, or watching the sun and the moon in their courses, could have failed to gain from such contemplation some vague idea of an almost immeasurable vastness in Creation, held together in a perfect beauty and order; and so have extended far beyond the earth its conception of the creating and sustaining Sovereignty of God. The adoring wonder of the eighth and nineteenth Psalms, and the more meditative utterances of the Books of Job and Proverbs, show how powerfully this irresistible conviction told upon the imagination, and through it both upon the mind and upon the heart. But still all this was but as a faintly luminous background to the more vivid realization of God on this our earth. The very revelation of God, through the voices, which 'without speech or language' told of 'His glory and the wonder of His works,' was but a part of His dispensation to man, leading up naturally to the plain and explicit revelation in 'the Law of the Lord.' And so from it the soul came back without shock or bewilderment, to acknowledge God's 'visiting' and 'regarding' man, as having dominion over the works of His hands, and illuminating every human soul by the light of

His special Revelation of Himself. Even in the days of St. Paul, although in the Greek schools of Philosophy—not least that of Alexandria, with which we know that Tarsus was closely in touch—Astronomy, under the guidance of Hipparchus and Ptolemy, had advanced far towards the knowledge of our own Planetary System, and the observation of the numbers and arrangements of the fixed stars; yet still it is to be remembered that in the Ptolemaic Astronomy the earth was looked upon as the centre of that nearer system, with no notion of its immeasurable insignificance in comparison with the Sun, and that of the vastness of the stellar multitude of suns and systems numberless, there was as yet no adequate conception. Substantially, therefore, in this matter the Apostolic age stood very much on the same ground, as the greater simplicity of earlier generations. Still in all the material creation the earth was acknowledged without hesitation, as the true central sphere of the exhibition of the Power and Wisdom and Love of God; and this conception of it in the natural order led on without difficulty to the place of humanity, as the head of that natural order, in the new and supernatural dispensation, which began in the Incarnation of the Eternal Son.

It was rather in respect of the spiritual Creation, that the thoughts of men then gained the idea of vast extension of God's Sovereignty beyond this earth and its life. Man stands in his complex nature on the frontier between the psychical and the spiritual world; as below him animal life extends downward in minute and countless gradations to its crudest forms, so above him the spiritual life was seen as stretching upwards, in order after order of superior being, towards the unveiled Presence of God. Gradually through the Old Testament itself we can trace the fuller development of the first simple conception of these angelic orders; in Jewish thought succeeding, the imagination delighted to go beyond that which was revealed, and to picture to itself 'thrones and dominions and principalities and powers' of the celestial hierarchy—the Diviner antitypes of the hierarchy of God's kingdom upon earth. Yet still, as was natural, even this higher creation was largely viewed in its relation to this our world: the angels were recognised as God's ministers to it—now 'shouting for joy,' as 'the morning stars sang together' over the new-born earth—now swaying the powers of terrestrial Nature—now ascending and descending on God's messages to man, to the chosen family, to the chosen nation, to all the nations of the earth—till at last that angelic service came to its full culmination in the ministry to the Birth, the Life, the Passion, the Resurrection of the Incarnate Son of God. While, therefore, the very belief in this higher world gave a wonderful expansion and exaltation to the sense of God's Sovereignty, and of the manifold Power and Wisdom in which His infinite greatness expressed itself to all His creatures, still man did not entirely lose himself in the contemplation of it: he was not bewildered, but simply cheered and inspired; for he felt that even through it God was ordaining a ministry for his salvation, and so could believe that even this higher world of being was 'gathered up in Christ' the true Son of Man.

But to us all this is changed. Step by step, as Science has enlarged our vision, the infinite vastness of the material creation has grown, and still grows, upon us. Our earth is known as but one, and far from the largest, of the planets, circling round the greatness of the Sun; in itself a specimen of but one stage in the evolution of worlds out of primeval nebula; the whole solar system but one of a host revolving round a central sun, and this itself again but one of a countless multitude of heavenly bodies, so vast, so immeasurably distant, that the mind fails to gain any conception or even imagination of the infinite greatness of the whole. Yet it is a whole; through all, so far as our Science extends, by telescopic vision, by mathematical calculation, by spectroscopic analysis, the same material laws rule, which we know more closely upon earth. And, though we have no real knowledge, or even capacity of sure inference, beyond this, yet the imagination cannot resist the belief, that everywhere, as here, the higher laws of animal and spiritual life must somehow fulfil themselves in an appointed development; and that man may well be but one of many orders of rational and moral beings, belonging, not like the angels, to a supernatural sphere, but to the natural order, of which we see but a small part here [1].

[1] The controversy raised many years ago by Dr. Whewell's 'Plurality of Worlds,' was singularly interesting and instructive—showing, as it did, on the one hand, the scantiness or absence of evidence of habitation of the other bodies of our system; and, on the other, the irresistible

So partly through knowledge, partly through this all but irresistible inference, there comes upon us a bewildering sense of the vast unity of the universe. Nor is this all. As we extend through the whole the idea of slow growth through countless ages, which Evolution brings home to us in relation to the earth, there is added to the sense of vastness of space an equally bewildering conception of an almost infinite duration of time, hardly distinguishable to our finite minds from the eternity of existence, which ancient speculation attributed to the Universe. But, beyond this, from the same idea of Evolution—involving to many minds the conception of an immanent power, however originated or infused, in that universe, which is gradually developed, under these great pervading laws into matter, life, spiritual being—there grows also upon us the temptation to a Pantheistic worship of this immanent power—this Soul of the Universe—this half-personified Nature—as if it was not only a reality, but the supreme and ultimate reality. It is, of course, no new worship. What is it, after all, but the old Pythagorean conception, which Virgil has embodied as in immortal verse [1]? But it comes upon our larger know-

power over the imagination, and through it over the intellect, of the suggestion through analogy of a development there, under different conditions, indeed, yet essentially not unlike our own.

[1] Principio coelum et terras, camposque liquentes,
Lucentemque globum Lunae, Titaniaque astra,
Spiritus intus alit, totamque infusa per artus
Mens agitat molem, et magno se corpore miscet.
Inde hominum pecudumque genus, vitaeque volantum,
Et quae marmoreo fert monstra sub aequore pontus.
(Aen. vi. 724–729.)

ledge now with overwhelming force. Those who just catch and reflect the spirit of the age, tell us (like M. Renan) that a vague sense of infinite space, infinite time, infinite being diffused through both, is to supersede what is held—strangely enough—to be a poorer and shabbier belief in Creationism, referring all to an Infinite Personal Mind and Will, and is to satisfy, by a corresponding vagueness of wonder and awe, the inherent instinct of worship in the soul.

Let me repeat once more that this Pantheism has never really maintained itself, as a living and working force of belief, especially when we emerge from the schools of speculation and imagination into the realities and needs of every-day life. Against it there rises (as has been said) a double protest from mind and heart—from the strong inherent consciousness of our own personality, and with it of conscious will as the one true cause, that we know, and of conscious design as the guiding force of action,—from the homage of the conscience to Righteousness alone, which cannot accept a Soul of this world, so strangely compacted of good and evil, as its supreme moral authority. And this intellectual and moral sense of our own personality leads us to the worship of a Divine Personality, and to it alone. Nay, the very increase of our knowledge of the laws of order and growth in the Universe, by testifying to the spiritual greatness of the mind in us, compels the belief in a Divine Mind, of which ours is but the image, as the Source and Maker of these laws. It is a strange shallowness, as well as profanity, to acknowledge that the heavens declare the glory of the finite discovering mind of Kepler or Newton, and to deny their witness to the glory of an Infinite Creative Mind of a living God.

But, even if we rise out of this dream to grasp what the waking reality of life demands, and, passing through immanence of power to the origination and guidance of that power, ascend through stage after stage of Law, to the final belief, old as humanity itself, in a true First Cause, which is the source of all this infinite vastness and complexity of Being; still the bewildering awe of its greatness remains undiminished, if not enhanced. Just as the loftiness of some supreme mountain-peak most grows upon us, when we rise up to it over ridge after ridge of lower heights, so through this process of thought the infinite greatness of the Supreme Power impresses itself upon the soul more and more; and thus when the mind returns upon itself, upon its own littleness, and the littleness of the earth which once seemed so great, the cry 'What is man?' sounds with a new intensity and depth of meaning. Men find it harder now, than the Psalmist found it, to add 'that Thou so visitest,' 'that Thou so regardest man,' 'to crown him with glory and worship.' 'Tush' (say they) 'how shall God perceive us?' Can there be knowledge, care, love, of such infinite littleness in the Most High? Even if He does vouchsafe to humanity some fragment of His universal Providence, men ask still more emphatically, when the doctrine of the Incarnation is presented to them, 'How can we conceive that the Infinite Godhead could deign to tabernacle in this pigmy humanity of ours, on the earth, which is but a speck in the great heaven of the Universe? Is there not here, in a moral, instead of a material form, a perpetuation of the old exploded Ptolemaism, which makes the earth and man the very centre of all the works of God?'

The difficulty is, indeed, as has been truly said [1], one of the imagination rather than the reason. For to a Mind, really infinite, it is clear that no expansion of scope implies imperfection in consideration and care even of its least work. In measure we can realize this in ourselves. Even in our finite nature we see that the slightest action is characteristic, or, in other words, that in the slightest work the essential character of the worker is expressed; and the highest wisdom and genius show themselves especially in the capacity of uniting grasp of the idea and the leading principles of a great whole with minuteness of provision for accuracy and perfection of detail—whether in completeness of mechanical design and artistic conception, or in the subtler completeness of foresight and influence, which belong to leadership of men. If from our own finiteness we turn to the vastness of the material world of Nature, the microscope has been said in this respect to correct the telescope; because, while the latter extends our vision of the grandeur of Creation, the former shows us a perfection of usefulness and beauty in the

[1] See Dr. Martineau's Essay on 'God in Nature'; where he examines the growth of our conception of space and time, and correlation of forces in Nature, and shows that it is merely to imagination, not to reason, that they create any difficulty in the 'religious interpretation of Nature,' through which 'the world reports the Power, reflects the Beauty, spreads abroad the Majesty of the First Cause.'

minutest organism, which—however it may have grown to be what it is—yet bears, as it is, the impress of a creating and sustaining purpose. Nor need our sense of the material littleness of humanity lead us to forget the truth of the old saying that 'Nature conceals God; man reveals him'—that His highest attributes are brought out, not by the beauty or majesty of Nature, but by the spiritual life in humanity, which is the 'broken light' from Him. Hence in the spiritual world it is but reasonable to ask simply whether through our intellectual and moral nature we have a sufficient positive witness of 'God with us'—whether the truth of the Incarnation establishes itself to us as, both historically and ideally, the crown of His revelations of Himself to men—without allowing ourselves to be troubled by bewilderment as to the infinite greatness and variety of His relation to all His creatures. Here 'egoism is the true modesty.' It is wisdom to know in part, and in part truly, without obscuring the reality of such partial knowledge by the sense of our ignorance of the Universal. If God 'fulfils Himself in many ways,' He does not the less perfectly on that account fulfil Himself in each.

But it is a fatal error to slight the power of Imagination, either as a potent factor in human action, or as giving a certain power of insight to human thought; and so this extension of our knowledge of the immeasurable greatness and variety of Creation may well force us to enquire more earnestly than of old, whether there is any corresponding phase of the doctrine of Christ, which bears upon the being of this vast Creation as a whole, up to which, therefore, this growth of Science leads our faith.

(II) Now, in spite of this great expansion of thought, the old saying remains as true as ever that

'The proper study of mankind is man'—

man in himself and man in relation to God. In the outer circles of our knowledge of the universe, the light is dim and scanty, disclosing to us only a few vague general laws of material being, with which we have ourselves no close concern, and under which we have no practical energy of influence. As we pass inwards through our own system of worlds to the earth our habitation, our light grows brighter and clearer, and this vagueness is exchanged for an ever-increasing definiteness and richness of knowledge; while the power and duty of acting with conscious purpose continually increases with it. At last we come to the inmost sphere of humanity—our own individual humanity and the collective humanity of our race—and there, through the added intuition of the inner consciousness, the light is at its clearest intensity; and the sense of responsibility for our own action assumes an imperious tone of moral command, because the power of such action becomes more absolute. Spiritually, as well as physically, that which is nearest, though least in itself, becomes for us greatest to the mind and dearest to the heart.

Naturally, therefore, in a Revelation which addresses itself to man, and which, though it diffuses an intellectual light, has beyond all else a moral and spiritual purpose, the main tenour and direction of thought look to humanity. The earth in the whole order of its past Evolution, and in the Laws through which it is sustained now by the Divine Wisdom, is viewed mainly as ministering to man, at once its highest creature and its lord. Even the greater Creation, beyond, above, around it, is conceived, as at once influencing the outward life of the earth and man, and manifesting to the soul, in the vision of its Design and Beauty, the handwriting of the message of God. It must be so: for if it were not so, there would be no correspondence with the actual conditions of human thought and life. Accordingly, when that Revelation has its consummation in the Incarnation, the pervading idea is of its bearing upon the humanity, which the Son of God deigned to assume. It is as giving life and guidance to that humanity, that the Headship of Christ becomes an ever-recurring phrase, a household word in the family of God, first as the life of each man's individual being [1], next as the indwelling life of the whole Catholic Church, coextensive in idea and promise with all humankind [2].

But although this is so, and although (if we may venture thus to speak) it ought so to be, yet there is an element of larger scope in the Revelation of Christ, forming the background rather than the foreground of the Divine picture, yet necessary to its completeness as a whole. It is the truth of the Headship of Christ over all created being—the 'gathering up of all things in Him, both which are in heaven and which are in earth.' It is wrought out for us mainly in the later books of the New Testament, corresponding to these

---

[1] See 1 Cor. xi. 3. [2] See Eph. i. 22, 23.

later years of the Apostolic age, when the preaching of the two lesser and closer Headships had done its work, and individual souls, drawn one by one to Christ, made up already the body of an organized and growing Church in all provinces of the civilized world.

It was, it would seem, mainly to meet the theories framed, and to solve the problems raised by human speculation, that this largest Christian conception was brought out. The Gospel, now emerging into a position of living power and authority, which even the world could not ignore, came necessarily into contact with all the higher thought of the day—a day (be it remarked) as busy in cosmological speculations and mystic theosophies as our own. It could no longer be despised as a mere Eastern superstition; it was seen to enshrine, not only a strong moral enthusiasm, but a mysterious wisdom. Had it not (men began to ask) some philosophic significance? How could it be interwoven with mystic speculation as to the origin of being? How could the idea of a Redemption of the world—in the recognition of which the thought of the age, strongly affected by Christian influence, differed from the philosophies of days gone by — be wrought into these speculative theories? How could Christianity in all its aspects be harmonized with the laws of the actual world, as yet discovered or surmised?

In that enquiry we trace the germ of that extraordinary development of various speculations which we call Gnostic—subtle, comprehensive, mystic, often fantastic —as ingeniously elaborate, as obviously artificial, as the cycles and epicycles of the astronomy of old days, or the last shadowy imaginations of modern theosophy. Their very name implies that they arose first from an exaggeration of knowledge above the place, which it rightly occupies in the harmony of the full Christian life, and next, from a disinclination to bound its capacity of extension within the limits of faith in the Revelation of Christ. So, venturing to enter boldly the regions of mystery, the Gnostic theories concerned themselves with two great questions, which have exercised men at all times, and strongly exercise them now—the speculative question, how the Absolute Eternal Being can so enter into relations with the finite, as to become really the First Cause of all creation, and the Life of all finite beings—the moral question of the cause of the existence of evil, physical and spiritual evil, in the world and in man, conflicting, as it obviously does conflict, by negative hindrance or by positive antagonism, with the superior power of good [1]. Gnostic Cosmology sought to answer the one question by the interposition between the In-

[1] 'Two Metaphysical problems may be particularly specified as those which Gnosticism borrowed from heathen philosophy, and to which the Christian Revelation was made subordinate—the Absolute Existence and the problem of the Origin of Evil.... The search after an Absolute first principle, the enquiry how the Absolute and Unconditioned can give rise to the relative and conditioned, is one which, when pursued as a theological inquiry, almost inevitably leads to a denial of the Personality of God.... The other great problem, the Origin of Evil, naturally assumes a similar character.... The Personality of God having disappeared, the personality of man naturally disappears with it.... Contemplated from this point of view, evil is no longer a moral, but a natural, phenomenon; it becomes identical with the imperfect, the relative, the finite. ... Religion and morality become nothing more than curious questions of Metaphysics.' (Mansel's *Gnostic Heresies*, Lect. i. pp. 11–13.)

finite and the finite of a series of emanations—angelic in its Jewish forms, impersonal *Aeons* [1], ages (that is) of time, strangely metamorphosed into beings or personifications of the Divine—in the more purely Gentile forms. Gnostic Dualism explained the other by an inherent evil in the world of matter [2], either a force of passive resistance to the Spirit, or a force of positive and turbulent antagonism. Under both aspects Gnosticism endeavoured to weave Christianity into its own philosophic schemes—now (as in Valentinus) seeing in its Author but one of many emanations from God—now (as in Marcion) shaping it by mutilation and perversion to express the ideas of Jewish or Gentile mysticism. Against the first beginnings of this 'Science falsely so

---

[1] The system of Aeons is perhaps set forth in its wildest luxuriance of speculation in the theory of Valentinus—'filling the supermundane region with a succession of Aeons or celestial beings, the ideal prototypes of things imperfectly realized on earth.' (See Mansel, Lect. xi. pp. 166–183.) His whole system was 'an Eclecticism derived from various sources . . . from the Platonic philosophy . . . from the pantheistic philosophies of India . . . from the Judaism of Alexandria.'

[2] 'The evil in the world' in this theory 'must be due to the Creator of the world; it must be inherent in the world from the beginning—the result of some weakness, at least, or some ignorance, if not of some positive malignity, concurring in its first formation. . . The Creator of the world, the God of the Jewish people, may be regarded merely as an imperfect, or as a positively malignant being. . . He may be an emanation from the Supreme God, imperfect but still a servant of God . . accomplishing the Divine Purpose . . blindly and ignorantly. . . Or he may be a being hostile to God; either the offspring of some power alien from God and antagonistic, . . . or at least one so far degenerated from the original Source of good, that his imperfection becomes in result an actual contrariety to good.' (Mansel's *Gnostic Heresies*, Lect. ii. 19, 20.)

called' the true Christian teacher necessarily protested with all vehemence, as destroying both the simplicity and the solid reality of the Gospel. But yet we can see that it was overruled to minister to the fullest development of the Christian truth itself, by forcing him to pass in thought beyond the limits of the earth and humanity, and to proclaim the one Eternal Son of God, as not only the Saviour of men from evil and the Conqueror of death, but as the Head, the indwelling Light and Life, of all created being, 'summing up all things in Himself'—even the spiritual Creation above man of 'thrones and principalities and powers' in heaven— even the natural Creation below man, in the visible realm of the earth and of all that surrounds it in the greater universe.

Now in our own days, just as in the Apostolic age, it seems to me that the large extension of scientific discovery, and the still larger expansion of scientific speculation, force us to dwell more than we have yet done on this largest conception of the Headship of Christ. True it is that this modern advance in enlargement of thought is widely different in character from the old; while yet, in the luxuriance of the ancient speculation, we constantly come across fantastic difficulties and fantastic theories to meet them, which remind us of the philosophies of our own day. But our modern thought deals, so far as it assumes scientific form, with the material, instead of the spiritual Creation; although, by a singularly striking and instructive reaction, it seems to have stimulated a new curiosity, a new boldness of theosophic speculation, a new growth of mystic fancy, in respect of immaterial powers, laws, beings, not dreamt of in the merely physical philosophy. But yet this distinction, which naturally arises out of that direction of the expansion of modern thought, which has been already referred to, does not prevent its having the same effect in suggesting, almost requiring, this enlargement of our faith; nor does it prevent the old truth of the Apostolic age, from giving the answer, which this modern thought demands.

(III) We have but to consider more in detail, what that answer really is, and how it grows out more and more definitely, with the development of Christian doctrine, through the later books of the New Testament. We must see that, to meet our new conditions of thought, no new doctrine has to be added to it, even by inference; only that which perhaps to earlier ages sounded but as a majestic burst of adoration, becomes now a Divine philosophy of plainly necessary truth.

In St. Paul's teaching it belongs mainly to the Epistles of the Captivity—naturally more meditative in the enforced silence and retirement from the active work of Evangelism—naturally having the character of a profound teaching to disciples already won, in a Church already developed, rather than of the earnest, practical, impassioned pleading of the preacher with those who needed to be drawn to Christ. True that in his first teaching of the Greek mind at Corinth, he had summed up all worship, in the consciousness as of 'the One God the Father, of whom are all things and we unto Him,' so of 'the One Lord Jesus Christ, through whom are all things and we through Him[1].' True that in the Epistle to the Romans his view of the Redemption of Christ extends beyond humanity to 'the whole creation,' as groaning and travailing in pain together, and holds out 'the promise of its deliverance from the bondage of corruption into the glorious liberty of the children of God[2].' But now these earlier indications of larger thought are wrought out into detail.

In the great Creed of the Godhead and manhood of the Lord Jesus Christ, drawn out in the Philippian Epistle, His exalted majesty of Salvation is viewed as receiving the due homage, and therefore as affecting the being, not only of man, but of 'things in Heaven and things in earth and things under the earth.' But it is in the other Epistles of the Captivity that the great conception unfolds itself.

In the Epistle to the Ephesians the leading idea of the unity of all men, Jews and Gentiles alike—in that Catholic Church, which in itself extends beyond the earth, because it starts from the eternal predestination of God, before humanity was, and draws its life from Him who is exalted at the right hand of God above all heavenly powers—naturally expands, as in the text, into the grander idea of His sovereign and eternal relation to all created being, both in heaven and in earth, summed up in His Divine Personality.

More distinct and explicit still is the enunciation of the same great truth in the parallel Epistle to the Church of Colossae, where clearly some Judaic—perhaps

[1] 1 Cor. viii. 6.   [2] Rom. viii. 21.

Essenic[1]—form of Gnostic speculation had sought to fuse in a vague mysticism the grand simplicity of the Headship of Christ, and with it the reality of the universal Mediation, from which there flowed out to all men deliverance from sin and death. There the Lord Jesus Christ is set forth as the perfect Image—(that is) the perfect manifestation of the Invisible God; in whom 'dwelleth all the fulness,' all the Infinite Attributes 'of Godhead,' and that 'bodily,' working visibly through a true humanity; and accordingly His relation to the whole universe, drawing its being from God, is wrought out with deliberate and emphatic explicitness. 'First begotten,' He is of the Father 'before all creation[2],' 'through Him,' and 'for Him' all the universe was created in its beginning'; 'in Him' now in its full development it consists, holding together its manifold unity of life; on Him rest both its material and visible existences, and its higher spiritual orders of being, the mysterious thrones, and principalities, and powers, far above us in heaven, as truly, though not as closely, as the order of humanity itself, gathered into a nearer unity with Him in the Church on earth[3].

Clear again is the same order of deeper thought in the Epistle to the Hebrews—evidently belonging to much the same period, evidently bearing the impress of the Pauline teaching; and perhaps this identity of idea is

---

[1] See Lightfoot's *Epistle to the Colossians.*
[2] Without entering on any etymological and grammatical reasoning, the whole context shows that we must so render the πρωτότοκος πάσης κτίσεως of the original.
[3] See Col. i. 15, 16-19; ii. 9.

the more striking, because the special object of the Epistle, and the special phase of thought which it addresses, are plainly different. There again the declaration of Christ, as 'the brightness of God's glory and the express Image of His Person' is drawn out into the same relation to created being; 'through Him the worlds were made'; 'by the word of His power they are upheld'; above all, even the highest angelic creation, He is exalted as the true Son of God; to Him is applied the language of the ancient adoration of the Eternal Source of Being, who made both the earth and the heavens in the beginning, and who shall endure when they all shall wax old and perish [1].

Then we have but to pass on through another generation to the close of the Apostolic age, and hear how in the final utterances of St. John, the same truth grows out to a calm and majestic completeness, and is clenched (so to speak) by its expression in the very name of the Christ—as 'the Word of God' in the mystic visions of the Apocalypse, as 'the Word of Life' in the profound teaching of the Epistle, as 'the Word,' who 'in the beginning was with God and was God' in the yet profounder Prologue to the Gospel, enshrining the Supreme Truth, which the whole record of that Gospel is designed to unfold and illustrate.

THE WORD—it is indeed 'the Name above every name,' above even those titles of adoration at which we have already glanced, in a twofold fulness of meaning. It takes up and crowns with a Divine perfection two distinct lines of thought. In it there is, on the

[1] See Heb. i. 2–4, 10–12.

one hand, the completion of all the teaching and the interpretation of the Old Testament, both on the 'Word of the Lord,' as the full manifestation in the realm of matter and in the realm of mind of the Invisible Godhead, and on the Eternal Wisdom 'from everlasting, from the beginning or ever the world was' working, when 'He prepared the heaven .... gave a decree to the sea, and appointed the foundations of the earth[1].' On that side it brings out the Manifestation of the Living God, transcending, infinitely transcending, all His Creation, which in idea is of the essence of Theism, and which, as realized by the sense of a living relation of the soul to Him, is of the essence of all vital Religion. Into it, again, are taken up those Alexandrine speculations—half Jewish, half Platonic and Stoic, which we read (for example) in Philo—of the Λόγος, not so much an express Word revealing the transcendent Godhead, but as an indwelling Reason of God, energetic in all the laws of the material and spiritual Creation—speculations which, as the Jew or the Greek in him prevails, hover (so to speak) between a true Personality of indwelling Being on the one hand, and a mere personification of the Ideas and Attributes of Godhead on the other. On this side it recognises that immanence in created being of a Life, gradually unfolding itself under an inherent Design of purpose, into all the manifold forms of material, psychical, spiritual being, which is the 'higher Pantheism' of

---

[1] See Prov. viii. 22–31. The whole chapter is a magnificent completion of the personifications of the Divine Wisdom, which we read in the earlier chapters.

philosophical Science [1]. In this (as has been truly said [2]) 'The Christian doctrine of God brings together two one-sided views. Religion demands as a condition of its existence a God who transcends the Universe; philosophy as imperiously demands His immanence in Nature.' 'The unsolved problem of Platonism, which is the unsolved problem of the non-Christian philosophy in our day, is met in the Christian doctrine.'

And the consequences of both these ideas, united in Him, are clearly drawn out. If we look to the Gospel, He is, on the one hand, 'in the beginning' before all Creation, and in that Creation 'all things were made through Him, and without Him was not any one thing made, that hath been made.' 'In Him was life,' the sole inherent Eternal life, expressed in the very Name Jehovah. On the other hand, that life is made 'the life of men,' an indwelling light—the light of mankind in its entirety, and the individual light, which lighteth every man—so that even the supreme mystery of the tabernacling in human flesh, fore-ordained from the beginning, is but the new and transcendent perfection of that light and life

[1] See Westcott's *Gospel according to St. John*, Introd., pp. xv–xviii. His conclusion is that mainly St. John's doctrine is the development of the Hebraic doctrine of the Word—'the fulfilment of the three distinct lines of preparatory Revelation, which were severally connected with the Angel of the Presence ... with the Word of God ... with Wisdom'; but that secondarily the speculations of Alexandria—mingling (as in Philo) 'the Stoic, the Platonic, and the Hebraic currents of thought,'—'quickened and developed elements, which might otherwise have remained latent.'

[2] See Mr. Aubrey Moore's singularly able and suggestive Essay on 'The Christian Doctrine of God,' in *Lux Mundi*.

indwelling in humanity [1]. If we turn to the Epistle, we are taught how the three great Aphorisms, 'God is Light,' 'God is Righteousness,' 'God is Love,' which trace up all good to the Eternal Source of Being, are fulfilled in His true Godhead; and yet, through all these, He is shown as by His Incarnation indwelling in the souls of men, and implanting there the likeness of those very attributes of God, in earnest now, in perfection hereafter [2].

So was gradually unfolded the largest and deepest truth of Christ, to meet the needs and enquiries of that Apostolic age, which has been held to be a kind of epitome of the whole future history of the Church. As the centuries rolled on, and Christianity asserted its world-wide power, over the thought as well as the life of men—in its Creed and Theology over the critical or mystical speculation of the East, as in its Catholic unity over the social organization and order of the West—its greatest thinkers drew out more and more the meaning of this complete Scriptural teaching; till St. Athanasius, in the great struggle on which the very life of Christianity hung, put (so to speak) the finishing touch to the ever-increasing realization of this great truth. Pleading with the educated Gentile thought of his day, he sets forth to them the origin and continuous life of all created being, in 'the Holy Word of God, almighty and all perfect,' who 'having entered upon all things, and having everywhere unfolded His power, and enlightened all things visible and invisible, holds

---

[1] John i. 1-4, 13.
[2] See 1 John i. 5-7, compared with ii. 9-11; iii. 2-10; iv. 8-21.

and binds all together into Himself, leaving out nothing destitute of His power, but quickening and sustaining each thing separately, and all as collected in one.' To that Creative power he refers in detail all the elements of material being—cold and heat, moisture and dryness—as blended by it into a harmonious whole; in obedience to the Word he tells how the sea holds its place, and the earth brings forth her produce. Lastly, summing up all, he concludes that 'as a musician, having tuned his lyre, and harmonized together the high with the low notes, and the middle notes with the extremes, makes the resulting music one; so the Wisdom of God, grasping the universe like a lyre, blending the things of air with those of earth, and the things of heaven with those of air, binding together the whole and the parts, and ordering all by His Counsel and His Will, makes the world itself and its appointed order one in fair and harmonious perfection; yet He Himself, moving all things, remains unmoved with the Father[1].' It would be difficult to express more forcibly and more completely the conception at once of transcendence and immanence in the creative power of the Word of God.

(IV) Not unlike this is the expansion of Christian thought, suggested in our own day by the rapid enlargement of our scientific knowledge of the universe and its pervading Order—its transcendent First Cause and its immanent Life. That tendency has been expressed in the well-known saying, that, in contrast with

---

[1] See St. Athanasius' *Oratio contra Gentes*, referred to and partially quoted by Mr. Aubrey Moore in his Essay on 'The Christian Doctrine of God,' in *Lux Mundi*. See Note G.

the natural currents of thought in mediaeval times, and in the period which began from the Reformation, we have now to pass from the Christology of St. Peter and St. Paul to that of St. John, from 'Christ risen' as our King, and from 'Christ crucified' as our Saviour, to 'Christ the Incarnate Word of God,' in whom all things and all beings consist. In that saying there is, as in such sayings generally, only a rough approximate truth. It is evident, even from the references already made, that the whole Christology of the New Testament is substantially one in its essential idea, wrought out in a continuous development. It is certain that, in realizing our own relation to God, all these phases of Christian faith must coexist and interpenetrate each other. The deepest student of the mysteries of God is at the same time the sinner, whose eye must turn to the cross, and is ever on the way to that shadow of death, which is lighted only by the Resurrection. But still the saying is so far true as this—that our point of view is necessarily modified by our enlarged Science, which is as a schoolmaster to bring us to understand the true meaning of this universal Headship of our Lord Jesus Christ, over the whole vastness of created being, and through all the ages from the beginning to the end of time; while yet throughout we retain that ineradicable sense of our own moral and spiritual personality in the close personal relation to Him, which the text expresses as giving us in Him our own inheritance of God [1].

---

[1] 'In every age the theory of the Divine Economy will present itself under an aspect corresponding with the general aspect, under which the whole finite order presents itself. It cannot but be that the

What is the full meaning, and what the actual power, of this universal Headship we do not know, and we cannot expect to know, with the same clearness which attaches to His Headship of our own individual soul, or His Headship of the Catholic Church. For these appeal to our own moral sense; they belong to our own spiritual life; they concern our own salvation. Without the knowledge of these, through mind and heart, we cannot rightly live or die. The larger truth seems rather to meet the needs of our intellect and imagination; and to teach us through both the lesson mainly of wonder and adoration. It is sufficient to know of this vast material universe, that all in the past was called into being 'through Him'; all in the present consists in its marvellous order 'in Him'; all in the future shall work itself out 'unto Him,' to fulfil His purpose, to manifest His glory. It is sufficient to know that of all the spiritual order—as of men and angels, so of any other races of rational creatures, which the far-off orbs of heaven may contain—He is both the Light and the Life—the Light of the intellectual, the Life of the moral and spiritual being. It is sufficient to know that the immanence of Divine Power in all creation, which our

views, which are entertained of the relations of man to the earth on which he lives, of the earth to the universe, of the period of human life to the measurable period of the existence of the objects of sense, should affect our views of the Redemption and Consummation of man, not in essence, but in mode of apprehension. . . . The sovereign pre-eminence of Scripture, as the vehicle of spiritual knowledge, lies in this,—that it finds fuller interpretation from growing experience.' (Westcott on 'The Gospel of Creation' in the *Epistles of St. John*, p. 305.)

Science seems more and more clearly to disclose, comes from the Omnipresence in it of a Divine Personality, after the distinct image of which our own personality was framed—the Presence of the true and Eternal Son of God, at once dwelling in it, and yet infinitely transcending it. It is sufficient thus to feel of all the immeasurable vastness of the universe, what we know more clearly of our own life and the life of humanity— that (according to the old theological distinction) all things are 'from the Father' by transcendent Will, all things 'through the Son' by indwelling Presence, all things 'by the operation of the Holy Spirit,' working out the realization of that Presence, and for this brooding over the face of material creation, as well as moving in the heart of the spiritual. If we can believe these truths in broad, majestic outline, even though all details be to us unknown or dimly seen, then we can go on in willing and hopeful sympathy with every advance of the knowledge of Nature in its largest sense, with every new discovery of the vastness of the universe, and the manifold unity of the Power, gradually developed in it through immeasurable time into infinite variety— sure that in this immensity we shall neither lose ourselves nor lose the knowledge of God, because everywhere we find the Presence of Him, in whom is the life of our own souls, and the corporate spiritual life of the Church of Christ.

All this belongs to the truth of the Presence of Christ in and with the universe from the beginning; but, as we pursue in faith this line of thought, we shall, I think be led naturally to infer, although we cannot pretend to know, that even the Manifestation of the Son of God in our flesh, which is the supernatural crown of God's dispensation to humanity, and which therefore primarily and properly concerns humanity, may yet have some larger bearing also on this larger order of things. For, in respect of our humanity, that deeper teaching of the New Testament, at which we have glanced, represents the Incarnation as having close connection with the indwelling in it from the beginning of the Word of God. It passes on without break from the life-giving power, flowing from that indwelling to all creation, to tell how the 'Word was made flesh and tabernacled visibly among us'; so that men in Him actually beheld the Divine glory, and had revealed to them, through the only-begotten Son, the Father, whom no man hath seen, or can see. Even the redemptive power of that Manifestation, while it properly concerns men, and most closely those who have the first-fruits of the Spirit, is spoken of as secondarily touching 'the whole creation'—evidently by the context the whole terrestrial Creation—waiting in eager expectation for its final consummation. If now to us the sphere of this indwelling power is seen to extend itself even to the starry walls of the Universe—the *flammantia moenia mundi*—must not the belief in some larger significance of the crowning Epiphany of the Incarnation expand with that expansion? We note that this Manifestation is presented to us under two aspects—two distinct phases of 'the great humility'—the one, which the humility of the Incarnation and the corresponding glorification of the Ascension bring out to us, and which, as being simply the crown of God's self-revelation and the perfection of His image in humanity, seems to be the fore-ordained gift to humanity in itself —the other in the greater and sadder humility of the Atonement, offered in the Passion, sealed as accepted in the Resurrection, which clearly is the gift of God's unspeakable love to humanity as sinful, for its salvation both from sin and death. We may perhaps conceive—as religious thought has delighted to conceive—that man's spiritual condition, as fallen in sin, although capable of redemption and renewal to repentance, is darkly exceptional among other bright orders of God's rational creatures, who are still, as He made them, 'very good'; and that accordingly the manifestation of 'Christ crucified' belongs properly to man, and through man to the terrestrial creation, of which he is the head and the lord, and which, as in some mysterious way it was overshadowed by his fall, so shall partake of his redemption. It may be so; whether it is so, we cannot know. But in any case the brighter and larger aspect of the Manifestation remains, untouched by this limitation, in its universal scope of bearing upon the whole creation of God.

What that bearing is, we can but infer—with the reverent caution of imperfect knowledge—from analogy to that effect upon humanity, which we do know more clearly. For in regard to man we are taught by His own word to believe, not only in a subjective effect through the knowledge and love of faith upon every believing soul, but in a deeper and wider objective effect upon the condition and nature of all humanity.

Now in respect of the former effect, we find that the Revelation of Christ is certainly spoken of again and again in Apostolic teaching, as extending its rays of light far beyond the sphere of human nature. It is a Revelation of God's Infinite Wisdom and Love, before all the higher orders of rational beings; it is that which 'the angels desire to look into'; it is that which 'before principalities and powers in heavenly places makes known through the Church the manifold wisdom of God, according to the Eternal purpose, which He purposed in Christ Jesus our Lord[1].' May we not, as Butler suggested long ago in respect of the manifestation on earth of the Moral government of God[2], 'enlarge our notions of the plan of Providence,' in its relation to all rational beings, 'in some sort proportionably,' (to use his own words) 'to what late discoveries have enlarged our views with respect to the material world'? May we not extend the declaration of this illuminating function to the whole order, whatever it may be, of God's rational creatures? Nay, if on such high matters reverent speculation be allowable, may we not go further still, and conceive that in some way the objective reality of the Incarnation may have its wider effect, known or unknown, on all creation, which we see more and more clearly to be in all its parts one continuous whole—on the spiritual creation, as having closest likeness to man—even on the material creation, as closely linked with the spiritual. May it not possibly even have its analogies in other spheres of being,

---

[1] 1 Pet. i. 12; Eph. iii. 10, 11.
[2] See Butler's *Analogy*, Part i. c. 3.

and so, all-perfect as it is to us, be the revelation in humanity of some transcendent Law of Manifestation of the Godhead to all His creatures, which fulfils itself everywhere in His own appointed way?

But, however this may be, certainly every way the Light and Grace of the Eternal Son of God, incarnate in our nature, are seen to extend through all the whole sphere of being. He is exalted that, in the largest sense of the word, He may 'fill all things.'

(V) What is to us the spiritual effect of this Revelation of Him? Not (I think) unlike the power of that mysterious vision of Him in the Apocalypse, which so grandly closes for us the story of His plainer manifestation on earth. It does not tell directly upon thought and conscience, like the record of His perfect word and life here; it does not speak to the heart, like the lifting up for us on the Cross, of His infinite love; it does not, like the Incarnation, bring home the mystery of 'God with us' in such close and living power, that it can be the main strength of our faith in the communion of God with man, which makes the sacredness of this present life. But it tells, as a great strain of Divine music, upon the Imagination—that faculty in us, which so strikingly links together the clear light of understanding and the glow of passion—so as to stir through it 'thought beyond our thought' and feelings spiritualized above mere emotion.

That spiritual effect has, as has been already said, its special value, as (so to speak) consecrating our modern enlargement of thought; which in itself is apt to be somewhat dreamy and self-forgetful,—somewhat too far removed from sympathy with the needs and emotions of actual human life—somewhat dulled as to keenness in the right human sense of the horror of evil and of 'hunger and thirst after righteousness.' It is not enough to muse, or even to wonder, in the sense of the Infinite; although no doubt, wonder (as Carlyle has taught us) is a preparatory condition of insight into the heart of things. Marvellously that wonder should be stirred in us—though we have been warned that its capacity is not always preserved in Scientific study—as we gain clearer and clearer glimpses of the vast and manifold unity of the Universe, and these, moreover, glimpses, which only show us how beyond the circle of our knowledge it stretches immeasurably into the unknown. There falls on the soul a silence of bewilderment and awe, which is a natural preparation for reverence and worship. Yet in itself it is but a preparation: the vague so-called 'worship of the silent sort,' of a reverent Agnosticism, unable either to discern or to articulate, is no living worship at all; for worship implies communion of human personality with some Personality Divine. As Dr. Arnold once said, with the keen insight of strong common sense, it fuses the faith in God into something like the vague admiration, with which we gaze at a beautiful sunset. But, as we search into the infinity around us for something more definite and living than this, the cry rises more than ever; 'Oh that I knew where I might find Him!... I go forward, but He is not there; and backward, but I cannot perceive Him.' Then comes to us in this darkness the light of that Revelation of Christ, which shows Him in personal relation to all this infinity. When by it we can find Christ in it all—when out of the unspeakable glory, we see the Face that we know, and hear the Voice that we love—then only does the preparation for worship complete itself in the reality. God is known, as well as dimly felt, as through all and yet above all; and, like the elders in the Apocalypse, we see in the exalted majesty of heaven the Lamb slain for us, and so we can fall down and adore in an intelligent and articulate worship Him who liveth for ever and ever.

Nor should we omit in this connection the lesson taught us as to the right attitude of the soul towards our Lord Himself. It is well that we realize His perfect humanity, having sympathy with all the trial, all the weakness, all the suffering of our own. Through it 'we come boldly to the Throne of Grace' in faith; through it we learn the lesson of love to Him who so loved us. But there is, as the needful complement to this, the lesson of adoration—sometimes, as it would seem, but imperfectly learnt by those who think of Him only as the Son of Man. The sentimental familiarity of some modern forms of address to Him has been noted, as strangely in contrast with that Apostolic practice in the New Testament, which never, except for special reason, uses the simple 'Jesus' of the Gospels, without attaching to it some phrase of reverence, if not of adoration. What can more effectually rebuke that over-familiar tone of thought, than the vision opened to us of Him, as exalted not only over humanity, but over all the immeasurable vastness of created being—

receiving, as of right, a share in 'the glory and honour and power' belonging to Him who 'created all things, and for whose pleasure they are and were created'?

But, beyond this satisfaction of the Imagination, and this lesson of reverence, there are also other lessons to be read to the intellect from this knowledge of Christ as over all Creation. In it we find God in the universe, and we find man.

We find God. We know how the ineradicable conviction of a Divine Will and Purpose of Wisdom and of Love, both in the perfection and in the beauty of Creation, is apt to be troubled—partly to the intellect by the sense of mystery that we cannot fathom in its Laws—partly, and more seriously, to the moral sense, by the intolerable presence of evil, in suffering and sin and death; which, though there is now (in reaction from shallow Optimism in the past) a tendency to exaggerate it, as not only resisting but overmastering the Divine Law of good, is yet only too real, both as a burden and as a perplexity. But, when we see in all things the Christ whom we know, these contradictions are hushed. When we are sure that in all Creation work that very same Wisdom and Love, which He has Himself shown, in the bright flashes of beneficent miracle, and in the steady radiance of His life on earth—like what we know in man, but rising above all that here limits and degrades it—then all the bewildering mystery of our Natural Theology vanishes. When, moreover, we can feel that in the great order of the world there must be the foresight and the remedy of all those mysterious evils, under which all creation suffers, because it is ruled by Him, who came down from Heaven to take them away by the sacrifice of Himself—who still, by His Divine Intercession in Heaven, and His guidance of His Church on earth, is overcoming all that militates against happiness and goodness—then, if we still feel the moral burden of mystery, we can bear it in faith, and see on the horizon the light of a rising hope. Our Lord's miracles on earth are Epiphanies of this double truth. So far as they are miracles of creative power, and of mastery over Nature, they are (as St. John teaches us [1]) simply Epiphanies of His glory over all the world. But the miracles, more frequent and dearer to His Divine mercy, are the miracles of the healing of body and soul, and of the raising of the dead; and these are cheering Epiphanies of the victory of that Divine and all-pervading glory over pain and sin and death.

Nor must we omit that last lesson, which is taught us in the closing words of the text. In this knowledge we find man. If we can see Christ in all creation, then in Him the soul finds itself, as having in Him the sure and certain inheritance of a true sonship of God. It is not lost in the vastness and complexity of Nature; it is not a mere instrument in the hand of irresistible force; it is not a mere bubble, to form and burst on the stream of time. As has been already said, there is in the soul itself a continual witness against these dreary notions; and the power of that witness ought to be strengthened, in proportion to the increase of its power of discovering in all the vastness of the universe

[1] John iii. 11.

the laws and forces which rule it: for such power surely indicates some likeness to the supreme Author of all. But, when we know in that Author the Christ, who has lived and died for each one of us, and who draws each to the Godhead through Himself in an individualizing tenderness of love—who has told us that in His Supreme Majesty, still bearing the marks of His Passion for us, He watches over and pleads for the very least of us, and so orders all things as to prepare for each an appointed place with Himself for all Eternity—then the conflict of the two voices within us is set at rest. Infinitely little in ourselves, we are infinitely great in Him. The old confidence of the Psalmist receives a new strength of meaning: for we know that the Godhead itself in Christ has 'visited and redeemed His people.'

There is somewhere a famous picture of the Christ in His glory. It is the face of the Divine Humanity which we know and love so well, and by its own spiritual power it draws to Him the whole mind and heart. But yet there is a new thrill of consciousness of the infinite greatness of His majesty, when, looking closer, we see that the glory round His head is made up of myriads of angel faces, all catching and reflecting His light, in proportion to their nearness, till they fade away into immeasurable distance. So is it in the line of thought opened to us in the text to-day, when we see, gathered round our dear Lord and Master, all the various cycles of being in their infinite and perfect order —all seen as centred in Him—all, whether near or far, showing by reflection something of His glory. For thus the whole sphere of being is to us alive in many phases and gradations of worship ; and by that universal worship, while we still know and trust and love His perfect humanity, we learn afresh to adore the fulness of the Godhead in Him.

LECTURE V.

CHRIST AND HUMAN SOCIETY.

We, being many, are one body in Christ, and everyone members one of another.—Rom. xii. 5.

IN relation to the truth expressed in these words—once a new revelation to the world of human brotherhood, now an accepted commonplace of Christian teaching—we may consider another exemplification of the witness of Science to Christ, as having the effect of elucidation, bringing out with new clearness and brilliancy certain old truths of the Gospel message, and transferring them (so to speak) from the background to the foreground of Christian thought. Of such elucidation we have already seen one most striking example, in the wonderful light, thrown by modern discovery or inference of the vastness of the natural and spiritual universe, on the Apostolic doctrine of the Christ, as not only the Light and Saviour of humanity, but the Head of all created being, 'gathered up in Him.' We have now to examine the same elucidatory witness to Christ, as borne not by the Science of the Universe, but by what we have learnt to call the Social Science of humanity.

(I) We have in this to contemplate a unity, infinitely narrower in its scope, but yet one far nearer and dearer to us, telling, moreover, not only on the intellect and imagination, but on the conscience and the heart—one which, therefore, calls upon us to know it and to serve it, with a call of imperious moral urgency. Never has that call been more urgent than in our own days. No one, I think, who reads with any insight the signs of the times, will doubt that one great burning question, which our modern civilization, if it is to live, must resolutely and wisely answer, is the question how human society can be really One Body, while yet it has 'many members'—each in some sense complete in itself, and each, for the discharge of its proper function, needing to retain its own freedom and individuality. St. Paul once answered that question by the simple words 'in Christ.' The answer has been taken up and wrought out in all the Christian centuries; and, while it is necessarily unchanged in its essential meaning, it has worn to each generation an aspect corresponding to the social knowledge and the social needs of the age. Now that to us this knowledge has been greatly widened and deepened—now that these needs have been most formidably intensified—ought we not to find that the old answer has assumed a new clearness and depth of meaning?

It has been said (as by Laveleye) that from that answer many of the chief modern schemes for the regeneration of society have, consciously or unconsciously, caught their inspiration [1]. It is (I think) certain that

[1] 'The ideas and sentiments, which have given birth to Socialism, were deeply engraven on our minds and hearts by Christianity. . . .

in our own country Christianity—not least as embodied in a Church claiming to be national—is now more than ever challenged to show that this answer has both a theoretical sufficiency, and a practical reality of meaning. The challenge may be sometimes ignorant and impatient, assuming that to deliver a social gospel is the sole or highest mission of the Church. But it at least implies a belief that our Christianity has such a gospel; and, moreover, that, in order to proclaim it with power, it only needs to be more thoroughly Christian—more Christ-like (that is) in primitive simplicity of idea, both of the brotherhood of man and of the Fatherhood of God [1]. All men will allow that it must be fairly met.

Every Christian, who understands and accepts the teaching of his Master, is at heart a Socialist; and every Socialist, whatever may be his hatred of religion, bears within himself an unconscious Christianity.' (Lavelaye's *Socialism of To-day*, English translation by G. H. Orpen, p. xix.) The accuracy of the remark plainly depends on the sense in which the word 'Socialism' is used. If Socialism be defined (with Proudhon) as 'aspiration towards the improvement of society,' it is obviously true; if (with Adolphe Held) as 'demanding the subordination of the individual to Society,' it will not be accepted without some discrimination: if we take M. Lavelaye's own definition, that it aims at introducing 'greater equality in social conditions, and realizing these reforms by law,' it must necessarily generate in application much difference of opinion among those who, as Christians, equally desire the well-being of human Society. There are few subjects on which it is more necessary to begin by defining our terms.

[1] From some recent experience I know how strong is the feeling on this matter among working men. All directly anti-Christian movement has been largely superseded by Socialistic aspiration and agitation, and a demand from the Church of an energetic 'Christian Socialism.' So far as I observe, if the Church is attacked, it is as owner of property in land and endowment. If Christianity is distrusted it is on the ground that our actual Christianity is very

My contention is that it can be met hopefully, if it be met thoughtfully, not by superficial inference from this or that doing or saying, but by going down to the root of the matter. The true social doctrine of Christianity cannot be rightly estimated by taking, for example, the free community of goods, in the first enthusiasm of the infant Church at Jerusalem, as a type of universal Christian obligation, in face of the distinct evidence, that it never extended to the Churches even of the Apostolic age; or by applying the letter, as distinct from the spirit, of the Sermon on the Mount, to social conditions and needs, utterly unlike those for which it was spoken; or even by taking the life, which our Lord saw to be needful for Himself and His immediate disciples, in the discharge of their unique mission, and enforcing it literally on the whole body of His future Church. From each of these indeed, we learn great lessons of principle, bearing upon the true idea of Christian unity; and we are taught also how under similar circumstances it ought to be practically exemplified. But the idea must be thoughtfully considered in itself; and, when it is so considered, in relation to what Social Science— not, perhaps, without receiving, directly or indirectly,

imperfectly Christian; that, after so many centuries, its moral and spiritual influence has failed to redress social evil and injustice; that, in fact, it has allied itself too much with the world as it is, not as it ought to be. There is, at the same time, much of vehement, even passionate, denunciation of the whole existing condition of society, showing a deep-seated discontent, indicating again and again an impatience of gradual development, avowing distrust of purely moral influences, and a desire to right all supposed wrongs, either by almost despotic law, or by revolutionary violence.

some guidance from it—has brought out to us as to the actual Laws of human society, I believe that here once more Science will be found to be 'a schoolmaster to bring us to Christ.'

(II) 'One Body and many members'—the metaphor is probably as old and as universal as human language itself. But, old as it is, the tendency of modern thought, finding everywhere real analogies underlying such metaphors, is increasingly to regard it as conveying an objective reality of meaning. Just as Physiological Science draws an analogy between the growth of an individual being, and the Evolution of the whole sum of Organic Life, so Social Science inclines to apply to what it calls the 'Social Organism' the laws discerned in individual growth and life [1]. This application must, indeed, be made with certain reservations, for no metaphor drawn from a single organism can adequately express the free individuality of each human soul, coexisting with the unity of the whole society [2]. But the comparison goes as far, as any such comparison can

[1] See, for example, Mr. Herbert Spencer's Essay on 'Progress.' (*Essays*, vol. i. pp. 8–61.) His contention is that 'the law of organic progress,' traced in the growth of the individual being from the ovum to full maturity, 'is the law of all progress,' both of human society, and of the world of its material environment; and that 'this uniformity of procedure' 'in Social Evolution' 'is a consequence of some fundamental necessity.'

[2] This imperfection is implied by the variety of metaphors, employed in the New Testament to express the unity of humanity with and in Christ,—the Body and the members, the Vine and the branches, the building and the chief corner-stone, the husband and the wife. Each brings out to us some peculiar feature of the truth, to which all bear generally a common witness.

go, in expressing what instinctive human consciousness declares, that our nature is at once individual and social—each man, as a distinct member, having an inner world of thought, conscience, will, in which, so far as humanity is concerned, he is absolutely alone, and yet all being bound together into one body by a subtle network of spiritual ties, through which there thrills one common life. Civilization, which is the growth of humanity, has always been recognised, as developing both elements of this certain, though mysterious, antithesis, by free individual cultivation, and by harmony of all individualities in the citizenship of a great commonwealth, ultimately coextensive with humanity. But, while this antithesis has always been thus acknowledged in general, it is clear that at different times prominence has been given, even to excess, to one or other of its parts.

Looking only to our own country, we cannot but see how, in the England of old days, both under the feudal system, and the first growth out of it of the kingly power, the dominant idea was of the unity and authority of Society, both as a whole and in its lesser social forms. The unit of Society at large was not the individual, but the lesser society of the family or the class; at every point individual action, social, political, commercial, was always regulated and limited, often overborne, by Law. This social condition, moreover, was accepted as natural, because felt to be needful. Loyalty to the supreme authority became a ruling passion, showing itself in forms, which seem to us excessive and even fantastic; and its exuberance is all the more remarkable, when we note that it often belonged to periods of great enterprise and mental activity. Even in the religious life the same leading idea asserted itself as supreme. The Church was looked upon not so much as One Body of living members, but rather as a great 'City of God'— a Kingdom of Christ under authorities ordained by Him, in a great hierarchy culminating in His Vicar on earth—having right and power to rule not only individual action, but individual thought and faith: and it has always seemed to me significant that, even within that general authority of the Church, the life of stricter submission, as in monastic communities, to an absolute rule, in which all individual freedom was merged, was held to be, as indeed it was called, the true 'religious life.'

Then came, in the Renaissance of the sixteenth century, the revolt of Individualism against this all-pervading power of Law—the assertion of liberty, in idea and thought against the iron symmetry of Scholasticism, in action against social and political despotism, in faith against infallible and absolute Church authority. Gradually that assertion won its victorious way—not, of course, without conflict, even of political and religious civil war, but happily in our country without extreme vehemence of revolution; and for some three centuries there was a continual advance of Individualism—free trade and competition in our commerce—'civil and religious liberty' (to use the common phrase) in our political life, restricting within the narrowest limits the regulating action of law—the conception of religion commonly called 'Protestant,' as a spiritual force essentially personal, in which the Headship of Christ Himself was felt as a direct Headship over the individual man, and the very idea of the One Body in Him, though, of course, it could not be denied, was suffered to fall into comparative abeyance—to imply, indeed, little more than the religious association of individual Christians, like-minded to one another, for mutual encouragement and edification.

But now in our own days the Social problem has evidently passed into a new phase. This change of idea, and still more of feeling, arises from many causes. First—perhaps most obviously—from bitter experience of the fruits of an excessive Individualism; partly in the development of the natural inequality between men to extremes of contrast between individuals and classes, which are fairly appalling, and of which we feel that they cannot and must not endure; partly in the growth out of excess of free competition of grave moral evils— selfishness, untruthfulness, adulteration of goods, dishonesty of reckless speculation, antagonism of classes and cruel struggle for existence between men—which impair both individual character and national loyalty. It has arisen, again, through the disentanglement in our political life of the assertion of civil and religious liberty from the movement towards democracy, which was formerly allied, and in removal of class privileges and restrictions, even identified with it, but which is now assuming towards it a position substantially of antagonism, because naturally inclining to sacrifice the individual to the community. But I think that it owes much, perhaps most, of its power to deeper Social

Science—revolutionizing the hard and narrow conceptions of the old Political Economy [1]—which studies humanity as a whole, having its laws of corporate growth, moral as well as physical, coming down from the past to the present, to which individuality must submit, and ought to submit freely. From all these combined influences there has grown upon us a strong conviction that in some way the old truth—that Society is one Body, though having many members—must be made new, as a living reality. 'Socialism' (it is commonly said) 'is in the air'; and if by Socialism is meant, as should be meant, not this or that theory of method, but the strong universal sense that what may be called broadly the Socializing forces, of Law, Cooperation, Public Spirit, have now to be guarded and

---

[1] 'The wisest Economists of our time' (says M. Laveleye), 'have recognised, that the exaggerated, though often well-founded, criticisms passed on our social condition by Socialists, have been the means of producing undoubted progress in Political Economy.' He instances the recognition by Economists of the function of human laws of justice, as well as 'natural laws' of tendency, and of the infinite importance, not only of the question of production of wealth, but of the question of its right distribution. (Laveleye's *Socialism of To-day*, p. xliii.) It is seen that 'the present distribution of wealth is perilous, alike to those who have and to those who want.' It is felt, as was truly and eloquently said by the President of the Economic Section of the British Association in 1889, that 'Every year economic problems become more complex; every year the necessity of studying them from many different points of view, and in many different connections, becomes more urgent. Every year it is more manifest that we need to have more knowledge, and to get it soon, in order to escape, on the one hand, from the cruelty and waste of irresponsible competition and the licentious use of wealth, and on the other from the tyranny and the spiritual death of an iron-bound Socialism.'

strengthened, the saying is true. Nor can I think it a mere accidental coincidence, that in our religious thought and action there has been a corresponding revival of what has been not untruly named 'Catholicism'—the belief (that is) in the corporate life through the Indwelling of Christ in the Church itself —a life which has come down to us in unbroken continuity through all ages since the Day of Pentecost, and which implies some authority of direction and regulation over individual action and faith. For religious thought has necessarily connection, in various degrees of power, with the whole of man's life. In this case it would seem that the religious sense of unity preceded, and in some degree stimulated, the secular; and certainly the question for the Church now is how the two impulses can rightly be harmonized together.

But, while there is, and while (if I may venture so to say) there ought to be, this changed direction of social thought and aspiration, yet, here as always, it must be clear to any thoughtful mind, that the past cannot be ignored in any of its parts, and that any attempt to go back to the old condition of society, as strictly organized under an almost absolute rule of law, must be a fatal anachronism. The assertion of liberty of thought, conditioned only by the laws of truth and righteousness, has been victoriously made once for all, and is being clenched every day by new intellectual enterprise and discovery. It can never be unmade; and, within limits, and those wide limits, it must carry with it freedom of word and freedom of action. We, least of all, can forget this in England. I do not think that we have yet unlearnt the teaching which bids us glory in

> '... the land, which freemen till,
> Which sober-suited Freedom chose,
> A land, where, girt with friends or foes,
> A man may speak the thing he will.'

For indeed it is deepened to us by thoughtful study of the appointed order of being. We must see that through such freedom, in spite of its errors, its vagaries, its intestine conflicts, it is God's will to rule man—neither by His Providence absolutely determining our action, nor by His Spirit over-mastering and enforcing our wills. All despotisms, which attempt what He Himself will not do, are, therefore, necessarily unnatural, retrograde against the progress which He has ordained, and, as being unnatural, doomed to failure—whether the failure of disruption by revolutionary violence, or the worse failure for a time of a lethargic and deadening success.

Least of all, as it seems to me, can such usurpation maintain itself now, in respect of that religious sphere of life, which brings out most strongly and directly the inalienable freedom of thought and conscience. In reaction against excessive religious Individualism, with its inevitable conflicts and uncertainties, there has been (as we know but too well), even in some of the noblest minds, an eagerness to find and to obey implicitly some voice of command, absolute as claiming infallibility, before which the dread responsibility of freedom may be laid down. But this spiritual despotism can maintain its claim only by declaring war against the invincible elements of human progress—delivering itself (to use a celebrated phrase) 'from the yoke of history'—resisting (that is) the irresistible law of fact, seeking to ignore or undo the irrevocable past. Whatever, therefore, may be the religious destiny of the future, it seems impossible that religious despotism—whether in the hands of a single man, or a class, or even the whole body—can ever wield over individual freedom the power, which once it exercised in the imperfect civilization of days gone by.

But perhaps the lesson, most urgently needed for our own times, is that which bids us remember that in this matter it makes no essential difference, whether this despotism is one, which, as democratic, each man has helped to make, and in which he has some infinitesimal share. Despotism, however originated, and wherever seated, is despotism still. In its democratic form, if it is mitigated to each man by the consciousness of his own consent to it, and his own power, however insignificant, in guiding it, yet, on the other hand, it is, in its daily pressure upon individual freedom, the most ruthless of all despotisms, alone untempered (to use the old proverbial phrase) 'either by epigram or by assassination,' and acting with a force, which collects and concentrates, not only the wisdom and the goodness, but the folly and the wickedness of humanity. Rightly (to continue my former quotation) are we warned to beware lest

> 'banded unions persecute
> Opinion, and induce a time
> When single thought is civil crime,
> And individual freedom mute.'

Yet, all the while, it is just that 'single thought,' spoken by the tongue of 'individual freedom,' which has in the born leaders of mankind, initiated all the chief steps of the intellectual and moral progress of humanity. It is always the few who lead, while the many have but to listen, and to judge whether they can accept and follow. Even in that necessary task of judgment, what fatal error and wrong has the world seen! If the vision of Truth and Goodness calls out Hosannas to-day, what of the 'Not this man, but Barabbas,' on the morrow? But, to go beyond that function—to claim by force of law, or at times lawlessness[1], to direct, control, enslave individual freedom—to refuse it all wide scope of exercise, within the limits of moral right and respect for the rights of others, whether of individuals or of the whole community—this is a fatal and disastrous usurpation, sinning against the true law of humanity. Under whatever grand names, with whatever high and generous hopes, it may advance, we have learnt not only from true science of humanity, but from terrible or disheartening experience, that, now at any rate, such usurpation cannot stand.

No! the unity of human society, which our age needs, must in some way recognise and conserve the freedom which has been won; and it follows from this that,

---

[1] It is notable that the lawlessness, apparently an increasing lawlessness, which is so ominous a feature of the present day, is not so much the lawlessness of individual self-will or selfishness, as the lawlessness of combination, fighting for the supposed rights or needs of class, party, or section; and that it shows itself most violently, wherever there is, rightly or wrongly, some distrust in the honesty and energy of the administration of law.

while it will, of course, use law, both coercive and directive, and claim that obedience to it be unhesitatingly rendered, it must rely mainly on influences, which tell on the individual by free conviction, moulding public opinion, fostering public spirit. In this direction, as in all others, it must decline to revert in the maturity of civilization to the reliance upon that overmastering force of Law, which was the rightful schoolmaster of simpler and cruder ages of society. It must aim at harmonizing together the Individualism and Socialism, which are really correlative, but are hastily assumed to be antagonistic to each other [1]. It must recognise, as the actual facts of human nature demand, at once the natural equality of all, in regard of indefeasible human rights, and the natural inequality of all, in respect of gifts, powers, opportunities. It must be something higher and more spiritual than those schemes for the reconstruction of society, which avowedly rely on material change and improvement, as the one thing needful, supposing that change of circumstances must in itself surely change the man. It must have as its

[1] I venture to quote on this point from a Paper at the Church Congress of 1890:—'Is this true Socialism irreconcilable with right Individualism—as is sometimes plainly declared, more often tacitly and practically assumed? The answer to the question is given by a glance at man's nature, which is obviously at once individual in free will, thought, conscience, spiritual aspiration, and social in the existence and in the recognition of all the ties of which we have spoken. Harmony, not antagonism, must be the law of the relation of these two forces, both equally natural, both inhering in one indivisible nature. Freedom is license, when it breaks these living ties: unity is despotic tyranny, when it does not merely condition, but ignores or crushes, freedom.

ideal 'that in free and generous co-operation each shall offer the fulness of his own life, that he may rejoice in the fulness of the life of the whole body.' Where shall the spirit of such unity be found? How shall the metaphor be realized of One Body with many members —each free and complete in itself, and yet all thrilled by one nervous energy, one life-blood from one heart?

(III) To that question it is historically certain that Christianity once supplied, as in the text, a very strong and practical answer. No one can doubt that it changed the Brotherhood of humanity, from a theory and an aspiration into a living reality. On all hands men are asking, Has it lost its force now? Is it still to solve the old problems in their new shapes, or is it to be superseded by some newer Gospel of idea, some newer enthusiasm of energy?

In order to reply to this question, it is necessary to see clearly what its theory of human unity is—what is meant by 'One Body in Christ.'

Unity in Christ is ultimately unity through Him in God. In the Baptism which is its appointed means, each individual nature is baptized into the Name—that is, into the Nature—of the Father and of the Son and of the Holy Ghost. So, and so only, is it 'engrafted into the body of Christ's Church.' In the Incarnation the Eternal Son is revealed as gathering all humanity into Himself, that He may make it one in sonship of God; in the Atonement, as lifted up that He may break the bonds of sin, and draw all the individual souls of men, as by a spiritual gravitation, to Himself and to the Godhead through Him; in the Resurrection and Ascension and the Mediatorial Royalty, as continuing till the end of the work so begun in His manifestation here, till it shall be completed in the restitution of all things at His Second Coming to judge the earth. This is the primary and direct unity of all souls in Him, as He Himself taught it, when He said, 'I am the Vine; ye are the branches.' Secondary and indirect, although most real, is the unity of all with one another.

Clearly is that order marked in the text—the diametrically contrary order to that of most Socialistic schemes of ancient or modern days. They are, like Plato's, 'Divine Republics;' in which the direct unity of all with one another—in part by the constraining force of law, in part by an enthusiastic cultus of humanity—is the one thing needful; and relation of the soul to a Supreme Power, if recognised at all, is put far away in some mysterious background—at most allowed to affect the inner life, in no sense conceived as ruling the course of human society. This, on the other hand, is a well-centred 'Kingdom of God'—'One Body' in the Headship of the Son of God and Man. Each through that Headship has his individual life 'hid in God'; all through that same Headship are members one of another.

How striking an illustration there is of this conception of human unity, in its analogy to the Law, which in the physical universe binds our system of worlds together! Under that Law there is at every point for each body the great central attraction of the sun, source to all of force, as of light and life; and yet, lest all should be drawn into it, and absorbed in its vastness, there is also at every point the velocity, tending (as we say) to 'fly off at a tangent'—to move (that is) as for the moment each body would move freely, if it were left to itself alone : and this balance of the uniting central force and the free centrifugal velocity is so absolutely predominant in its importance, that by it, roughly yet substantially, the orbits may be determined, in which all move side by side in a wonderful order. Yet, when we look more closely, we see that, subordinate indeed, but co-existent with this great central attraction, there is on each body a multitude of lesser attractions from all the other bodies of the system—proportionate (I may remark) not only to their greatness, but to their nearness; so that all in their motion form one great whole, continually acting and re-acting upon another, and so modifying, but never impairing, the effect of the primary law, under which the great ruling power is centred in the sun. Central force, free energy, mutual attraction —these, and these in this order, are the great ideas which emerge, when we study the system of which our world is a part. As we realize them, is not a new force given to the familiar metaphor in which the old prophet speaks of Christ as the 'Sun of Righteousness,' drawing all to Himself by moral attraction, along the living cords of Truth and Love? yet, so that at every moment each has also an impulse to move freely by self-determination of will, thus 'conscious,' at all times primarily, at some critical times exclusively, 'of God and his own soul'; and so that all are bound in a network of spiritual ties to one another, and, even in this lower sense, 'no man lives or dies to himself'?

Such certainly is the conception of the One Body in Christ; and that it is not to remain a mere abstract conception, but to be realized in practical energy by all, even the simplest of His disciples, He has Himself taught us in the 'Great Commandment' of Love. For love is the realization of unity with self, with man, with God. In the second great Commandment He implies, and so allows, 'the love of self'—the devotion (that is) of each soul, with a sense of duty and even of enthusiasm, to the man's own personal freedom and rights, to his happiness and perfection—in which we trace what has been called 'the will to live,' and the survival, rationalized and tempered, of the great Law, under which Organic Life has had its evolution of progress towards higher forms [1]. In that same Commandment He emphasizes the love of Man, but under the form of 'the love of our neighbour'—the love, that is, of all men, but of all in their various orders and degrees of connection with us. We see, moreover, that, while He clearly implies here what is taught everywhere—as by His word, so by His example—that in degree it is to rise above the love of self, and to call for willing self-sacrifice, yet, in the words 'as thyself,' He distinctly teaches that

[1] In this respect Christianity, recognising all the facts of human nature, stands in contrast with transcendental theories of 'Altruism.' Self-love (as Butler taught us long ago) is not 'selfishness,' in the common sense of the word, till it assumes an unrighteous and unnatural dominance. To brand with that name the desire for individual perfection, as crowned by the Christian hope of a personal immortality, surely argues a strange ignorance of what humanity really is, and of the duty to self, which is implied in the existence of a true personality, having capacity of spiritual perfection.

it is of the same kind, at once instinctive and rational, moving on the same moral level, to temper the love of self and harmonize with it, not to destroy it or overbear it as by an essential superiority. But the key to the right relation and harmony of both these secondary forces He gives us in the supremacy of the First Great Commandment of the love of God, embracing the whole mind of the intellect, the whole heart of affection, the whole soul of moral being, and the whole strength of practical energy. That love of the Supreme Power—as distinct from the wonder, and awe, and the obedience of submission in fear, which result naturally from any adequate conception of it—had for Israel its inspiration in the sense of a free covenant with the Lord Jehovah. But, in the perfection of that covenant in the Lord Jesus Christ, it became a 'new Commandment.' To use St. Paul's striking phrase, 'The Head of man is Christ, and the Head of Christ is God.' The Brotherhood of humanity in Christ—the only Fraternity which really conserves liberty—depends absolutely on the realization through Him, for each and all, of the Fatherhood of God.

(IV) How then did Christianity proceed to embody that idea in practical reality?

First of all unquestionably by the creation of a Catholic Church, in which all peoples and all generations should be one. I use the word creation; but, like other forms of Divine creation, it was a growth, evolved out of the idea itself. Nothing can be more unhistorical than the fancy (as, for instance, of M. Renan) that the main conception of the first preachers of the Gospel was the formation of a great world-wide empire over human thought and action. What was the actual fact, as we read it in the pages of the New Testament? 'They determined not' (as St. Paul himself testifies) 'to know' and declare 'anything save Jesus Christ,' as God in Man. The Catholic Church was but the natural extension of His humanity—the πλήρωμα (so He was pleased to consider it) 'of Him that filleth all in all[1]'; its unity was not made, but grew out of the unity drawing all souls to Him.

And I may note in passing that, whenever in Church history that true order of Apostolic teaching has been forgotten or obscured—whenever the first object has been to form a Kingdom over men, and to win souls to it, instead of simply ministering the light and grace of Christ, and leaving it to Him to win the souls for whom He died—whenever its unity has been made to depend on outward bonds, however sacred, or even on direct subordination of the soul to the voice and will of the whole community, expressed through some form of absolute authority—then the true Christian ideal has been marred, with results invariably of corruption and disaster. The new Comtist 'Church of Humanity' has been described by an acute critic as 'Catholicity without Christianity,' that is, without Christ. May not its idea have been learnt in some degree from perversions of the true Christian idea, which practically put Catholicity first, and Christianity only in the second place?

It is only in the Catholic Church that the true

[1] Eph. i. 23. 'The head' (says St. Chrysostom on this passage) 'is the complement of the body and the body of the head.'

Christian ideal of the unity of all mankind is completely set forth, and, in spite of the imperfections of sin and error, gradually realized in anything like fulness. Necessarily (as St. Paul shows us in the great passage of his Ephesian Epistle [1]) the soul of that unity has its inner life in the communion with the One Spirit, the One Lord, the One Father, of whom the One Baptism testifies; and it shows itself through those spiritual energies, which in our common humanity underlie all individual and natural peculiarities—the 'one faith,' the 'one hope,' the one love, which is 'the bond of peace.' And 'of these the greatest is love'—love to God in Christ, and through Him to one another. For love is the free recognition of unity, the free spirit of sacrifice, which at once realizes self and loses self [2]. Old as man himself: for is it not what we significantly call 'humanity'? yet undoubtedly a new creation in the life of the Church of Christ.

Necessarily the ideal of Christian aspiration is to extend this spiritual unity, as 'Catholic,' over all the world, so that it may interpenetrate the whole human

[1] Eph. iv. 4-6.
[2] At the same time the definition of Christian Love always implies that it is to be harmonized with Truth or Righteousness. The likeness of Christ is to St. Paul, the 'being true in love,' and to St. John, with characteristic variation, the 'loving in truth.' (Eph. iv. 15; 2 John 1.) In relation to some of the enthusiasms of the day, it is necessary to emphasize the truth, that love to man, whether to individual or collective humanity, cannot rightly overbear truth and righteousness. Sir Walter Scott's Jeanie Deans, who will not lie even to save a loved sister, is a truer ideal than the modern heroine, who would despise such restraint, and for such an end would cast all truth to the winds.

society. Just so far as this is in degree realized—as races professedly Christian are, directly and indirectly, Christianized—as through them races still heathen (mostly the weaker subject-races of our modern world) are drawn into the Christian family—it is certain in fact that man is united in a spiritual brotherhood, the only such brotherhood which the world has seen.

But, while this is the supreme ideal of Christianity, yet secondarily its power is felt in the recognition and regeneration of all the natural forms of unity—the family, the city, the nation, the race; and it is to be noted, that, following out the idea implied in our Master's description of the love of humanity as the 'love of our neighbour,' Christianity has stood forth boldly, in contrast with many socialistic theories, to recognise and guard the sacredness of these lesser unities within the greater unity of universal brotherhood. How largely in this respect its position is justified both by historical experience, and by scientific study of the forces of Heredity, will be plain to most observers. But of the fact of this graduated social action of Christianity, harmonized with its universal enthusiasm of humanity, there can be no doubt. Not by accident—not merely (I think) for the sake of convenience—has even the Church unity itself incorporated these natural forms into its own higher life: so that the family becomes 'the Church in the house,' the city the parish or diocese, the nation a national Church, the whole race, actually or potentially, the Church Catholic. It has done this, because a Supernatural Force always harmonizes and assimilates to itself whatever is natural.

But, independently of this incorporation, Christianity, ideal and actual, has always manifested a deep interest, an effective influence, in respect of all these forms in themselves, and testified that each, as one body, ought to find its unity in Christ [1].

We know commonly, yet we hardly realize in its fulness, the exalting effect on the life of the family of that Christian teaching, which (as in the same great Epistle of St. Paul) hallows all domestic relationships, as reproductions of the Divine relations to man—the marriage, from which the family takes its rise, as the type of the mystical union of Christ with His Church—its fatherhood of authority and love, as a delegation from the Fatherhood of God—its brotherhood as a miniature of the brotherhood of humanity in the house of the One Father—even its service (once a slavery, now through Christian influence, a free service) as a not unrecognised part of the universal service of God [2]. Under that high religious sanction the sacredness of the home has grown up among us: by that sanction against individual lawlessness, against low materializing ideas, and against socialistic encroachments, it is mainly guarded still. The living inspiration of this teaching has done what could not be done, either by the enlightened sense of expediency, or the strong coercion of Law, or even the philosophic sense of the creation of high moral relations

---

[1] I may perhaps be allowed here to refer to a fuller treatment of this subject which I have attempted in *Lectures on Christianity and Socialism* (Cassell, 1890).

[2] Eph. v. 22—vi. 9; Col. iii. 18—iv. 1; Comp. 1 Pet. ii. 18—iii. 7.

through that which serves for the physical propagation of the race[1].

Less direct and powerful, yet not less real, this social influence of Christianity over the larger and looser unity of what we call 'neighbourhood'—whether the neighbourhood of locality, most felt in old days, or the neighbourhood of class, strongest in our own. With regard to the former, we know how, not least in our English history, the Church of city or village, in setting forth the light and grace of Christ, has necessarily become the centre of the secular life of the community, and of all the energies of local sympathy and fellowship and charity which bind it together. With regard to the latter, we know how in old days the Guilds of common handicraft or commerce or art were distinctly hallowed by religious influence—as crafts or 'mysteries' (to use the old London civic term) 'in the Body of Christ.' Of such religious relation the traces are unhappily but faint in the corresponding associations of our own day. Yet the sense of it is not extinct. As the Church enters more and more into the consciousness of her social responsibilities, there is a growing tendency in these associations to revive in-

[1] It is a significant fact, that at the very time of the first birth of Christianity in the great Roman Empire, the Emperor Augustus—a cold and far-seeing politician—felt so strongly the need of raising and defending against a growing corruption the sanctity of the family, that he sought vainly to protect and revive it by force of stringent law; and his favourite poet, himself only a genial easy-going man of the world, mourned over the degradation of the home by an 'age prolific of evil,' and told how
'Hoc fonte derivata, clades
In patriam populumque fluxit.'

formally the old acknowledgment of religious sanction. Certainly, in all class-aspirations and class-antagonisms, there is urgent call to the representatives of religious ideas to intervene, especially in the cause of the weak: and to that call there has been in response a marked inclination—sometimes in details wise, and sometimes unwise—to enter upon the region even of 'business,' and to claim in it recognition of the obligations of Christian unity.

Certainly when we pass to the greater and nobler unity of the Nation—although the old theory has broken down, which, in England at least, made Church and Nation coextensive, and added, as a matter of course, to the natural unity into which all were born, the higher unity into which they were born again—still the phrase 'National Christianity' has an informal but substantial meaning, which is indicated by the blazon of the Cross on our banner, and the expression of our loyalty in a 'National Anthem.' English Christianity has unquestionably moulded English history and English character; just as our English Bible, and in less degree our English Prayer-Book, have coloured English literature. It must be so; for Christian faith cannot but tell with power both on the loyalty, which is here the analogue of loving reverence for Fatherhood, and the patriotism, which expresses the Brotherhood of the whole nation. How remarkable it is that, while the first preaching of Christianity, in its strong emphasis of individuality in Christ on the one hand, and Catholic unity in Him on the other, seemed to leave no room for the development of the lesser unities of human society yet national unity has grown up with unsurpassed vigour in Christendom, and has resisted all efforts to crush it in the name of a larger unity, whether civil, as in the Empire, or spiritual, as in the Church of Rome! How infinitely stronger now the conviction of the two correlative truths, which St. Paul united together[1], but which opposing parties have held in separation, even in mutual antagonism—that the civil authority, as 'an ordinance of God,' has its sacredness, which calls for the loyal duty for conscience sake of its individual citizens, and as a 'minister of God' has its responsibility of duty to every one of them, which it cannot arbitrarily neglect! How significant, if we consider it, the demand—although it may be sometimes in practical form unwisely made and unwisely answered—that in all our intestine conflicts, Christianity shall step in, and cry in the name of national unity, as consecrated by God's Law, ' Sirs, ye are brethren. Why do ye wrong one to another?'

But it is when we come to that unity of all humanity, which is the leading idea of all true civilization, that this social influence of our Christianity is most clearly felt. The old cry, 'Am I not a man and brother?' now somewhat hackneyed and conventional, but once living and powerful, as the cry which shattered the slave-trade, was the watchword, not of mere philanthropy, but of the Christian philanthropy which recognises a brotherhood 'in Christ.' Still the truth which that cry expresses is, we believe, the inmost spirit of all true civilization. It would be, indeed,

[1] Rom. xiii. 1, 4.

folly to deny or undervalue the other unifying forces, which grow with the growth of the world—the material bonds of physical communication and commercial intercourse—the intellectual unity of common knowledge and culture—the political unities, which are aggregating great masses of men under the supremacy of a few dominant races. But in all these, there are but too obviously elements of selfishness, and therefore of disintegration and conflict; and even at their best, they lie more or less on the surface, touching mainly the outward life, and not piercing to the heart of things. The one force of unity which, if we were only true to it, would be pure from all disturbing elements, and would go to the very root of human being, is the Christian claim for our Lord and Master of the whole humanity for which He died; for through Him the unity of man is centred in God, and its bonds, being spiritual, are therefore universal.

Yes! and in spite of the sins of actual Christianity—its defect in energy of sacrifice, and the marring and paralysing effect of our wretched religious divisions—we may boldly say that it is this Christian enthusiasm, which is the inspiration, not only of the continual extension of His Church, but of the sense of moral duty and love, even beyond the reach of this extension, to all who are our brothers in the family of humankind. As beyond the pale of actual conversion there extend the Fatherhood of God and the salvation of Christ, so there exist for us the duty and enthusiasm of brotherhood in the 'service of humanity.' What a strange delusion it is—not only unphilosophical in itself, but contradicted by the emphatic witness of history—to suppose that this service stands in contrast, even in antagonism, to 'the service of God'! It should be especially the one main force in that work which is so essentially Christian—the securing to the weaker subject-races of the world something at least of the justice, the protection, the beneficence, from the stronger, which is indeed the true 'humanity,' but which has to wage so hard a war against the inhuman struggle for existence of individuals and of races. It should be so; and in measure it is so. The ruling races of the earth are clearly the European races—not least the English-speaking race. The one voice, which has constantly proclaimed and enforced on those ruling races their duties to the weaker races of the earth, brought under their influence or dominion, is the voice of Christianity. It has had its failures in fighting against external forces of evil—against commercial selfishness and political greed—against the false science, which calmly assumes that the black or red man must perish before the white man's presence, when, in fact, he perishes by the white man's sin. It has had its worse failures, through internal fault of its own error and timidity, and the unreality of so much of Christian profession. But look only to the aggregate result of the power over the world, even of our own English race, and examine the actual history of its growth. No impartial student will fail to see that here the supreme influence has been that of Christianity, and that the beneficent character of that power on the whole is a proof, that here Christianity has not spoken and laboured in vain.

So in respect of these two actions—the creation of the supernatural and purely spiritual unity of the Catholic Church, and the breathing new life into all the forms of natural unity—Christianity accepts the growing light, and even the bolder and more philosophical theories, of Social Science, as leading up to Christ. From that Science it has learnt much in both these directions. The study of humanity, individual and collective, teaching the correlation and right order of its various elements, physical and spiritual, has certainly aided it greatly in laying hold of the whole for Christ—body, soul, and spirit all consecrated to God in Him. It is not, indeed, always easy to harmonize rightly these two parts of the Christian duty of witness to Him. Perhaps at this moment there is some tendency—in reaction against excessive neglect in the past—to emphasize even disproportionately the second, till it rivals or supersedes the first in its place of primary dignity. To give way to that tendency would be, I hold, a fatal error. If the clergy in their ministerial duty, and the Church in her collective witness, should allow devotion to what are called 'social subjects' to set aside or obscure their primary charge—which is to draw individual souls one by one to Christ, and to advance the corporate spiritual life of the Church, through the light and grace of God—it would be a treason to their high calling, and a neglect of the wisdom of right proportion taught by the Master Himself; ' These things ought ye to have done, and not to leave the other undone.' But in that right proportion, both these forms of witness have their proper function ; and both, if they are to be true and effective, must keep a firm grasp of the essential principle, involved in those famous words, 'One in Christ.'

(V) For that principle is fruitful in practical deductions.

First, with whatever form of human unity, higher or lower, we are concerned, it teaches us that it must have its centre in God, as revealed to us in humanity through the Lord Jesus Christ. Each soul must realize, as the dominant conception of its life, the drawing to this Divine Centre—in a free obedience to a Divine Law, even if it rise not to the higher consciousness of a Divine Spirit. In that consciousness is the strength of true Christian Individualism; in the resulting unity with others, so drawn to the one centre, the bond of the Christian Socialism. The 'manliness,' which I take to be right self-assertion—the secret of freedom, energy, progress, and the 'humanity,' which is right self-sacrifice—the secret of unity and stability —meet together under this supreme devotion, and, we believe, under it alone. Revolt of either from it, whether in the Stoic worship of self or the modern worship of society, is equally an idolatry; although the former be of the baser, and the latter of the nobler sort. Here, as in all else, not only is the Life of Christ—hid in God, yet laying hold by sympathy of all humanity— our true ideal, but the reproduction of that life in us is the very soul, as of our individual, so of our social being.

Next, it is clear that Christianity must be essentially a thing not of the Law, but of the Spirit.

Of course it will hold with St. Paul that 'Law is

good, if it be used lawfully,'—that is, in its right secondary place, and as a means to a higher end. The extent of that use, moreover, will vary under different conditions and in different times. About the first and most permanent function of Law there can be no division of opinion. It must act, and that sternly and decisively, against all unrighteous selfishness of the strong, whether of individuals or of combinations; as shown either in crime and fraud and oppression of the weak, or in evasion of the public burden, which the responsibility of wealth and strength lays upon them. It must in this view, for example, be used to enforce on the property which it protects, the duty which it owes, both to those with whom it is immediately connected, and to the public service, especially that of the poor and weak. It must equally be used to protect against violence the individual freedom of labour, and the individual property which, directly or indirectly, results from it. Other functions of law may be less unquestioned, and certainly need more caution and self-restraint in working. But few will doubt, that, in the present condition of civilized society, Law may be rightly used to secure for the mass of our people such right material environment of life, as may give fair scope to their higher humanity, and such help in education and culture as may foster it,—supplementing always, and not superseding, their own self-help. Perhaps (although in this we touch more controverted ground) it may with this view find it necessary to interfere by regulation and restriction with commercial and social life, and, acting in the name of the State, to supersede in some fields both individual action and free co-operation. The tendency in our day has been, and still is, towards a larger measure of this action of 'State-Socialism[1].' It may, as seems to be generally thought, continue to advance, or, like excessive Individualism, by experience of its insufficiency and its evil, it may provoke reaction. But clearly, from a Christian point of view, all this is a question of policy, not of principle. How that good may be best secured will be, of course, matter of opinion, on which each man must take his own course after serious thought, agreeing to differ with others, and believing them to be not less earnest than himself. But it is fatal to the life of the Church of Christ, if it can be justly accused of lukewarmness in sympathy with the masses of His people. We may say that while recognising that in law interference, whether with rich or poor, should have to prove its necessity, and justice be done to all alike,

[1] On this action of the State, and on the actual extension of it in the England of to-day, see Mr. Sidney Webb's *Socialism in England* (Sonnenschein, 1890). His conclusion is that (see pp. 15, 16) 'The progress of Socialism in England has been, and is still being, accomplished in four chief directions:—1. Constantly increasing restrictions on private ownership of land and capital (Factory Acts, &c.). 2. Gradual supersession of private industrial ventures by public administration (telegraphs, municipal tramways, parochial schools). 3. Progressive absorption by taxation of unearned incomes (rent and interest) and "rent of ability" (income tax, taxes on real property, &c.). 4. The supplementing of private charity by public organization, aiming at raising the condition of the "residuum" (public education, improved dwellings, &c.).' He assumes—I think, hastily—that all this indicates progress, not to the right control and balance, but to the extermination, of Individualism, and 'the realization of the Socialistic ideal.'

yet Christian influence, in framing and administering it, will hardly be true to the spirit of Christ, if it does not look with chief thought and favour on that which tends to the good, not of the few, but of the many.

But still the Christian Socialism, unlike the chief socialistic schemes of the day, will place its chief reliance, not on the compulsion or the authoritative direction to be gained from Law—nor, it may be added, even on voluntary co-operation for mutual advantage, useful though it is, and capable of a far larger development than it has yet attained—but on the free self-devotion of the spirit to the common good, and that, moreover, as swayed not by a simple enthusiasm of humanity, but by the true enthusiasm of obedience to the Spirit of God. For this is the 'Law of liberty,' as in the Sermon on the Mount it is placed in contrast with the harder Law of Sinai, laid on 'them of old time.' That Law—in itself, and as embodied in the Life of Him who spoke it—must still be our guide, in its spirit rather than its letter, in essential principle, which is eternal, rather than in the practical details, which vary with the time [1]. In itself it is the freest and gladdest of all devotions, because entering most fully into the Divine blessedness of giving. Yet in the world as it is, it involves necessarily in different degrees, through struggle with the antagonistic forces of evil and selfishness without and within, some cross of sacrifice.

It is, again, a part of this leading idea, that Christianity teaches us to depend mainly for true unity and progress of society on moral and spiritual forces. No

[1] See Note H.

sane man will disregard the reacting influence of the material environment of life; no one, who looks at the condition of our own English society, will doubt that much, very much, has to be done, in order to make it for the mass of our people worthy of a Christian civilization. But even the soundest Pagan philosophy, through one great master of Greek thought, declared that in the true welfare of individual or collective humanity, first is to be placed the moral force of character, and only in subordination to it the outer environment—the βίος τέλειος—which is necessary to give it scope. It would be retrogressive, indeed, for those who speak in the Name of Christ to fall below that Pagan teaching, by accepting the theories, which so loudly proclaim that for social regeneration we need nothing but 'sweeping economic change,' which must carry with it—to use their own curious and instructive phrase—'political, ethical, technical, and artistic changes'; and for this, perhaps not unnaturally, rely on the swift coercive action of law, national or international, backed by physical force.

Christianity must read to the world a higher lesson. Conscious that the true strength against all evils is in living moral principle, it has laid upon it here a twofold duty. It has to foster that strength, first and best, by the development of the higher spiritual life of Love to God and Man in itself, as it is 'hid with Christ' in the soul, as it is diffused by His Presence through the whole body of the Church—sure that, wherever it is real and deep, it will show how to deal rightly and nobly with all the practical questions and duties which present themselves. But it has also, in the second place, boldly to proclaim and strongly enforce that moral principle in its direct practical bearing on the problems, and especially the antagonisms, of our present Society—to get rid of the inveterate error, showing itself but too often in all classes and in all schools of opinion, which holds that the religious can be separated from the secular life, and that the Christian principle, acknowledged in the individual, domestic, ecclesiastical spheres, is to be ignored in the realms of business or of politics. In regard to these questions, its concern is, not so much with details of special economic and social arrangements, which need to be dealt with by experts, but with the moral obligations of duty and love, which should underlie and determine them; in these its proper task is to speak out, at once with authority and with persuasiveness, to all parties—the few and the many—the representatives (for example) both of Capital and of Labour—not only in the name of humanity, but in the name of God. It will not speak in vain. In spite of a natural impatience of what seems to the hasty to be but a slow, indirect, transcendental process,—an impatience, which ought to be, but too often is not, corrected by historical experience, both of the failures of mere legal compulsion, and of the victorious strength of idea and spiritual enthusiasm —Christianity must still be true to its Master's method[1].

---

[1] Some of the most thoughtful of Socialistic leaders see clearly that trust must be placed not in revolution, but in the evolution of the natural and gradual progress, which they believe that they can discern, towards the realization of their ideal. But even they seem inclined

As it was with the monstrous wrong of slavery—destroyed slowly but certainly, by the declaration 'Not a slave, but a brother beloved in Lord'—so must it be now, in the warfare against all the lesser wrongs which disgrace our modern Society. The weapon, not carnal but spiritual, is mighty for the pulling down of strongholds.

In part, the trust in this moral power is justified by experience. History, and most of all the history of Christianity itself, tells us plainly what an age like ours should be the last to question—the living power of moral idea, enthusiastically accepted, to disintegrate strongly compacted systems of injustice and oppression. We need but open our eyes now to the causes of our social dangers, in order to see plainly that to generate a higher moral life of duty and love—even to root out a few gross moral evils, such as drunkenness, impurity, cruelty, falsehood, dishonesty—would do infinitely more to drive our dangers and difficulties away, than those 'sweeping material and economic changes,' and that, in truth, these changes themselves would really follow, while they cannot lead and determine, moral regeneration.

These leading principles of the unity in Christ we all, I suppose, recognise clearly in respect of the spiritual unity of the Church. But I would plead, that

<small>in detail to assist Nature too much by artifical enactment; and in the rank and file of their followers there is far too much of this impatience of this slow victory of idea—hardly to be wondered at among the uneducated, suffering under the pressure of severe hardship, and perhaps injustice, but shared, and even fostered, by those who should know better.</small>

in all problems which present themselves to us, in relation to the natural forms of human unity, still the concern of Christianity, as Christianity, is not properly with their material and economic, but with their moral aspects, and with these lower elements only so far as they subserve the higher. Those, who strive in any way to speak and act avowedly as Christians and as Churchmen, must never for one moment interfere with the supremacy of this moral witness; either by confusing it with lower and more doubtful issues, or by allowing these to absorb their minds and engross their chief practical energies. As we clergy individually have often deliberately to limit our freedom of commercial and political action, lest it should practically interfere with our spiritual efficiency, so (I think) the Church, as such, must beware lest, plunging, perhaps with imperfect knowledge, into struggle and controversy on these lower issues, she imperil her powers to do that for which she exists—to minister the Light and Grace of the Lord Jesus Christ. She is called upon, we know, —sometimes even in the tone of menace—to redeem the time and to seize critical opportunity. Be it so. Yet, after all, as Archbishop Leighton warns us, it is possible so to speak to our times, and the questions which engross them, as to forget to speak to the eternity of Divine Truth and Grace, which, just because it has its fulcrum in heaven, shows its power to move the earth.

Thus the growth of Social Science, forced upon us by the growth of urgent social needs, still bears to Christianity what I have called the witness of elucidation. It seems not indeed to demand for Christianity a new Social Gospel, but to bring out into new light the full meaning of the old. The Social Gospel, in its practical application, can never go beyond the idea so forcibly expressed in the Apostolic exhortation, 'Owe no man anything, but to love one another.' 'Owe no man anything'—in this we have enunciated in the widest universality the principle of absolute Truth and Righteousness, which, according to the old Platonic definition, proclaims that each has a work to do for society, and bids him do it freely and earnestly, at once realizing self, claiming his own freedom and right, and yet only that he may really obey that appointed service. In the 'But to love one another' there is the acknowledgment of the one debt which can never be fully paid—the enunciation of the yet higher principle of a willing self-sacrifice by each of his own pleasure, fame, power, even (so far as may safely be) his own individual rights, that he may sink himself in the cause of unity, of progress, of peace.

That Social Gospel has been, we know, preached at all times with various degrees of earnestness and power. But in its ordinary proclamation we may, I think, trace two defects, which the deeper study of Social Science should help us to correct. The first is that—perhaps naturally—emphasis has been laid too little on the strong conviction of duty, which appeals mainly to the conscience, too exclusively on the love, which touches the heart—the 'new commandment' of the Gospel—and on this, moreover (as the very limitation in common parlance of the glorious title of 'Charity' shows), in its power to create those countless works of beneficence to the poor, the weak, the suffering, the sinful, which are rightly held to constitute one glory of a Christian civilization. There are many, who in these days are apt indignantly to repudiate all acceptance of these works of Charity, insisting that, if Society was what it ought to be, they would never be needed, and that it is sin against right dignity and independence to recognise in them charity, as distinct from duty. But such assertion argues but little knowledge of human nature and human life. While these are what they are,—subject to distress and weakness and sin, full of necessary, because natural, inequality, swayed by sentiment as well as conviction —these works of mercy will always be necessary, and always blessed 'both to him who gives and him who takes.' Surely there is a true social philosophy in St. Paul's teaching, that, while each man should 'bear his own proper load,' as his share in the burden of humanity, yet that, when it becomes a heavy crushing burden, disproportioned to his strength, then we should 'bear one another's burdens and so fulfil the Law of Christ[1].' It is a savage independence, which would refuse the gifts of mercy in their right function as degrading; for there is a blessedness in rightly receiving, as true, though not as great, as the blessedness of giving. It is simply an inexcusable slander to look upon them as bribes to avert spoliation, a 'ransom' (to use a singularly unfortunate phrase) paid as to a natural enemy. Yet they may have been un-

---

[1] Gal. vi. 5, 2. The word is φορτίον in the former verse; βάρος in the latter.

v.] *Defects in popular Christian Teaching.* 215

consciously made a substitute for a wider and deeper view of the true Christian ideal of 'Truth in Love,' in which the massive framework of duty is clothed in the warm flesh and blood of sentiment, and which teaches us, not merely to relieve existent suffering, but to remove the causes which produce it. So far our popular Christianity may well have failed to grasp the whole truth of the matter, and have given just occasion to reproach.

But the second defect in the proceeding of our Social Gospel is that, under both its aspects, it has been perhaps too Individualistic. It has taught duty and love in all personal relations with an unequalled power; it may not have brought them out sufficiently in relation to the whole community. I am not sure whether this has not been in some measure true, even in respect of the great spiritual unity of the Church of Christ. But I cannot avoid the conviction of its truth, in respect of the secular unities of class, of country, of race. Has our Christianity failed to give sufficient sanction and inspiration to that which we ordinarily call 'public spirit'—a spirit compacted of the sense of public duty, and the self-sacrificing enthusiasm of humanity—which resolves at any cost, except that of justice, to root out from our social system everywhere all elements of injustice, class selfishness, hardship, and of which surely, even if it rise to no higher service, our Master would have said that it was 'not far from the kingdom of God'? If that be so—and were it not so, I doubt whether men would be crying out for new Social Gospels—then here also Christianity may owe a debt to the deeper Social Science, which has taught, and almost forced, us to see more clearly what our old Gospel really implies.

In one sense that lesson has been pondered already in the Church. By many utterances, both of individual leaders of thought and of corporate Church opinion, from the irresponsible Church Congress to the Lambeth Conference itself, it is plain that it has awakened the conviction, that the Church, while it is her first duty to devote her main effort to the fostering of the spiritual life in Christ, for the individual soul and for the whole Body, yet is now especially called to claim for her Master the whole of human life in all its social relations, and to bring the moral principles of the Gospel, which is her charge, to bear more effectively upon a civilized society, still, after eighteen centuries, so imperfectly Christian. It is strongly felt that there must be distinction, but no separation, between the religious and secular life; there must be no surrender of the world of commercial, social, political energy to anti-Christian or non-Christian laws; there must be no occasion given, even to slander, for representing our own Church as the Church of the rich and the cultured, and not the home of universal human brotherhood. But on these grave matters it is not enough to feel strongly, without thinking as deeply and seriously as we may. We shall not have learnt the whole lesson, unless we endeavour, under such guidance as the text gives, to see what 'One Body in Christ' really means—what are the great irreversible laws of human society, which it indicates. It was shrewdly said that one of the most dangerous of cries was the cry that 'something must be done,' without being sure what that something should be. Perhaps even more dangerous is the advice 'to let things alone' when they ought not to be let alone, and to drift on without thinking at all, in indolence or cowardice, till the crash comes.

Hence it is that we have to examine seriously, as Christians, what the Christian Law of society is; and when we do this, we shall once more be led from Christianity to Christ Himself—to read in the spirit of the Sermon on the Mount the great social lesson—to see in the relations of His life to men the great social ideal—to recognise in His Mediation, known or unknown, the great bond of all human society. While it is by the expansion over all the world of the Catholic Church that we seek to realize the highest and deepest unity in Christ, yet we have to enter, more fully than we have yet entered, into the meaning of those great words—which must have some measure of fulfilment now, as an earnest of the perfection of the hereafter—that 'the kingdoms of this world are become the Kingdom of the Lord and of His Christ.' By acting on that conviction, we shall, as we believe, translate into a Divine reality the laws of human society, which our Science teaches, and even the aspirations of which Socialistic dreams are the vague and fantastic expression. Therefore we dare not rest, until, even in what men call secular life, we have done what we can to claim those kingdoms for Him.

LECTURE VI.

CRITICISM AND THE SUPERNATURAL.

Prove all things ; hold fast that which is good.—1 Thess. v. 21.

(I) THE command thus addressed by St. Paul even to the immature Christianity of Thessalonica—in direct reference (as the context shows) to the prophecies, which claimed to set forth a Supernatural Revelation of God—may well be our guide, in passing from the confirmatory and elucidatory witness of Science, to consider the effect of its distinctly critical relation to the Gospel of our Lord Jesus Christ. For it describes to us with incisive brevity the only kind of criticism, right in principle and likely to be fruitful in results, when we have to deal with a great power, which has proved itself in any sense a reality. It is the criticism, first, which claims, not to discover, but to 'test' all things—taking the thing criticized, as it actually presents itself, and not reconstructing it out of our own discovery or imagination. It is the criticism, next, which, until it is forced to an opposite conclusion, holds (with Richard Hooker) that whatever has spiritual life and power in it cannot be 'wholly compacted of untruths' but must have in it something 'which is good,' and which it is therefore worth while 'to hold fast.' It is, moreover and above all, the criticism, which performs its two functions simultaneously, not waiting in suspense till the whole conceivable work of testing is over, before it proceeds to grasp anything firmly, but at every point laying strong and enthusiastic hold of whatever, so far, it has found by trial to be good, living in it by strong sympathy, and making this experience of its inner meaning a means of advancing towards larger knowledge. For so only can we avoid the purely negative condition of bewildered intellect and moral impotence, in which

'the native hue of resolution
Is sicklied o'er with the pale cast of thought.'

Only under these conditions is a critical mind or a critical age capable of the strong energy and enthusiasm, which, after all, are nearer to the heart of human welfare and progress than the keenest criticism. Better it is for ourselves and for the world that we hold fast an imperfect Creed, than that we stand apart, 'holding no Creed but contemplating all,' and cultivating the critical faculty to excess, till we are afraid of ourselves. We have learnt (I think) that this is the only criticism of much worth in dealing with great human things. We must not forget the lesson, when we deal with things which claim, and not without some *prima facie* evidence, to be Divine. Clearly in the text Holy Scripture not only permits, but commands, the use of such criticism as this, not so much perhaps for the origination, as for the confirmation, of Christian faith.

I do not indeed mean that for the great mass of men

obedience to St. Paul's exhortation issues, or ought to issue, in abstract scientific criticism. They inherit their Christianity, as they inherit their civilization, from the past; and they have it brought home to them by the teaching authority of the present. For themselves they have mostly to be content with practical test. If they find that this Christianity of theirs gives them light on the great questions, which every man must ask himself as to his own nature and destiny—if they find that it gives them the capacity of a victorious moral strength and enthusiasm—if they find that it satisfies their spiritual aspiration after the Infinite and Eternal, which is, indeed, the thirst for a living God —they mostly rest on this, and are content to go no further. There is sound reasonableness in this contentment. It shows the strong practical wisdom of the blunt, almost humorous, reply of the blind man at Siloam to the captious questions of the Pharisees, 'Whether He be a sinner or not'—whether He fulfils, or fails to fulfil, your abstract tests of a mission from God—'I know not. One thing I do know, that, whereas I was blind, now I see.' There may be in many things an 'encircling gloom,' and that gloom peopled with strange, fantastic shapes, but through my Christian faith, I find for practical guidance and comfort a 'kindly light';

'And in that Light of life I'll walk,
Till travelling days be done.'

But, while this is the necessary attitude of most men, as individuals, towards great principles of Truth, whether they are presented to them on the authority of Revelation or Science itself, yet we may rightly claim the words of the text, as not only allowing, but welcoming, the most searching criticism of Gospel Truth, and implying that it has a true function to perform for humanity, as a whole, through those who are in each age its leaders of thought. Not least in our own age must that function be recognised; not least here, in one of the great representative homes of Science and Philosophy.

It must, no doubt, depend on certain spiritual conditions. We do not forget what the same inspired teacher of the Gospel elsewhere declares—that the natural or 'psychical' man, having in him no tincture of spiritual insight, cannot receive or judge of the things of God[1]. In this, indeed, he enunciates a general mental law. All criticism must be wholly negative, and therefore either barren or destructive, which has no agreement on first principles with that which it attempts to criticize, and therefore must have unconsciously prejudged the case, as unworthy of serious investigation. Who would accept criticism on a great symphony from a man who had no music in his soul, or listen to the mere mathematician, to whom a masterpiece of poetry 'proved nothing'? For right criticism there must be some preparation of sympathy—unknown to the science, which is narrow and partial in its views of truth, having lost by absorption in itself all sensibility to great realities outside its own immediate line of investigation. This is the kind of Science which, in relation to spiritual truth, St. Paul would have designated

---

[1] 1 Cor. ii. 14.

as 'falsely so called,' and to which he knew that the Gospel of Christ must necessarily seem foolishness.

Thus a Science essentially materialistic—either in theory or from that absorption in purely physical investigation, to which we are peculiarly liable in the present scientific division of labour—cannot effectively criticize that which it utterly ignores, as lying wholly beyond its domain of Matter and Force. A Science, purely Psychical, looking upon humanity as merely one element in the great system of Organic Life, and ignoring in it anything differing in kind from the senses, the instincts, the appetites, the passions, which we share with the brute creatures, is equally incapable of judging of what claims to be spiritual. Clearly the Science, which is to criticize here with any hope of positive results, must be so far in harmony with fundamental ideas of Christianity, as to recognise the supremacy of the spiritual element of Will, Reason, Conscience, Love, as in man himself, so in the Supreme Power which rules humanity, and to understand, moreover, that, in the search after it, right function must be assigned, not to the pure intellect only, but to all these spiritual faculties of our nature. The universal witness to these truths in the soul of man is (as our Lord Himself teaches) the conviction of the Spirit to the world, preparing for the knowledge of God in Him. Only when that witness is received and realized, is the man in any degree what Holy Scripture calls a spiritual man, and so capable to some extent of judging from without of what must be 'spiritually discerned.' I say 'to some extent'; for it is only from within the pale of the fuller gift of the Spirit to the faith of believers, that he can grow into the fulness of their meaning, and find for himself the truth of our Lord's declaration, that thus what is otherwise 'hid from the wise and prudent' is 'revealed to babes.' To use the words of the text, it is only by 'holding fast,' through mind and heart alike, what has been partially known by test, that the soul comes to the knowledge of the inner reality of truth.

(II) What then is the right critical function of this higher Science in relation to Christianity?

To criticize is, first, to distinguish—to distinguish in a complex reality what is primary, essential, eternal, from what is secondary, accidental, temporary. So we find out what is the essence of the thing itself, making it what it is—as distinct from accessories not necessarily peculiar to it, which have gathered round it, and which can be, and perhaps at times should be, stripped off. That office of criticism—to use again a quotation from the Bampton Lectures of 1884—should tend, in its application to Religion, 'to aid Religion in clearing her own conceptions'; 'to make perpetually clearer the true meaning of the Revelation itself'; 'to interpret better the message, which' it believes men to have 'received from their Father in Heaven.' Largely (I think) has that function been exercised in our own age, by believers and unbelievers alike, and it is impossible to doubt, that it has before it a fuller and still more useful development.

To criticize is, next, to test. When this first duty of distinction has been discharged, and the root of the matter made known to us, it has then to go on to the work described in the text—to test or prove it. It must try to discern, first, whether it is a reality,—whether (that is) what it declares as truth is a real truth, accordant with the great laws of being—whether the power which it claims to wield is a real power, able to guide, to rule, and to exalt humanity. Next, it has to see whether under both aspects it is sufficient for the purpose, which it professes to serve, and adequate to the claim of a Divine Origin and spiritual supremacy made for it. In respect of Christianity this comes very nearly to the judgment on its double claim to be at once (to use the common phrase) Natural and Supernatural—Natural in its harmony with what we can discover elsewhere of the Laws of the working of the Supreme Power over the world and man—Supernatural in going far beyond this, both supplying the key to the inner meaning of what such discovery has partially revealed to us, and advancing to regions which it cannot even profess to enter.

(III) To the critical faculty in man, in relation to these two main functions[1], consider how Christianity presents itself, first as an actual, then as an ideal Christianity.

It is essential to note that it comes to us first, not as

[1] The former is κρίνειν; the latter (as in the text) δοκιμάζειν. Much error in criticism results from confusion of the two functions, or inversion of their right order. Clearly we must know the essence of a thing, before we can tell whether to accept or reject it; otherwise acceptance or rejection of what is accidental or subsidiary may be made wrongly to apply to the thing as a whole.

a doctrine or an idea, but as an actual and living Force. In the individual experience, it is felt as exercising a real power over the soul, and so over the life. To the scientific observation of the world, it is seen as a power or life, certainly in many respects unique in history. The Church of Christ presents itself to our sight and to our thought as a unique spiritual society, which has grown continuously through eighteen centuries from small beginnings towards a world-wide expansion. It claims by the title of 'Catholic' a future coextensiveness with humanity itself in all countries, all generations, all phases of character; in part it already justifies that claim, by moulding, directly or indirectly, the growth of modern civilization, dominating the leading and conquering races of the world, and through them acting on all humanity, as the one continually advancing and aggressive religious force. The power, which it exercises over its members, is certainly an intellectual, moral, spiritual power, with which none can compare, in which they who, like the great Napoleon, best know what are the capacities and limits of earthly empire have recognised a spiritual royalty, differing from these not in degree but in kind. But even beyond the bright circle of its direct spiritual sway over men—as the author of the *Gesta Christi* has so strikingly shown—there is a diffused light of larger indirect influence upon the whole civilization of mankind in thought and action, so that the very principle of self-sacrifice for others, which we significantly call 'humanity,' has by universal acknowledgment gained through it a new power.

There is, moreover, in it by its very nature a force of diffusive energy, through which it not only lays hold of those without its pale, and draws them to itself or rather to its Head, but extends to them, while they still remain without, the rights of brotherhood, and spends itself in labouring for their protection, their happiness, and their goodness.

There it is—this living phenomenon of actual Christianity, as a great fact of which critical investigation must take serious account, and moreover as a unique fact, demanding some unique explanation[1]. Other powers—other great religious powers—of course, there are; but none like this. It is unlike the Judaism, out of which it grew, in its capacity of world-wide extension; it is unlike the iron system of Islam, which was in all its best parts a growth out of Judaism, in recognition of the Divine in humanity, and so in power of harmony with knowledge and progress; it is unlike the Buddhism, which broods over the unprogressive races of the East, in being a religion of hope and energy and not of despair and passiveness. It stands

[1] The conclusion of *Ecce Homo* is as true as it is striking. 'The achievement of Christ, in founding, by His single will and power, a structure so durable and so universal, is like no other achievement which history records. The masterpieces of the men of action are coarse and common in comparison with it, and the masterpieces of speculation flimsy and insubstantial. ... Who can describe that which unites men? Who has entered into the formation of speech, which is the symbol of their union? ... He who can do these things can explain the origin of the Christian Church. For others it must be enough to say, "The Holy Ghost fell on them who believed." No man saw the building of the New Jerusalem; ... *it descended out of heaven from God*' (p. 330, ed. 1866).

alone in both inspiring and developing the good in humanity, and grappling with the evil; it is the one Religion which has power to adapt itself to all races and to all stages of civilization, and to speak with spiritual efficacy in all the tongues of men. Accordingly by universal confession it is the embodiment of the only religion, in the ordinary sense of the word, which has a vital and victorious power. What—Science must ask—is the secret of that extraordinary power? What is the essential basis, on which this imposing superstructure is raised?

The answer would be given at once on the authority of the Master[1]. It rests upon a Divine Revelation of Truth—the truth of God and the truth of man: the one condition of membership is a Creed, which is simply the acceptance of that truth in faith; its individual subjects are at once disciples and in degree Apostles, learners and teachers of that accepted truth, by the combined powers of mind and heart and spirit; the charge, by a spiritual necessity laid upon it as a Church, is to hold the truth fast, and proclaim it to every creature. Other religions may possibly consent to be stiffened into systems of morality, or sublimed into nebulous enthusiasms. Christianity never, till it has ceased to be what it is.

In this Truth is enshrined the Ideal Christianity, by which the actual Christianity is guided and is determined. It has grown to be a vast and complex body of truth, having relation to every direction of thought, and moulding every form of intellectual activity; for

[1] John xviii. 36, 37.

it professes to be at once individual and universal, teaching to each the wisdom, which is the knowledge of the true end and perfection of his own life, by glimpse of the Wisdom of God—the Law Eternal, that is, of His dispensation to all humanity. As its spiritual power over humanity extends, its very Creeds have grown from original simplicity to elaborate subsequent development; it has produced in all languages a splendid literature of its own; it has coloured the whole literature of the races over which it has exercised power: it claims in its philosophic aspect, as Theology, to be the Queen of Sciences.

But all this vast system of truth is centred on one Book, which has grown up through the centuries, in many ages, by many hands, and these often unknown, into a marvellous unity, and which by its variety is (so to speak) in touch with all the various phases of human literature—history, law, poetry, philosophy—all subordinated to one purpose, the manifestation of the Will and the Nature of God. That in its intrinsic character, and the world-wide spiritual power with which it speaks in all the tongues of men, it is a Book of books, far above all others, no thoughtful man can doubt. Perhaps its uniqueness is best seen by comparing it with the other great religious Books of the world—venerable though they be, and having gleams in them of the Divine light, that lighteth every man—which the scholarship of our own day is busy in reproducing and criticizing. With one partial exception—and that a book, which has borrowed in idea from the ancient Scriptures, and claims relation to them—they are virtually dead, and it is living. For it the Church of Christ makes everywhere in different forms a claim, the tremendous character of which is often lost to us by familiarity—the claim which we express in the well-known declaration that it contains for all men and for all times 'all things necessary to salvation'; and the very word 'salvation' implies at once a Gospel of regeneration of the Divine image in humanity, and a Gospel of deliverance from that power of sin and death, which to all other forms of thought is simply a hopeless and awful perplexity.

There, again, stands out the even stranger phenomenon of this Ideal Christianity—challenging once more the enquiry, 'What is the central secret of this extraordinary life? What is the ground of this extraordinary claim?'

Now it is clear and it always has been clear, that—as was so strikingly shown in the Bampton Lectures of last year—Christianity, whether ideal or actual, is, in a sense to which no other religion presents analogy, Christ Himself. So has it been from the beginning, and must be till the end of time. We cannot go beyond what St. Paul said of old. It is not that He gives but that 'He is made to us,' 'Wisdom' to the intellectual, 'Righteousness' to the moral, 'Sanctification' to the spiritual element of man's nature, and so finally 'Redemption' from the evil which darkens and perverts them all[1]. Of the actual Christianity, He is acknowledged as, by His indwelling, 'the Life'; of ideal Christianity He by His Manifestation is the Light. But yet I venture to think that the effect in our days

[1] 1 Cor. i. 30.

of the wonderful growth of critical power, in its first function of distinction and insight, is to bring out with new vividness this original and undying truth. If by the principle of Idolatry is meant—as I suppose should be meant—the resting on any means of manifestation of God, instead of passing through it by spiritual intuition to God Himself, it has helped us against the two subtle forms, in which alone it is now possible.

Thus Historical Science has studied and analysed the actual Christianity, the Church of Christ in all ages. It has bidden us look through the visible developments of law, system, ritual, to the inner spiritual force, which gives them life; it has distinguished in it the obviously human element, with all the imperfection and evil clinging to it, which it shares with other great world-wide powers, from that element, which is its peculiar characteristic, clearly unique and claiming to be miraculous and Divine. It makes us see plainly that this inner reality is, in spite of all imperfections, accretions, superstitions, the reproduction in the individual and the community of the Life of Christ Himself; it prepares the mind, though of course it cannot teach it, to accept the only adequate explanation of this universal reproduction, which Christian faith gives, in the indwelling Presence by grace of Christ in His people.

So, again, our literary and critical Science examines the Holy Scripture which is the embodiment of the Christian Truth. It distinguishes in it also, by an insight of which past ages had no conception, the human element of imperfection and progressiveness from that which claims to be Divine—the essential truth itself from the forms in which it has been conveyed, and which by their very variety bring it into living contact with all phases of human consciousness. And the result is to make us see clearly that the one key to its right interpretation is the knowledge of the central Manifestation of Christ Himself—His Life, His Word, His Person—that on this ultimately must rest the plenary authority, claimed for Holy Scripture—that in relation to this all other parts stand simply as preparatory or explanatory, and only in that dependence can be rightly understood and reasonably reverenced.

In both cases it seems to me plain that, in its critical aspect, Science is the schoolmaster to lead us from Christianity to Christ Himself. It forces us to put aside all other enquiries for the supreme question— 'What think ye of Christ? Who and what is He?' In some sense it prepares the way for Faith, by showing us that for ourselves this question means, 'Have we ground for the absolute faith in Him, once expressed by St. Peter, as having perfectly "the words of eternal life," which necessarily implies the further conviction that He is "the Son of the living God".'

(IV) But this power of distinctive insight in scientific criticism, when it has thus brought us face to face with the supreme question, must also go on to define for criticism itself both the method and the limit of its further duty, of proving or testing the answer which Christianity gives.

Christianity, thus centred in Christ, presents itself, as I have said, under two distinct aspects—as at once Natural and Supernatural; and it would seem that in the function of criticism towards it there is a corresponding distinction.

Whether Christianity is Natural it seems to have a full right and power to judge. That it is thus Natural —in harmony (that is) with what we can discover of the Laws of the Supreme Power over the world and man, and actually with them a part of the 'Law Eternal' of all being—is the great argument of Analogy. That argument is necessarily as old as Christianity itself. It is implied by the very fact that in Holy Scripture the Manifestation of Christ is described, as ordained from before the foundation of the world, and actually embedded in the whole history of humanity—as the consummation up to which all led beforehand, and by which all that follows is to be determined till His Second Advent. It is implied by our Lord's own use of teaching by Parables, in which the laws of the Kingdom of Heaven are illustrated, and in measure represented, by the laws of the natural world. The saying that 'Christianity is as old as the Creation,' which was once crudely used to depreciate its supernatural authority, is now seen to be but a perverted statement of the claim, which is implied in the beginning of its Scriptural record from the first origin of this world.

But there have been epochs—epochs of great advance in the knowledge of Nature and its Laws—when this argument has assumed a special importance. One such epoch followed in England the great discovery of Newton, giving predominance of interest to the study of physical Science, affecting also the prevalent forms of metaphysical and moral Science. It was then that the argument was wrought out by Butler, in relation to the knowledge and the philosophy of his age, in that great book, of which I hold it entirely an error to suppose that in its essential force it is, or will be, obsolete. In another such epoch we are living now—an epoch of a yet more extraordinary advance of the same study under different aspects. For us, therefore, once more the argument of Analogy starts into a new prominence; and, as I venture to think, with an even greater advantage than in Butler's day. True it is, that he was allowed to assume, with a freedom denied to us, a personal and intelligent Author of Nature. But then by the Deism of his age this assumption was made somewhat barren. Nature was looked upon as a great machine, set going once for all by its Author, and then left to work under fixed laws of uniformity, of which Miracle was clearly a break, to be proved, if possible, by evidence against inherent improbability. We have learnt to see that in Nature there is not uniformity, but continual growth and development of an indwelling Life, always producing out of the lower the higher forms of being—that at each great epoch in this development, there comes in a new force, which in comparison with the lower form of Nature preceding is supernatural—and that what we call the miraculous in the Manifestation of Christ presents itself to us as a supreme new creation, rising above the old, yet connecting itself with it, using all its laws and forces, while it brings in a new and Diviner power of its own. It is plain, I think, that this larger scientific view of Nature diminishes greatly, if it does not altogether remove, the dead weight of antecedent improbability, against which the argument of Butler had so laboriously to struggle. In some of my previous Lectures I have tried to suggest to you certain points, in which it absolutely confirms by analogy the great doctrines of the Gospel.

Accordingly, as it seems to me, the whole tendency of the scientific criticism of our own day is to conclude, that, while, of course, there are points in Christian doctrine, on which it cannot pronounce at all, and which appear to it as mysterious and unreal, and while there are other points, which seem abnormal, and therefore constitute to the critical mind difficulties of belief, yet that, as a whole, Christianity is emphatically Natural. The old objections or scoffs against it as an unnatural and unphilosophical superstition—contradicting both Natural Science and Natural Theology—are nearly dead and gone. Its moral and spiritual power, alike over the individual man and over human society, is acknowledged as the greatest that the world has seen. Its system of truth is recognised as containing the highest conceptions yet attained of God and Man. Its Author is reverenced as the greatest Son of Man, who has created for all time a new ideal of humanity, and who, in respect of our moral and spiritual life, is, in the well-known words of John Stuart Mill, so accepted as an universal guide, that by His teaching all men may translate abstract moral idea into concrete living reality. Accordingly in relation to the Supreme and Absolute Being, it is largely acknowledged that the alternative is between Christianity, and a vague Pantheism or dreary Agnosticism; and, moreover, that, if Christianity is to endure at all, it must be the full Christianity of Holy Scripture and the Catholic Creeds, and not the diluted and attenuated Christianity, which in the worship of reason, and in the fear of mystery, has been substituted for it. So far the attempt of critical Science to test all things has certainly brought men, with some degree of faith and reverence, face to face with Christ; and we, who believe that, when lifted up to the thoughtful gaze of men, He will fulfil His great superhuman promise, and 'draw all men to Him' in a deeper and more absolute faith, so far may 'thank God and take courage.'

(V) But this acceptance of Christian Life and Idea and of Christ Himself, as simply occupying the highest place as yet known to us in the Natural scale, is like the 'philosophical devotion,' which Gibbon notes in Alexander Severus; it may prepare for Christianity, but it is not Christianity, and ought never to assume the name. Evidently it can have no finality about it; it can justify no absolute faith or devotion: it never could have had the power or the right to claim the whole world of humanity for its Master. Christianity is nothing, if it be not Supernatural, or (if you will) miraculous—if it is not (that is) the revelation to the world of a new Life and Light brought to it in Christ, differing, not in degree, but in kind, from all others in the Natural scale—and if accordingly it does not acknowledge in its Master an 'only begotten Son of God,' in a Sonship essentially and infinitely exalted above the sonship of humanity at large [1].

[1] The definite Ὁμοούσιον, as contrasted with the vague Ὁμοιούσιον, of the Arian controversy.

Such it unquestionably was from the beginning. Nothing is historically more certain than that its first preaching to the world rested on the great visible miracle of the Resurrection, with the Ascension as its necessary consequence, without which St. Paul so bluntly declared that the faith in it was a delusion, and the preaching of it a lie [1]. Nothing is clearer in the New Testament than the teaching that this is but the visible outcome of the yet greater invisible miracle of the Incarnation—that through this He, who was but 'made of the seed of David according to the flesh,' is 'declared to be the Son of God with power[2].' Nothing, again, in the whole Gospel record is plainer than the constant declaration, almost as a matter of course, that from this invisible miracle flowed, so to speak, naturally in the Lord's earthly life what St. John calls Epiphanies of His Divine Glory, in the lesser miracles at once of power and of love, which He made an integral part of His Ministry. The miraculous character attaches to the Manifestation of Christ as a whole; what we commonly call miracles are simply visible flashes from time to time, by which it was His will to disclose the Divine light through the veil of His humanity. To deny these things, or to explain them away, is simply to substitute for the historic Christianity a new religion or religious philosophy under the old name [3].

[1] 1 Cor. xv. 14, 15.   [2] Rom. i. 3, 4.
[3] 'On the whole' (says the author of *Ecce Homo*) 'miracles play so important a part in Christ's scheme, that any theory, which would represent them as due entirely to the imagination of His followers or of a later age, destroys the credibility of the documents not partially

Now what is the attitude of Scientific criticism towards this assertion of the Supernatural?

I am old enough to have seen it pass through at least three phases. In my younger days the whole question was considered on the basis, on which it was placed by the scepticism of the old Deistic School and the answer of Paley, reproducing with transparent clearness and thoroughness some part of the deeper treatment of the same question by Butler[1]. It was on all hands acknowledged, by the broad common-sense of the eighteenth century, that miracles, as disclosures of the working of a Supernatural Power, presumably Divine, were the natural credentials of Revelation; although they were treated too much in isolation from other elements of that Revelation, and in themselves not sufficiently viewed as forming a whole, and having relation to the great miracle of miracles. On this basis the argument on both sides rested. On the one side men urged the improbability of all that contradicted common experience, and the general insufficiency in such cases of testimony; on the other there was denial that such contradiction was overwhelmingly improbable, and the examination of the actual testimony of word and deed, of life and death, by which the Christian miracles were established as unmistakeable facts. In this phase of the

---

but wholly, and leaves Christ a personage as mythical as Hercules.' (Part I. c. 5.)

[1] *Anal.*, Part II. c. vii., where he speaks of 'Miracles and Prophecy'—i. e. miracle, physical and spiritual—as 'the direct and fundamental proofs of Christianity'; while he goes on to point out that these must be viewed in relation to the 'general scheme of Revelation,' and the 'whole argument for it in one view.'

controversy it was (I think) generally allowed that the defence was victorious against the attack. Then came an entire change of critical attack and defence. All examination of testimony was put aside as futile by a high *a priori* reasoning that miracle was simply impossible, because it implied deviation from irreversible 'Laws of Nature' (under which, it seemed, the Deity, if indeed a Deity there were, was bound, like Darius under the laws of the Medes and Persians), and that, indeed, this grand unchanging uniformity was the best, perhaps the only worthy, expression of a Supreme Mind; so that the apparent occurrence of miracle would only encumber and weaken the evidence of a Revelation from God, which it had been supposed to strengthen. But these imposing assumptions have, I think, been fairly exploded—by none with more brilliant and unanswerable force than by Mozley in his Bampton Lectures of 1865[1]. On the one hand, it is seen that the so-called 'Order of Nature,' so far as it is discerned by observation, amounts simply to a statement of constantly recurring facts in the past, and, as such,

[1] It is, of course, clear that the masterly argument of Mozley's Second Lecture (taking up the reasoning of Hume that observation shows us only antecedence and consequence, and can tell us nothing of cause), is largely an *argumentum ad hominem*, addressed to that school of thought, which professes to rest only on observation and deduction from it, and to decry all metaphysical idea. So far it is unanswerable. Its effect, therefore, is, first, to drive the mind to recognise the necessity of an assumption of a ruling idea, lying beyond such observation and determining it; and then, if that necessity be recognised, to show that faith in a living God is the only assumption which really satisfies it, and to examine the witness borne to it by that direct exhibition of Will, which we call Miracle.

can have no determining force and no necessary anticipation of the future; that the very conception of unchanging Cause, and the consequent explanation of regularity, require something beyond mere observation; —something of necessary assumption—something, which (as we have seen) is called by the physicist himself an 'act of faith'; and that, if this something be supplied by what properly deserves to be called faith, the personal consciousness of a Supreme Personality—if (as the very use of the words 'Laws of Nature' in its proper sense implies) we come through that faith to the conviction that these laws of Nature are what we properly mean by laws—(that is) expressions of a Supreme Will—the whole argument of impossibility falls hopelessly to the ground. On the other hand, the somewhat transcendental contention that miracles are needless and useless, as indications of a mission from God[1], has been shattered by a simple appeal to the common sense, and the invariable experience, of humanity. So now the criticism of the real leaders of scientific thought has come back, although with far greater thoroughness and force, to the old ground. If

---

[1] 'The defect of Spinoza's view' (of the impossibility of miracle) 'is that he will not look upon a miracle as an instrument, a means to an end, but will only look upon it as a marvel beginning and ending with itself. "A miracle," he says, "as an interruption to the order of Nature, cannot give us any knowledge of God, nor can we understand anything from it." It is true that we cannot understand anything from an interruption of the order of Nature, simply as such; but if this interruption has an evidential function assigned to it, then something may be understood from it, and something of vast importance.' Mozley, Lecture I. p. 24 (ed. of 1867).

there be, indeed, a Personal God, the idea of impossibility or incredibility of miracle must fall. If there is to be a special Revelation of Him, the notion not only of the evidential uselessness of Miracle, but of any serious improbability must be surrendered: for any argument against Miracle from the analogy of the ordinary action of the Divine Moral Government must depend on essential likeness to the conditions and purposes of that action, and cannot apply to what is presupposed to be a unique occasion and purpose [1]. The whole question must turn once more on the adequacy of testimony in general, and of the Christian testimony in particular. The negative contention now is not that Miracles cannot happen, but that they do not, or did not, happen. It is supported by some general depreciation of the capacity of testimony, and much sceptical criticism of the special evidence of the Gospel record itself. It is this form of criticism alone, which is still alive and powerful: and it is, therefore, this that we are now concerned to meet.

But, has all this past criticism been futile? When the question thus returns to the old ground, does it come back unchanged? Surely we must answer, No; and see that this testing process has enabled us to get rid of much that is false or arbitrary in our own belief, and to hold fast that which in it is good.

Perhaps the effect may be described briefly as the discernment of a higher Law of Divine Order in Miracle itself.

That result shows itself, first, in the clearer idea,

[1] See Mozley, Lect. II. p. 47.

which we have gained of the essential character of Miracle in its relation to the Natural Order. The essence of Miracle lies not in its strangeness and its power to excite wonder, although wonder may be the first step to fuller knowledge and understanding—not in its indication of some forces at work, undreamt of as yet in our philosophy [1], although in this we take another step onward in the same course. It includes these things, but it is more than these. The essential point in Miracle, as our Lord Himself taught, is that it is a 'sign'—a visible indication of invisible and eternal reality. It is, as the very method of the record of Miracle in Holy Scripture might suggest, simply a plain and direct manifestation, in connection with known and declared purpose, of a Supernatural Will in Nature, which by those who believe in but One God, must be held to be, mediately or immediately, a Divine Will. Now as to that Will, I must hold (as has been already said) that our own human thought traces it ultimately as the great First Cause of all things, working through Nature's ordinary Laws. But to our human reason it works behind the veil, dimly seen through a series of 'second causes,' inferred, although with almost irresistible inference, rather than known. In Miracle it is plainly unveiled, so that he who runs may read it. In our Lord's miracles (for example), if the Gospel record be true, we see the plainest exhibitions of Divine Power, as a Power creative, a Power of rule over inanimate Nature, a Power of rule over humanity—

---

[1] This is exactly the inference drawn by Herod as to our Lord's miracles in Mark vi. 14, ἐνεργοῦσιν αἱ δυνάμεις ἐν αὐτῷ.

always directed by perfect Wisdom and Love. In all there is, therefore, (as St. John declares) a plain manifestation of the Divine Glory.

But more than this. Miracle is wrought through man, claiming to have mission from God; and in this aspect it is a sign, that his human will has a close and conscious harmony with the Supreme Will. We note in the course of Nature the action of this force of human will, to our eyes variable and original, yet of course necessarily subject to the Divine Will; we find it strong, just in proportion to its knowledge of that Will, and its conscious obedience thereto. Through these it becomes a real and powerful element, which works together with the invariable element of Natural Force and Natural Law, and within limits, uses these for its own purpose. We see it, moreover, as an advancing power, continually enlarging its province, as time rolls on, and as the higher faculties of our humanity are more and more developed. Strange new glimpses of the extent of that mastery of will, when exercised over weaker minds and wills, we are gaining in some of the researches of modern days—glimpses only as yet, mere promises of larger future discovery. Everything seems to indicate that in a humanity, perfect in itself and perfect in harmony with the Divine Will, such mastery might be also perfect over Nature and over Man. It is the supernatural fulfilment of this inference from natural analogy, which comes out to us in fulness in the miracles of our Lord, and in varying degrees in the miracles of His chosen servants before and after His coming.

For here all the limits, of which we are in our own imperfect experience conscious, are thrown down or thrown back: and the will of man, working under extraordinary knowledge of the Divine Will and obedience thereto[1], exercises a mastery to us certainly unknown, perhaps incomprehensible. How this operation of Divine Will, working through human will, effects itself—whether plainly through the instrumentality of natural forces, or by processes to us inconceivable—matters not to the essential character of Miracle. Nor, again, is it possible for us to determine in what forms, and on what occasions, it is credible that it should manifest itself. For of this we are no more able to judge than to determine why the same Divine Power should manifest itself under this or that form in Nature. Perhaps (to apply Butler's argument) we should expect to find things strange to us and unlikely in the one course of action, as we find them in the other—provided always that the manifestation of Supreme Will be not obscured. In regard, moreover, to this manifestation, since it is for the sake of men, we may expect that it will adapt itself at different times to different conditions and circumstances, so that in one generation it may take forms, which would seem trivial to others, but which were suitable to the stage of its spiritual education, and for the advance of that education in the knowledge of the Divine will. Since, again, it is made

---

[1] Such perfect knowledge and obedience our Lord declares, as the law of His own miraculous action. 'The Son can do nothing, but what He seeth the Father do. For the Father loveth the Son, and showeth all things that Himself doeth' (John v. 19, 20).

through men, may there not be here, as in Inspiration (which is, indeed, miracle in the realm of mind), the admixture of a human element with the Divine—a colouring (so to speak) of miraculous power by the medium through which it passes? In all these aspects, it is clearly seen, that it is with the reality of the manifestation of Divine Will and Purpose through man, rather than its form or method of working, that we are concerned. It is this which our critical thought is to test, and, so far as it discovers it, to hold fast.

But, again, this discernment of Law applies to the whole course of Miracle in itself, and gives a clearer idea of the right place and force of visible Miracle in the system of what claims to be a Revelation from God. We have come to see that it is a fatal error to judge of Miracle, as in itself and by itself a sufficient witness of Him. Miracle is always, as has been said, a sign of something greater than itself, with which it is indissolubly connected. But in relation to a Revelation it has a double significance.

It is a sign, as our Lord expressly taught the disciples of St. John the Baptist, preparatory (where such preparation is necessary) for the reception of a distinct word of teaching as from God—a 'Gospel preached to the poor' and simple. In that connection lies the essential distinction between Miracle in the Christian sense, and the strange unaccountable phenomena of physical and psychical agency, which are merely wonders and nothing more. Some of these have associations simply puerile or sordid; some are such, that, when thoughtfully examined, they may throw light on natural laws, both of the world's outward order, in which they occur, and of the minds which perceive them; but they certainly have no high moral and spiritual meaning for all mankind. That, seen in that connection, especially by the great mass of men, who are taught and influenced mainly through the senses, Miracle always has been, and always must be, most powerful, no one who knows human nature can doubt. The inference of Nicodemus, 'No man can do these miracles that thou doest, except God be with him,' is the expression of the common-sense of humanity in all ages. It may be true —and the dispensation of Miracle seems to suggest it— that this witness of Miracle will tell in different degrees of power on different ages of the world, on minds in different stages of culture and knowledge of God. But who can doubt that in some degree it must tell everywhere, while man is what he is—in the England of the nineteenth century, as truly, if not as powerfully, as in the Palestine of the first?

It is a sign, again, as He Himself also made it, of what is the invisible reality of the Divine work. The deliverance from bodily sickness and infirmity in the 'Take up thy bed and walk,' is a pledge and symbol of the invisible spiritual deliverance in 'Thy sins are forgiven thee.' In that light all careful study has recognised the symbolic appropriateness of our Lord's miracles, as acted Parables of His redeeming work. In that light a thoughtful consideration of the lesser miracles, wrought by His servants before and after His coming, would show that these also had a similar appropriateness to the character of the workers, and the special work for God, that they had to do.

Under both these aspects, moreover, we have come to see that Miracle belongs especially to what we may call epochs of advance and expansion in the progressive Revelation of God ; therefore in especial fulness to that Life, which was the transcendent completion of all the imperfect manifestations which had gone before ; therefore in measure to certain special and crucial occasions, both in the preparation for His coming, and in the extension of His kingdom. There is an economy of Miracle,—in Himself a self-imposed restraint,—in His servants a restraint, of which they themselves seem to have been conscious, as imposed from above.

But the sign has done its work, when it has pointed to the thing signified. The work leads up to the Word and the Life ; beyond this they must stand or fall (so to speak) by their own intrinsic power of Wisdom and Truth and Love, and by their harmony with all yet known of the Revelation of God. By that intrinsic character is decided the one choice, which remains to us, when supernatural reality of miracle in itself is brought home—whether to refer it to some erratic or evil power, as the Pharisees professed to believe that devils were cast out through Beelzebub, or to see in it the manifest working, direct or indirect, of the finger of God. Only by reference to that essential character of His Ministry is there force in our Lord's argument, that the supposition, involved in the cavil of the Pharisees, implies the monstrous conception of a 'kingdom of Satan divided against itself,' and so blindly serving the advancement of a true kingdom of Heaven.

But perhaps, above all, this progress in discernment of Law shows itself in the concentration of all our thought, in respect of this great subject, on that which must be its right centre—the Manifestation of the Supernatural in the Lord Jesus Christ Himself. It has often been noted that, in the recorded examples of Apostolic teaching, there is but slight and general reference to the lesser miracles of our Lord's life, while the whole stress of witness is laid on the reality of the great Miracle of miracles in the Resurrection; and the whole stress of argument on its signification of the true nature of Him who died and rose again. Surely there is in this a true insight into the heart of things. If in this the Christian faith is true, it is clear that through the Manifestation of our Lord on earth, we have entered upon a wholly new Supernatural order, in which, if I may so say, the manifestations of supernatural power are themselves natural. This consideration applies chiefly to the Divine Life itself incarnate in our flesh, but not exclusively. As there is a noonday, so there are a dawn and an afterglow of the Sun of Righteousness. If, before He came, we hold that for His Coming there was special preparation in the Divine Will and Purpose, it cannot surprise us, that from time to time, at great crucial epochs in that preparation—such as the era of the Exodus and Eisodus, and of the great Baal apostasy in the days of Elijah and Elisha—there should have been visible flashes of miracle, revealing the operation of that Will. If we believe that all which followed was the working out and proclamation of the great Supernatural reality, it cannot be strange to us, that, so far and so long as was necessary, the supernatural aids to such proclamation should have continued. We see what is the true key to the position—where is the true centre of the manifestation of the supernatural order. By it we judge of all the lesser parts of that order, utterly refusing to fritter away our strength in criticizing them as isolated phenomena. And the effect has always seemed to me to reverse the old proverb, so as to make the strength of our chain to be the strength, not of the weakest, but of the strongest link. For certainly it is here, where it is all important, that the great force of witness is gathered for us; it is here that we are best able to test truth, and to hold fast that which satisfies the test.

In all these three ways I cannot but think that ultimately, in spite of temporary obscurations and perplexities, our Christian faith owes a debt to Science in its critical function of distinction, for aiding us to rise to a worthier and truer idea of what we mean, when we proclaim Christianity as Supernatural. When that idea is clearly understood, many of the commoner cavils and denials answer themselves; the antecedent improbability of exemplifications of the Supernatural order at least so far passes away, that it can be readily overcome by force of strong testimony to its reality.

(VI) But now that the essence of the Christian assertion of the Supernatural is thus distinguished, as presented in the Life, Death, Resurrection of the Lord

Himself, what is the effect of criticism, when it goes on to the second function of testing its truth? The answer I would venture to give is this—that it seems in every way to be sweeping away all uncertainties and hesitations on either side, and to be bringing us face to face with the great alternative of faith and unbelief.

Thus it looks clearly and searchingly into the witness borne to the truth of that Manifestation—as it first flashed upon the world in the Apostolic preaching —as it is embodied to us in the history and teaching of Holy Scripture—as it is asserted in all the Creeds of the Church from the beginning, and implied in her whole worship and life. Knowing well the truth of the old motto *Dolus latet in generalibus,* it forces us to put aside the vague and sweeping generalities, both of wholesale depreciation of the value of all testimony, and of the attribution, questionable in point of fact, to the Apostolic age—the Augustan age (be it remembered) of the Roman Empire—of an eager undiscriminating credulity. It bids us look carefully at the special case—the definite character, circumstances, results, of the witness, as it is actually presented to us. Then, studying first the internal evidence, in the naturalness and graphic vividness of the history and of the Character, which is its centre—in the mingled loftiness and simplicity of the teaching—in the continuity and natural development of idea, which runs through the whole; and next, the external evidence, which, after much bold criticism in the opposite direction, now brings us to the conclusion that what we have in the New Testament, interpreted, as it necessarily must be, by subsequent history, is substantially the witness borne from the beginning, by those who (to use St. Luke's phrase) were 'eye-witnesses and ministers of the word,' I cannot but think that it has made, or is making, untenable the so-called mythical theory, of the gradual personification of an abstract ideal of humanity, or the gradual accumulation of imaginative and symbolic legend round a real but purely human life[1]. And, if this be so, it brings us (as I have said) face to face with the only possible alternatives—on the one hand of conscious legend, arising either out of sheer delusion in the original witnesses, or incapacity of understanding the difference between truth and falsehood, which it is hard to conceive intellectually, or out of sheer deception of the world, for purposes, perhaps great and unselfish purposes, of their own, which under all the conditions may be called a moral impossibility—on the other of that acceptance of the history as true, which is the backbone of the Creed of Christendom, and the basis of the unique and marvellous work which Christianity

[1] The crucial instance of this effect is found in the result of the criticism of the Fourth Gospel; of which so graphic and interesting a picture was presented in the Bampton Lectures of 1890 (*Modern Criticism and the Fourth Gospel*, by Archdeacon Watkins). That picture itself, even independently of all argument upon it, seems almost to decide the question, by the simple contrast of the multifarious critical theories of this century—in their extraordinary wildness and mutual contradictions, and their utter failure to see their way through the difficulties they have raised to an adequate constructive account of the thing criticized—with the simplicity of the faith in the Apostolic origin of the Gospel, which Church tradition has held from the beginning. The lecturer's conclusion is, I observe, that here at any rate 'the mythical theory is dead.'

has wrought in the world. The alternative is a great, in some sense a formidable one; and in the knowledge of this the mind is tempted to take refuge in some indefinite intermediate conceptions. But this cannot be. Clearly the matter is one in which no such halting between two opinions is, as a permanent position, possible, even if it be morally justifiable. If, therefore, we think it well to have the great alternative forced upon us—if we feel a strong conviction that, when thus thoughtfully considered, it must issue in the glad decision of faith—we may accept the position gravely and hopefully, and count that, even so, criticism has done unconscious service in leading men to Christ.

But criticism passes on, next, to study closely the actual substance of that to which witness is borne. It bids us throughout fix our eyes on the one great Central Figure, on which all the history and teaching continually rest. It bids us study deeply the Life, in word, action, character, of the Son of Man Himself, painted with that vivid reality of which I have spoken, and to mark its immeasurable exaltation above all other actual lives, still more above all ideals, which early Christianity was capable of framing. It bids us estimate it, not only in itself, but also in relation to the whole environment, intellectual, moral, religious, in which it appeared, and even in comparison with the lives of His chosen servants, whom He made His witnesses to the world. It acknowledges, as it must acknowledge, that the account of the inner secret of that unique Life, which is drawn out to us in the distinctive, yet concurrent, teachings of the

Apostolic Epistles, and which has been preserved and developed through the ages of Christian faith, is at least an intelligible and an adequate account; that, if it be true, the miraculous power over the material and the spiritual, with which the record declares it to have been clothed, is, both in itself and in the beneficence which directs it, at least appropriate to it, and (so to speak) natural; that the Resurrection and Ascension to the right hand of God are certainly its only worthy and adequate conclusion. It sees, moreover, that the declaration of this meaning of the story of Jesus of Nazareth was a power, which against all difficulties and antagonisms fairly conquered the world, and that the acceptance of it, as a living truth and a revelation of the Divine, has proved itself for eighteen centuries an ever growing and victorious spiritual force over all races of humankind. Then it is forced to ask, if this be set aside, if its solid reality be evaporated into legend and delusion, what other intelligible account can be put in its place; and certainly, as yet, in all the theories put forward it has never found an adequate answer. Their whole strength is in objection and destruction; in constructive power they are utterly weak. Yet it is a poor wisdom which only sees difficulties, and does not see through them to some tangible reality.

But yet this is not all. It teaches us to consider carefully the Word of the Lord Jesus Himself. We have learnt under its teaching to trace out that Word under various forms of revelation. We study it, as gradually wrought out in the Synoptic Gospels to the great climax with which the first Gospel ends. We study it, as it is reflected in various forms in the Acts and Apostolic Epistles. We study it, as it is brought out explicitly in its deeper teachings, not to the people, but to His disciples, in the Fourth Gospel. There we have been taught to note, not, as in the greatest of merely human teachers, self-effacement, but what has been called self-assertion, but perhaps would be better called self-disclosure—a claim, all the more startling from One, clothed in humility and living simply for self-sacrifice, of a Kingdom over all things in Heaven and Earth, a Priesthood of universal Mediation, a Nature One with the Divine. Then, seeing clearly that these things cannot be explained away, or referred, as the shallower criticism in days gone by referred them, to the pious imagination of those who came after Him, it has to bring home to us the most momentous alternative of all—the *aut Deus aut homo non bonus* of the often-quoted phrase. Either these great claims are true, or they are what we hardly dare to name—the wild dreams of a visionary enthusiast, the presumptuous ambitions of a nature, corrupted from its original nobility by success, with an element of half-conscious unreality necessarily mingling with these. There is no intermediate standing ground—and it is well that we should know it—between the action of the Jews, when, in face of that superhuman claim, they took up stones to cast at Him as a blasphemer, and the gradually deepening of the Apostolic faith to the final confession 'My Lord and my God.'

Lastly, in connection with this tremendous claim, it seems to me again that critical thought brings out to us more clearly than ever what is the real function of

Christian Evidence, in its bearing upon the fundamental and crucial question between the Church and the world as to the mysteries of the Gospel. It is not to give—what, indeed, man cannot give—demonstrative proof of those mysteries; but to ascertain whether we have sufficient grounds—grounds, of course, not merely intellectual, but moral and spiritual—for absolute faith in the Word of the Lord Jesus Christ. We have seen how the Law of Faith in general has shown itself to critical study, not only as a necessary practical factor in the whole conduct of life and in the constitution of human society, but as a chief means—perhaps the chief means of all for humanity at large—of arriving at ultimate truth, and especially moral and spiritual truth [1]. It has been seen that from the lesser and plainly limited applications of this Law in relation to man, we must ascend, if we believe in a Supreme Personal God, to the ultimate and absolute application of it to our relations with Him. So the true significance of the title of Christianity, as not a Philosophy but a Faith, comes out to us; when we see that the faith claimed for our Master is something more than this ordinary faith in man, increased, however immensely, in degree—that it is, indeed, the faith unlimited and absolute, which can be given only to God in man. Hence the true question of the acceptance of Christianity—by which I mean the historic and definite Christianity of the Creeds—is first, whether we can place this transcendent faith in the Word of Christ, as 'the Word of Eternal life' for all the children of men—spoken by His own lips, spoken in various tones in the

[1] See Lecture I. pp. 22–30.

Apostolic message, by which it was His will to evangelize the world; and next, what is the true nature of that Word, and how far all the elements, which make up the large and complex fabric of Christian doctrine, are really derived from it.

It is important that the crucial point at issue should be thus made clear, and not in any ways confused with those secondary considerations, with which nevertheless Christian Evidence has to deal. It is, indeed, well, in the largest sense of that analogy, of which I have spoken, to examine the harmony of the great truths of the Gospel with the Laws of Nature and Humanity—a true harmony, be it observed, as distinct from a mere unison, because in it the Gospel note rises supreme above all undertones. It is well also to seek to verify these truths by their living moral effects on the soul and on the world, and, indeed, only those who thus know them subjectively are likely to enter into their true meaning. But these two phases of Christian thought are (I must again remind you) subsidiary to the study of the one great question of the grounds of faith in Christ. If the answer to that brings us to rest on Him, then we sit at His feet, and learn what the New Testament calls the mysteries of the Gospel—secrets (that is) of the Divine Will and Nature, which are secrets no longer, although still for full comprehension they pass all knowledge, because they have been revealed through the 'mind of Christ.' How significant and typical those words of Martha, when, after revelation of one of the deepest of these mysteries, and the question 'Believest thou this?' she is content simply to answer, and our

Lord to accept her answer, 'Yea, Lord, I believe that Thou art the Christ, the Son of God!' However Christian thought may advance in knowledge, beyond what in those early days of discipleship was possible, its answer must still be substantially the same, and from that answer all else follows.

(VII) So, in all these ways, it seems to me that the criticism of our day, just because it is more than ever thorough, penetrating, unsparing, forces upon us the great alternative of Belief and Unbelief, not in this or that doctrine, but in the Lord Jesus Christ Himself. I do not disguise from myself the momentous character of that alternative—the struggle, even to agony, which it brings on many a thoughtful soul—the not unnatural temptation to shrink from it, occupying the mind provisionally with other and easier questions, or distracting it by practical duties and energies. But, believing (as I have already said) in our Lord's own promise, 'I, if I be lifted up, will draw all men unto Me,' I cannot fear the issue; and, although not without deep anxiety for individual souls, I would even thank the resolute and earnest questioning, which thus brings us face to face with Him. It has been often said that our age is apt not to go beyond the pathetic cry 'Lord, I believe; help Thou mine unbelief.' It may be so. But I note that the father of the demoniac boy in the Gospel was compassed round with this unbelief, from which he longed to be delivered, just so long he only had before his eyes the impotence of all earthly skill and love to relieve his child, or only sought aid from the imperfect disciples of the great Master; but, when he came to the Master Himself, saw

His face, heard His Word, then he could cry 'Lord! I believe.' If minds—perhaps especially the enquiring minds of this younger generation—vexed and bewildered by all the many critical questions and controversies, which darken the air, would only pass through them to the supreme issue, which they force upon us, and would turn from the complexities of actual and ideal Christianity to be face to face with Christ Himself—if they would but ponder His Manifestation in thought, try its practical power by even a tentative obedience, seek insight into its mystery by even a vague prayer to the Supreme Wisdom—I cannot but think that this experience would often be theirs also; and that, while still testing all things, which present themselves as revelations of truth, they will be able to 'hold fast the good,' in Him Who is the perfect Goodness.

LECTURE VII.

CRITICISM AND HOLY SCRIPTURE.

Search the Scriptures . . . they testify of Me.—John v. 39.

ONCE more in these words we hear that same demand of enquiry and judgment in things Divine, on which we dwelt last Sunday. But it comes to us now from a higher authority and with a greater definiteness. For it is the word, not of the Apostle, but of the Master Himself; and its definite application is to the Holy Scripture, the Charter of Christian faith. In the former clause of the text we must recognise a distinct authorization of Biblical Criticism; in the second an equally distinct declaration of the essence of the thing criticized.

To this search we must apply very emphatically those principles of true Criticism, of which we have already spoken. We must study Holy Scripture as it is, not as we may fancy that it should be or must be; we must be at least prepared to find that it has in it some inner life of truth and goodness; and, even if some things remain to us obscure and uncertain, we must hold fast, and so come really and deeply to understand, whatever we can grasp as true and good. The very tone of the text requires, with obvious right, that criticism, in virtue of these very characteristics, shall, while it is keen and searching, have in it some spirit of reverence and even of faith. For a Book, which has been confessedly unique in its spiritual power over humanity, has certainly a right to be examined with reverence, and with some predisposition, moreover, to believe that the secret of this supreme power is the utterance through it of what is in some supreme sense a Word of Truth, and therefore a 'Word of God.' Now it is (I think) beyond question that such criticism as this must find by its search through the whole texture of Scripture the witness of Christ, which He Himself promises. The one question is 'What is the authority of that witness? Has it a right and a power to draw to Him the intellect, as well as the conscience and heart, of humanity, that in Him they may have eternal life?'

In examining that great question between Faith and Unbelief, we have to see what are the main directions of enquiry in that Biblical Criticism, which has so wonderfully advanced to us both in scope and in power, that in many of its aspects it may be not untruly called a creation of the present century.

The first is 'What is Scripture in itself?' The next, 'How has it come to be what it is?' The third, 'What is the ground of its claim of authority?'

(I) What is this Scripture in itself? This primary enquiry, like all other enquiries into the nature of a thing, results first in analysis, examining and distinguishing its various elements; and then in synthesis, searching out the general principle of structure, which has bound them together as a whole. It is hard, I think, for men of the younger generation adequately to conceive the progress in this twofold enquiry, which has been granted to the critical study of the last half century. On the one hand, the sense of an infinite variety has grown upon us, against the inveterate habit of regarding the Bible as literally and formally one Book, the same in character and fulness of Revelation, wherever you open it. On the other, the clearer sense of unity has overcome, at least in great degree, the tendency to acquiesce from various causes in a piecemeal knowledge of the Bible, in isolated chapters and texts, with which no thoughtful man would be contented in any other book. In both these points the humblest student of to-day may have a degree of insight into the living reality of Holy Scripture, and the wonderful analogy in this repect between the Word and the Work of God, to which the greatest masters of Theology were strangers in days gone by. And we have come, moreover, to see more plainly, not only that both these characteristics exist, but that they are essential to any Book, which is to exercise an universal and permanent influence over man.

For its variety brings it into touch with all forms of human thought, and so with all ages and characters of men. It is a commonplace now to speak of the Bible as a literature in itself. But perhaps we hardly enter adequately into the full meaning of this familiar description, till we consider how that infinite wealth of human literature, which fairly bewilders us in the overwhelming growth of some great library, has, after all, a certain unity running through it. Its backbone, as we are coming to see more and more, is in History, past and present—the history of man, individual and collective, in his action and his thought,—the history of the earth, which by all its variety of treasure furnishes the environment of his life—the history, so far as we can read it, of the Universe, in its mysterious vastness of time and space, in which he loses himself in material littleness, and yet finds himself in the spiritual greatness of knowledge and understanding. Yet the very record of that history brings out necessarily the inner capacities of the humanity, which contemplates and records it, as, indeed, they express themselves in the very language of the record; and brings them out, moreover, as distinct, yet in the harmony of mind and heart and conscience and spirit. So, growing out of History, we have the purely intellectual element of Science, Inductive and Deductive, which discovers and systematizes the Laws, that underlie all history, and the Philosophy which correlates these discoveries together—in search, as the very name implies, for a Wisdom of Idea and Purpose pervading all. We have the aesthetic element of the Poetry and Art, which, alike in their discoveries and their creations, idealize the imperfect realities of life—discovering not so much wisdom and order, as beauty and grandeur —reflecting to us not so much the dry light of thought as the glow of passion, imagination, aspiration. We have the authoritative expression of Conscience, both in the wonderful fabric of human Law, restraining evil and enforcing right, and in the development of Morality, freely teaching and inspiring the principles which give life to Law. Lastly, since the mind and heart and conscience will not rest, except on some Ultimate Being, some Creative and Sustaining Power, some primal Source of Wisdom and Righteousness, known as personal, or by irresistible tendency personified, we have everywhere in all literature the expression of some Religion—'feeling after' (to use St. Paul's incomparable description) and in measure 'finding Him, in whom all lives, and moves, and has its being.'

Now, if this be so, what an immense significance there is in the unquestionable fact, which our modern Biblical Criticism has made so clear to us, that this sketch of the manifold unity in human literature is substantially a description of the structure of the Bible itself! Its backbone is certainly in the history, starting from the beginning of our world and leading up to the Manifestation of the Lord Jesus Christ, in itself and in its proclamation to mankind. Then out of this grow the declaration of Law, the insight of Prophecy and Philosophy, the Poetry of contemplation, love, adoration. Yet all is subordinated to the knowledge of God, in Himself, and in His relation both to the world and to the Soul. The Scripture is essentially an epitome of all human literature.

But it is something more than this, or it could rise to no Divine authority. Not less striking and instructive is the all-important distinction, which, indeed, makes the Book unlike all other books,—that this knowledge of God, instead of being looked upon as an ultimate mysterious result, up to which slowly, imperfectly, speculatively, all other lines of thought tend, is from the beginning set forth in a declaration of simple certitude, having authority at every point, yet growing in fulness and clearness, till it perfects itself in Him who is the Word of God. So it is not only the Omega, but the Alpha, by which everywhere these other lines of thought are themselves determined. In History, in Law, in Prophecy, in Psalm, the declaration of St. Paul at Athens, is the motto of all Scripture, 'Whom ye ignorantly worship, Him declare I unto you.' By thus keeping touch with all phases of human thought, it fastens (so to speak) the spiritual cords of knowledge and love into all varieties of human nature; by its own peculiar character of Revelation, it gathers them all into the hand of God in Christ, that He may draw all to Himself.

But, while in that marvellous progress of which I have spoken, our Biblical Criticism has brought out to us this variety, as its first and most obvious discovery, yet, in virtue of that last principle, it is equally certain that it discovers to us an underlying unity in Holy Scripture—not a dead, formal, unity as of some artificial work of man, but the living unity, at once of continuity and progressiveness, as in the growth of an Organic being. Again, it is obvious that familiarity obscures to us the extraordinary significance of this unity, between books separated from one another by centuries of time, by infinite difference of place, by not less infinite difference of tone and character, in the human authors, many of them to us unknown. For, in the conviction that there is this unity, all deep and thorough criticism confirms, as so often, the instinctive inference of common-sense. We know, of course, that, as in old days so now, there are the οἱ χωρίζοντες—those who would divide the indivisible whole—discovering or inventing inconsistencies, even antagonisms, as between the Old Testament and the New, so between the various books or sections of books in each, and mostly referring these to the introduction from time to time of wholly foreign elements. But theirs is not the criticism of the highest sort. In the cruder forms of old Gnostic days, it was abundantly shown by great Christian teachers to be both unhistorical and unphilosophical. In the subtler and more learned forms, which it wears now, it fails to stand before the more philosophical insight, which can look through superficial differences to essential principle. The progressiveness, which the Scripture itself declares, true criticism has certainly brought out with greater clearness than ever, in respect of knowledge, of moral teaching, of spiritual tone, of the conception by faith of God Himself. But that it is progressiveness, not breach of unity, is hardly questionable. That as the growth unfolds itself from the seed, it draws in nourishment not only from the heaven above, but from the earth beneath, in all the actions, and thoughts, and faiths of men, which make the history of the world, is true, and our increasing knowledge of that history makes its truth more obvious. In old time it assimilated such germs of truth as gave spiritual vitality to Egyptian or Assyrian or Persian religion; in later days it is clear that the Gospel took up much from the large speculation and culture of humanity in the Greek, and from the conception of an universal law of order and righteousness, which was the glory of the Roman. The one was undoubtedly wrought into the development of the Catholic Creed; the other into the development of the Catholic Church. But the inner life is still one, and it makes all its own, not by crude intrusion but by strong assimilation. From the days of Abraham to the manifestation of his seed on earth, that growth is traced as unbroken. It was by a true instinct that the world itself recognised in Christianity a growth from its old stock of Judaism; first, with contempt; then with fear and hostility; finally with homage and acceptance. The Christ Himself it saw to be, by no mere figure of speech, the 'seed of Abraham' and the 'Son of David.'

Nor is it less clearly discerned where the main secret of that unity lies.

Its subjective unity in one ultimate Divine authorship is, of course, largely a matter of faith. Criticism may deny, or refuse to consider, or explain away into vague generality, this faith of Christians in a Supreme Inspiration—whether of origination or selection it matters not—which has guided and overruled all these varieties of age and authorship to one Divine Purpose—so that 'the holy men of old spake as they were moved,' borne on the current of that Purpose, 'by the Spirit of God'—so that the unity is ultimately the unity in divers measures and manners of one Divine Voice. It may, I say, put this aside, though I hardly know what adequate substitute it can put in its place, as an explanation of what is undoubtedly an unique fact in the literature of the world. If (to use a well-known comparison) stones brought from various quarters, by various hands, in various generations, all fitted into one another, and grew into a structure of grandeur and beauty, who would explain this in any other way, than by the conviction that all these agents were under the guidance of one Supreme Mind, and intelligent instruments in working out one foreordained purpose?

But no thoughtful criticism can refuse to see the secret of the objective unity of the Revelation itself, in the undoubted gathering of all the lines of Scriptural thought, history, law, prophecy, into the Supreme Manifestation of the Lord Jesus Christ—all the rays of truth converging to Him through the ages before He came, and diverging from Him after His coming, to illuminate all the regions and all subsequent ages of the world. In spite of some recent statements to the contrary [1], it must seem to any criticism which looks to Holy Scripture as a whole, and is not diverted from this general view to minute examinations of detail, that this unity is not matter of faith, but matter of fact. It is hard to conceive how, even without faith in the Divine word of the text, it can fail to see that the ancient Scriptures in all their various elements really did testify of a

---

[1] See for example, in relation to Prophecy, Muir's summary of Kuenen's results in the English translation of the *Prolegomena*, where he says (p. xxxi), 'The traditional conception of the Old Testament Prophecy, as a testimony to the Christian Messiah, is repeatedly contradicted by scientific exegesis, and on the whole refuted.'

Messiah to come. Critics may differ as to the reality of special examples of this great anticipation. It may be true that the faith, which strongly realizes the glorious mystery of its fulfilment in Christ, has at times read some fanciful illustrations of it into the history or into the prophecy. It may also be true that, on the other hand, modern criticism has inclined to an arbitrary and unreasonable scepticism as to these time-honoured traditions, betraying a somewhat prosaic want of insight into deeper analogies, and strange conceptions of the power of very poor realities to satisfy the most glorious aspirations of the 'Oriental mind.' But of the fact itself there can surely be little serious question. Even if it could not be gathered from the Old Testament in itself, it must become evident to us, when we interpret it by the light of the Jewish history, which is itself confessedly unique in the history of the world. Still less can any one doubt that all the New Testament, like St. John's Gospel, is written that men might believe in Jesus of Nazareth as the Son of God, and that to this central truth it bears one witness in many tones. Men will differ in their judgment, whether this great pervading idea is a glorious dream, or the witness of a glorious reality. But surely it is there, and by it alone the Bible can be understood. It does not depend on the interpretation of this or that passage; it runs as an illuminating life through the whole body of Scripture.

It may seem, perhaps, unnecessary to dwell on what were in my memory novelties, but are now the accepted commonplaces of all Biblical interpretation. But in estimating the effects of Biblical criticism upon faith, it is right to take those effects as a whole. We must, of course, be aware that the very application of any criticism to Holy Scripture gives some shock to the old unquestioning faith, which holds it to be above all human judgment, and is content to listen to every sentence as a complete Word of God. We cannot fail to see that in the task of minute criticism there is some danger of frittering away the grandeur of the whole— perhaps of so busying ourselves in the dissection of the body of Scripture that we lose all conception of its soul. Nor is it to be denied that the actual results, to which criticism has been sometimes led, are justly looked upon as derogatory to the supreme authority of Holy Scripture. But these drawbacks, real and serious in themselves, are yet lost, as we believe, in the better fruits of Biblical criticism, taken as a whole. We must thoughtfully estimate—although, as I have said, it is hard so to do without long retrospection and comparison with a nearly forgotten past—the general effect of this first enquiry of criticism, in making the Bible infinitely more of a living reality to us, infinitely more comprehensive in its power over all forms of thought and progress, infinitely grander in the harmony, in which the dominant note is the Word of the Lord Jesus Christ Himself. So far, at least, the text has been fulfilled. Through such criticism we have 'searched the Scriptures'; we have heard in them many voices coming down to us through the centuries; but we find that all unite to testify of Christ.

(II) But, as in all other critical investigation, this

enquiry as to what Holy Scripture actually is passes naturally into the further enquiry how it came to be what it is—what has been the process of its gradual formation, and its establishment as an authoritative rule of Christian faith.

The enquiry has many phases. It is important to distinguish one from the other, and in each to see what conclusions are already accepted, and where the crucial point of controversy lies.

Thus, if we look at the Bible as a whole, no one doubts for a moment that there has been a growth in respect of what we now call the Canons of the Old and New Testaments—of the former through centuries, of the latter through at least two generations. On this matter the old tradition and the new criticism are at one. The one question which divides them is the question, 'Within what limits, by what authority, and under what determining causes, has this growth taken place, first in the gathering together of the books themselves, and then in their acceptance as a sacred and authoritative Canon?

When we turn, next, to the individual books, and enquire how they assumed their present form, a broad distinction at once makes itself evident, which must not be for a moment forgotten. These books fall into two distinct classes. We observe that, with but few exceptions, the books of teaching—the Prophecies of the Old Testament and the Apostolic Epistles of the New—declare their origin; that, on the other hand, the historical narrative generally, and, in some degree, the enunciation of law, the element of devotion, as in the Psalms, and of philosophical meditation, as in the Proverbs, are anonymous. On the former class of books, even if they draw from more ancient sources, there is mostly the stamp of unity[1]; in the latter clear signs of gradual accretion, as in the Psalms and Proverbs, or of compilation out of older materials, such (for example) as is implied in the Books of Kings, and expressly avowed in the Preface to the third Gospel. In both classes of books of the Old Testament, but especially in the latter, there are traces of what we now call editing in times subsequent to their original composition[2]. Now on these two classes of books arise two questions plainly distinct in their character and their significance. Can we accept, in the one case, the declaration of authorship as literal and genuine? Can we, in the other, trace the dates, methods and objects of the process, by which the books gradually assumed their present form? In both enquiries what weight are we to assign to ancient tradition, and what to internal criticism of the language and the character of the books themselves?

Into these main divisions fall the many enquiries as to the formation of Holy Scripture, which now present themselves in an almost bewildering variety. They are obviously of great and even fascinating interest. They have been made possible to us, as they were not possible to our fathers, by the marvellous advance of

---

[1] I speak, of course, generally, without ignoring such critical questions as those which bear upon the unity of the books of Isaiah and Zechariah.

[2] See (for example) the remarkable ethnographical and geographical notes in the book of Deuteronomy (Deut. i. 2; ii. 10-12, 20-23; iii. 9, 14, &c.).

VII.]   *The right principles of Enquiry.*   271

archaeological discovery, of historical and philological science. Perhaps at this moment they mainly absorb critical attention; so that, on both sides of the controversies which they raise, their importance, in themselves and in comparison with other forms of enquiry, is even exaggerated. That they have yielded much fruit already and will yield more, few can doubt.

It would be, of course, impossible to enter here upon any thorough examination of these questions, even if I were presumptuous enough to hold myself qualified for a task which requires the study of a life-time. On many points we must listen to experts with deference, although with some reserve still of the right and duty of intelligent judgment. But there are at least two leading considerations, by which, in order to form such judgment, we must test their arguments and their conclusions.

The first is this—that this branch of critical enquiry, which is properly historical, archaeological, and linguistic, must not be guided by any preconceived ideas—'prejudices' in the true sense of the word—derived from other considerations. It is rightly urged that we must 'take the Bible as it is.' On the one hand, it is obvious that we cannot allow our old traditional beliefs, or even our reverence for Holy Scripture, to blind us to conclusions from evidences, drawn from the character, the language, and the form of the Scriptural books, which in any other case we should accept without hesitation. We have already learnt that, in grace, as in nature, the Divine Inspiration expresses itself in methods, different from what we should have *a priori* expected. We have found that modifications in our conceptions of the human element involved in it are perfectly consistent with an unshaken faith in the Divine. Changes in our old traditional beliefs as to the date and method of the composition of the Scriptural books—unless they involve principles inconsistent with their authority, or imputations to them of untrustworthiness and insincerity—will be entirely consistent with faith in the authority and inspiration of the Scripture. It is right therefore that those, who firmly believe in this Divine Inspiration, should still examine the reasons given for such changes simply upon their own merits—judging each instance from the evidence presented, and distinguishing the different issues involved in different cases. To do this is not only a matter of critical honesty, but it is really an evidence of a faith, strong enough to stand trial and to be deepened thereby. But this same principle has an even more forcible application on the other side [1]. I do not mean only that there is, on this subject as on others, an instinct of innovation, quite as strong and arbitrary as any instinct of conservatism, and equally needing the control of thoughtful reason and judgment. The 'prejudice' to which I refer goes far deeper to the root of the matter. If we 'take the Bible as it is,' we cannot fail to see that it professes to be a Revelation of that Supernatural Order of things, of which we have already spoken, leading up to the supreme miracle of miracles, the Manifestation of the Son of God. If now we enter

---

[1] See Bishop Ellicott's *Christus Comprobator*, pp. 14, 15.

upon the enquiry as to its growth and origin with the fixed idea, that all miracle is incredible whether in the outer world of matter, or (as, for instance, in the predictive element of Prophecy [1]) in the world of mind—and that, accordingly, all record of miracle done, all prophecy which claims to look with supernatural insight into the future, must necessarily be the legendary growth of later times, or the invention of 'pious fraud' for the sake of edification, or history after the event, professing with scant honesty to predict it—if this be so, and in much of the new criticism apparently it is so—then such criticism cannot be impartial. Its conclusions, even on this point, will be warped, if not vitiated beforehand. For it has virtually to frame a new Bible in the place of the old. On the great question of the Supernatural we must make up our minds independently; how it presents itself for such decision in these days we have already tried to see. If we reject it altogether, we must, I think, regard the Scriptures, with which it is indissolubly interwoven, as having only a human authority and interest. But we cannot rightly take preconceived assumptions on the subject with us, when we engage ourselves in the detailed

[1] See, for example, the declarations of Kuenen. 'Israelitish prophecy was not a supernatural phenomenon derived from Divine Inspiration, but a result of the high moral and religious character attained by the Prophets ... which was itself the slowly matured growth of ages. The predictions of the prophets are nothing better than fallible anticipations of the manner in which they considered that the Deity must, as a necessary consequence of His character, as they conceived it, deal with the subjects of His government' (Muir's Preface to Kuenen's *Prolegomena*, pp. xxxvii–xxxix).

T

study of historical and linguistic criticism of the Scriptural record.

Nor, again, in the next place, is our criticism likely to be solid and enduring, if it fails to recognise the combined force both of external and internal evidence, and the power of each to correct the other. Probably in older times the balance may have inclined too much towards the former; tradition may have been accepted too unreservedly, without analysis and estimate of the correcting evidence presented to us in the books themselves, as regards both their language and their internal character. But I do not see how it can be doubted, that now by reaction this inclination of the balance has been somewhat violently and arbitrarily reversed. Traditions, however strong and consistent, are far too absolutely ignored. Internal criticism pronounces confidently, often on what seem to be largely conjectural grounds of its own, as to the date and authorship or compilation of this or that Scripture—as confidently, indeed, as if it had seen the various compilers at their work, had studied line by line the documents they used, and had collated the successive forms through which their productions passed. These critical conclusions and theories themselves need not unfrequently to be subjected to a somewhat sceptical criticism. They have to be balanced, even if proved to be sound, against external evidence. When they are thus resolutely tested, whatever in them is substantial will, of course, remain, but I believe that much, now confidently advanced as all but incontrovertible, will simply vanish away.

We have seen this, I think, already in respect of New Testament criticism. There the witness of external evidence was at all times seen to be exceedingly strong —in the all but unvarying tradition of the Church from the beginning to the great bulk of the New Testament, which, even without bringing in any belief of a special guidance into truth, it was impossible lightly to set aside. That tradition had, moreover, a simple, though all important, work of witness—merely to testify to Apostolic or quasi-Apostolic authorship of the New Testament books, and so to the fact that in them we have, directly or indirectly, the Word of the Lord Himself. But there came a time, when we saw that witness either assailed, or explained away, or still more frequently ignored and superseded, by a Criticism proceeding on the lines above indicated—disbelieving the miraculous and so forced to refer the Scriptural testimony to a later date, which might give time for myth and legend to grow up,—relying on the power of internal criticism, guided by arbitrary theories, (as in the Tübingen school) of tendencies and conflicts in Apostolic times, to disintegrate the Gospel narrative; to turn the Acts of the Apostles from history into an inventive Eirenicon; to pronounce confidently on the genuineness or spuriousness of this or that Epistle; above all to discredit the Apostolicity of the Fourth Gospel, the very citadel of the deepest Christian truth. What has been the ultimate issue of this criticism? It has necessitated stricter examination of the external evidence; and the effect, partly by deeper study, partly by new discovery, has been to test and immensely to strengthen it. It has taught or suggested some things in the history of Apostolic days, and the interpretation of Apostolic writings, which have enabled us to understand them better. But its own conclusions and theories are in the main confessedly obsolete; and the old traditional beliefs, which it attacked, remain substantially unchanged—only rectified in detail, and held with a more intelligent grasp of faith.

Now the critical controversy is transferred to the field of the Old Testament. It is a field in some sense more beset with obscurity and difficulty. It carries investigation back into distant centuries, in which historic light is dim, and the external witness of tradition necessarily far weaker than in the briefer and more historic period of the Apostolic age. For that investigation, moreover, we cannot as yet reckon (as in the other case) on the existence of an atmosphere of general knowledge, in respect of language and of substance, which may enable us to test, and where necessary to restrain, arbitrary boldness of theory and assertion in those who speak as experts in both. It needs that larger knowledge, not only of Hebrew, but of languages cognate to Hebrew, which is a thing of comparatively recent growth; it has far more numerous points of connection with the general history and thought of humanity in days gone by. It opens, therefore, a question, which will probably need a longer and more complex discussion, before it is set at rest.

In considering its spiritual importance, moreover, we have to weigh different considerations. It does not, of course, as in the other case, concern directly the citadel of our faith; it does not touch the reality of our Lord's Manifestation on earth; it does not deal with the truth of His Resurrection and Ascension. But its bearing on these is determined by such utterances as those of the text; in which our Lord (so to speak) clenches the conclusion, which might be suggested by the undoubted fact, that, both historically and ideally, His Gospel grew out of the ancient Covenant with Israel. However the Old Testament has come to be what it is, no man doubts that it is substantially the Scripture, into which He bade us search, to which He referred again and again as an authoritative word of God, and as in all its parts testifying of Him. So He made it an integral part of our Christianity. So His Apostles, taught by Him, dwelt upon it with unhesitating reverence as having Inspiration and authority. So the Church, resisting all attempts of old time to sever the two Testaments from each other, has borne the same witness in all ages, and must continue to bear it, whatever Criticism may discover or imagine as to its origin and its growth.

Now in this consideration there is a two-fold significance.

On the one hand, within certain limits, it has an effect of reassurance to those who are perplexed by these critical enquiries. So far as criticism leaves untouched the truth declared and implied in these words of our Master, it is obvious that we, who accept His Divine authority, can look on undisturbed, while it pursues its researches. However it grew up, the Old Testament is to us what He made it, and in this is the root of the matter. So far it is evidently true, that (as one of our leading critical authorities in England has said [1]) the conclusions of criticism 'affect not the *fact* of Revelation, but its *form*'; they do but 'help to determine ... the process, by which the record of it was built up; they do not touch either the authority or inspiration of the Scriptures of the Old Testament'; they 'pre-suppose that inspiration,' holding that 'the whole is subordinated to the controlling agency of the Spirit of God'; they do not affect 'the purposes for which our Lord appealed to the Old Testament, its prophetic significance, and the spiritual lessons deducible from it.'

But, on the other hand, there are certain developments of modern criticism, which it is hard for a plain man to reconcile with the acceptance of this authorization of the Old Testament by our Lord, as a part of His Divine Revelation. It is said, for example, in relation to prophecy, that 'it is the common conviction of all the writers of the New Testament that the Old Testament is inspired by God, and is thus invested with Divine authority. ... In accordance with this they ascribe Divine foreknowledge to the prophets ... they refer us repeatedly to the agreement between specific prophetic utterances and single historical facts. ... The judgment of the New Testament ... may be regarded as diametrically opposed to ours [2].' Yet, if the Gospel record is to be trusted, that judgment is simply the adoption of the teaching on this great subject of our

---

[1] See Driver's *Introduction to the Literature of the Old Testament* (Preface, pp. xv, xix).

[2] See Kuenen, c. xiii. p. 448 (English translation).

Lord Himself. It is again boldly contended, that, as almost a matter of course, all records of miracle must be held to be fabulous; principles and objects of composition are assumed for Scriptural books hardly compatible with historic or moral truth. How—except by derogation from His perfect knowledge or perfect truthfulness—can these be reconciled with the position, as authoritative and divine, which our Lord assigns to the Old Testament? It is on this, broadly considered, rather than on the interpretation, however important, of any words of His in relation to special passages, that our attention must be fixed, with a clear conception of the issues really involved. For certainly it goes to the very root of the matter; it does affect something more than form and method; it does bear on the whole question of authority to us. To minimize the significance of its assumptions, even in the interests of a troubled faith—to suppose that they can really fail to affect for ordinary minds its authority as a Divine guide of Christian thought and life—we must hold to be a serious error, in danger at least of incurring the censure on those who 'cry Peace, peace; when there is no peace.'

Now, as we examine not uncritically the process of this Old Testament criticism itself, we cannot but be struck with its strong similarity in principle to that criticism of the New Testament, which had its time of ascendency, and has now in the main passed away. There is in it the same ignoring of external evidence. Far, indeed, is the force of Jewish testimony from the overwhelming strength of that which witnesses to our

New Testament books. But yet, considering the tenacity of Eastern tradition, and the intense reverence of the Jews for their Scriptures—noting the indications in those Scriptures themselves of a gradual accumulation from early times of sacred books in close connection with the sanctuary—marking the significance of that well-known account given by Josephus[1] in the Apostolic age itself of the unhesitating belief of his countrymen, that with the prophetic succession the formation of the authoritative Canon of the Old Testament was bound up, and that with the cessation of prophecy it ceased—it must seem unreasonable to attach no weight at all to the tradition which ascribes large portions of Holy Scripture to Moses, to David, to Solomon, to Ezra; and to assume that, if some touches of legendary colouring has passed over this tradition, this argues an entire want of all historical reality[2]. There is again, as has been lately pointed out[3], a similar exaggeration of internal antagonism between the Priestly and Prophetic parties, and the reference to it of the origin—hardly a noble or truthful origin—of books composed for

[1] See Joseph. *c. Apionem*, i. 8; noting especially that he is enunciating not his own opinion, but the acknowledged faith of the Jews in general, and that he expressly excludes from the category of what is authoritative and Divine all later writings, 'after the reign of Artaxerxes,' διὰ τὸ μὴ γενέσθαι τὴν τῶν προφητῶν ἀκριβῆ διαδοχήν.

[2] Thus (for example) in relation to the work of Ezra, 'the later embellishments of the traditions which represent Ezra as the second author of all the books ... can only be accepted as signs of the universal belief in his labours, and ought not to throw discredit on the simple fact that the foundation of the present Canon is due to him.' Westcott on the CANON in *Dictionary of the Bible*.

[3] See *Christus Comprobator*, p. 17.

present purposes under ancient and venerable names. There is the same luxuriance of critical imagination, often without a shred of external evidence, assuming that, because this or that utterance would suit some historical period, therefore it must necessarily belong to it, and that, if it contains high and spiritual teaching, it must necessarily be brought down to later times[1]. There is the same tendency to disintegration, on grounds of superficial differences and real or supposed discrepancies of detail, in disregard of great underlying unity of idea: and the same confident assumption of certainty for these disintegrating inferences of at most probable speculation. All these similarities may well induce much hesitation in accepting sweeping conclusions, even if pressed upon us with a supposed *consensus* of critical authority. The experience of the past will teach us to pause, and rather induce expectation that, while these critical speculations will have their value, in clearing and (as has been said) 'rectifying[2]' our old traditions—while they may teach us much as to the

---

[1] With sincere respect for Dr. Cheyne's great learning and Christian earnestness, I cannot but trace some striking exemplifications of this arbitrary treatment in the Bampton Lectures of 1889 on *The Origin of the Psalter* (see, for example, the treatment of the date of Ps. cx. in Lect. I. pp. 20–29). The destructive result of his treatment, leaving to David, and even to the pre-exilian period, hardly a single Psalm, bears, I must think, an emphatic witness against his method.

[2] The phrase is Bishop Ellicott's in the *Christus Comprobator* (Sect. II). Of course, on the degree of this rectification there may be difference of opinion: but the phrase itself is simply a plea for due regard to the value of tradition, as modified, but not superseded, by the analytical method of investigation.

time and method of compilation of historical books, something as to date and immediate purpose of prophetic writings, something of the growth of the Psalter and the Books of Wisdom : yet, like the New Testament criticism—though, perhaps, after a longer time and greater difficulty, from the greater obscurity of the subject and less fulness of general knowledge thereupon—this criticism also will spend itself, and then pass away when it has done its work, leaving still the old belief substantially unchanged.

(III) But both these enquiries into the structure and growth of Holy Scripture have their spiritual importance to us in their bearing on the third supreme question on which Criticism has to speak. What is the distinctive and essential character of the Scripture itself—on the ground of which Christian faith claims for it a supreme authority, as at once holding the key to the inner meaning of other discoveries of Truth, and passing beyond them to mysteries of the Divine Nature, which they can at best infer in speculation or hope?

The enquiry is usually called an enquiry into the special Inspiration of Holy Scripture. The phrase, as a popular description, is well sanctioned by usage; and may even claim an Apostolic authority. But I venture to doubt whether it indicates the right method of investigation. In strictness—and of such strictness critical thought is more and more teaching us the importance—we ought to speak not of the Bible, as an inspired Book, but of the human authors of Holy Scripture, as inspired men, 'borne along' (to use St. Peter's phrase) 'by the Holy Ghost.' For inspiration is the action of the Spirit of God upon the living spirits of men. It is true that men are, on special occasions and for special purposes, lifted by the Spirit above their ordinary spiritual selves, and that these 'holy men of old,' in relation to the writing of Holy Scripture had, we may well believe, just that special exaltation, above what I may call the average inspiration of their lives. So much, indeed, seems to be indicated to us in the recorded spiritual experience of the prophets. True it is, also, that words become moulding influences over the thoughts, which they convey, and that the choice of words for things Divine needs a guidance from above, as truly as the choice of thoughts; so that there is a very true sense, though not its usual sense of dictation, in which we can speak even of 'verbal inspiration.' Under the consciousness of these two undoubted truths, we are justified (and indeed, as has been said, we are justified by Apostolic usage) in speaking popularly of Holy Scripture, in its present concrete form, as an inspired Book[1]. But the phrase is still in strictness incorrect, and, as usual, its incorrectness tells against clearness of idea. It tends to obscure the important truth, that the writers of Holy Scripture were not merely mechanical instruments, through which the Spirit of God spoke—the strings or notes (as old metaphor has it) struck by the Almighty Hand—the amanuenses writing (as in some well-known pictures) from angelic dictation. They were living and thinking men—moved, exalted, inspired by the Spirit of God, but living and

---

[1] 2 Tim. iii. 16, where the reference to the Holy Scriptures of the previous verse is obvious.

thinking men still, with all their peculiarities of age, race, character. The Divine impulse might overmaster, but it did not crush or destroy, individuality. The prophet did not rave in mere unconscious ecstasy, like the *Pythia* of Delphi. Not through human tongues only, but through human minds, did the Divine Mind reveal itself to the minds of His creatures.

For, in fact, we see that, under this popular phrase of the 'Inspiration of the Bible,' are included two distinct conceptions, which are properly called Revelation and Inspiration—processes not identical, but correlative or corresponding to each other. To convey truth from one mind to another needs first the presentation, manifestation, expression of truth by the teaching mind; this is revelation. It needs also the stimulation and enlightenment of the intelligence of the learning mind; this is inspiration.

If, therefore, we would describe the question before us accurately, we ought to see that the essential point is the claim of Holy Scripture itself to be an unique Revelation of God, while Inspiration is viewed as the power by which the writers of Scripture were quickened to understand and to declare it. This distinction of Revelation and Inspiration is no mere question of words. Upon some clear conception of it I believe that much depends, for the clearing away of many errors and difficulties, and for bringing out the essence of the great question here at issue between believer and unbeliever, between the Church and the world.

The distinction ought to be clear to us from our own experience of human teaching. Revelation to others is for us comparatively easy: inspiration of others infinitely difficult. The truth, which we ourselves thoroughly know, we can always reveal, by presenting, illustrating, enforcing it to others, so far as human language is capable of expressing it. But to inspire the minds of learners to receive it—to stimulate intelligence, to give insight, even to awaken interest—this we have to confess to be but slightly in our power, although even that slight measure of power is the highest quality of the teacher's art.

The distinction, again, is certainly marked out to us in Scripture itself, as in the recurring prophetic phrases, 'The Word of the Lord came to me': 'the Spirit of the Lord was upon me': 'it entered into me, as He spake.' 'The Word of the Lord came to me'—there is Revelation of Divine Truth, the clear disclosure of the Will and the Nature of God. 'The Spirit of the Lord was upon me'—there is Inspiration of him, who in old time was called simply the Seer[1], because his eyes were open to behold the vision of the Lord, in later times the Prophet, or Utterer, because charged and enabled to declare to men what he thus saw.

But, above all, in fulness and clearness comes out that distinction in the teaching of Him, who claims to tell not merely of the 'earthly things' of Manifestation of God to man, but of the 'heavenly things' of His Nature in itself. For in that teaching He speaks of Revelation as His own gift, to the world in measure, to the Church in fulness. 'I am' (he says) 'the Way, the Truth, and the Life'; 'The words that I speak

[1] 1 Sam. ix. 9.

unto you are spirit and life'; 'He that hath seen Me hath seen the Father.' The whole teaching is summed up in His Name, as 'the Word.' 'No man hath seen God at any time; the only-begotten Son which is in the bosom of the Father, He hath revealed Him[1].' But Inspiration—the 'bringing to men's remembrance' and understanding 'whatsover He hath said to them,' and the writing it through grace upon the heart—this He promises as the gift of the other Paraclete, who is the Holy Ghost[2]. It was by the harmony of the two Divine works that the Day of Pentecost became the birthday of the Church; the Ministry of the Lord Himself had been but preparatory for the spiritual harvest, which then suddenly sprang up. By that harmony now the continuing life of the Church is sustained. The Word and the Sacraments in the Church are the Revelation of God in Jesus Christ; the power to understand the one, and rightly to receive the other, is of the grace of the Holy Spirit. The individual Christian life is the knowledge and the reproduction of the Divine life of Christ; the power by which it is realized in its perfect harmony of truth, holiness, love, is the gift of Him, who is emphatically described as the Spirit of Truth, the Holy Spirit, the Spirit of Love. So it is that the Light of Christ has become the life of men, and the Word revealed has become the 'engrafted word,' growing into our nature and 'able to save the soul[3].'

But the significance of this distinction must be carried

[1] John xiv. 6, 9; vi. 63; i. 18.
[2] John xiv. 22–26; xvi. 13, 14.   [3] James i. 21.

Importance of this distinction.

somewhat further. For the full perfection of that harmony it is, no doubt, necessary that the two processes should not only correspond, but should (so to speak) keep pace, with one another. So it was with Him to whom was present the whole Truth of God and to whom was given the Spirit without measure. But for all others—so says our own experience, and so says the spiritual experience of the prophet, as recorded in Scripture—Revelation may often be larger than Inspiration; the truth (that is) revealed and uttered may be apprehended, indeed, but not fully comprehended, by the inspired mind. This belongs indeed to the general Law of the Divine intercourse with man. To have what Keble calls 'thoughts beyond their thought' is the especial characteristic of the great leaders of mankind — the privilege of intuitive genius, as distinguished from self-conscious talent. If Ruskin discovered in the works of Turner great aesthetic principles of which the artist professed himself unaware — if Coleridge discovered deep philosophies, underlying the creations of the unconscious genius of Shakespeare—it by no means follows that Ruskin and Coleridge were wrong. The truth, spoken, so far as it can be spoken, is a thing Divine and Eternal: the inspiration to understand, though it come from an equally Divine and Eternal source, is yet conditioned by the finite mind which receives it, and may have to disclose through many minds fresh depths in the truth, as the ages roll on.

But that general Law must have its highest and closest application in regard to Holy Scripture, in proportion to the fulness and depth of the Truth with which it has to do—in proportion also to the function, which it has had to discharge, not only to its own age, but to all the ages of the future. It is a great truth which is involved in the declaration that 'no prophecy is of private,' or personal, 'interpretation [1].' To know, for example, if we could know it, the exact conception of the truths, which they were inspired to utter, by Prophet or Psalmist, would by no means be necessarily to know the whole of the Divine meaning which that truth contained. The very use by the Apostles in the New Testament of Old Testament utterances—so often extending and idealizing them to a higher meaning—is singularly instructive on this point [2]. The truth itself was unchanged. It was the new Light of Christ, which disclosed the fulness of its meaning; it was the new inspiration of Pentecost, which enabled them to enter with new insight into that revelation. Their light and their inspiration were indeed unique, for the unique work which they had to do. But yet, just so

[1] 2 Pet. i. 20.
[2] These quotations seem to fall into three classes: first, quotations in the literal sense of the original, neither more nor less, as (for example) the quotation in Heb. x. 38 of Hab. ii. 4, 'the just shall live by his faith,' in the original sense of reliance on the strength and protection of God in time of trouble; next, quotations extending and idealizing the original sense, as the quotation of the same text in Rom. i. 17, where it is the motto of the whole Christian doctrine of Justification in the Blood of the Lord Jesus Christ; lastly, quotations, which are rather of the nature of application, as when in Rom. x. 6–8 the words of Deut. xxx. 11–14 are quoted with variation, and applied to the 'word of faith' in Christ, as contrasted with the external declaration of law. Of these probably the second class is the most numerous.

far as that light is shed upon the Church in all ages—just so far as the correspondent measure of Inspiration is given—we cannot doubt that we also shall be enabled, in that right development, which is neither invention nor accretion, to draw continually new wealth of meaning out of the treasure of the Eternal Truth.

But what is the practical bearing of this distinction? It seems to me to show that the really hopeful enquiry of criticism should be into Revelation rather than Inspiration—into the claim of the Christian Scripture to be the Truth of God, rather than into the question of the nature, method, limits, of the Inspiration given to its human authors. Truth is objective and so unchanging; that which claims to set it forth we may expect to be able to examine and to test. Inspiration is subjective; as such it must vary in form and degree; as such it can be fully realized only by the mind which receives it. Of it, therefore, we can hardly hope to discover an universal and comprehensible law. I do not, indeed, mean that it is not, naturally and rightly, a subject of speculation. There is much instruction in the contrast of the mechanical theory, which made its subjects mere instruments—their whole personality being absorbed into the Divine Inspiration—and the dynamical theory, which sees in it the regeneration and exaltation of natural powers, preserving in them the reality of personal character, and even the characteristics of race and an age. There is much to be learnt from the comparison and contrast of the special Inspiration of the writers of Holy Scripture with the general inspiration of humanity as such, and the fuller inspiration of redeemed humanity in the Church of Christ. There is much worth considering in the distinction, which has been drawn between the inspiration of origination of that which is new, and the inspiration of selection out of that which is old—an Ithuriel's spear of distinction between the true and the false. But what I would contend is that all this is matter of speculation, not of faith. The one all-important thing to us is to know whether we have in Holy Scripture a real Revelation of Truth; how it was given, through what forms or measures of Inspiration, is one of the secrets of God.

For that contention I think that I may claim the sanction of the deliberate action of our own Church on this grave matter. It is a commonplace to remark that in her authoritative documents there is nowhere laid down, explicitly or by implication, any doctrine of Biblical Inspiration. Various theories upon it have been held, and are held, freely and honestly, by her divines and her members. But on the reality of Revelation a pronouncement has been made, which for decision and definiteness leaves nothing to be desired—that in its entirety, 'the Old Testament not being contrary to the New,' it contains for all men and for all ages 'all things necessary to salvation[1].' For in this, and not in the other, is the true *Articulus stantis aut cadentis Ecclesiae*.

Once more, in the light of this tremendous claim, this search into the true nature of the Scripture leads

[1] See Articles VI. and VII.

us directly to Christ. For on what ground alone can it rest? Ultimately on this one foundation—the conviction that it contains adequately the direct manifestation to the world of the Word, the Life, the Person of the Lord Jesus Christ Himself. This manifestation is the central essence of the Scriptural Revelation. What St. John says of his own Gospel is true of all Scriptures old and new, 'These things are written that ye might believe that Jesus is the Christ, the Son of God, and that, believing, ye might have life through His Name.' As leading up to this, we understand the preparatory revelations of the Old Testament; as drawn from this, we accept all which makes up the manifold perfection of the New. In Him, and in Him alone, is the Revelation of God to humanity absolutely perfect, not only in the 'earthly things' of His visible working, but in the 'heavenly things' of His invisible Being. In Him, and in Him alone, dwells Inspiration without measure or limit, giving to His humanity—whatever may have been the mysterious limitations of its finiteness—the power to do that, for which the humanity was itself assumed—perfectly (that is) to know, and perfectly to declare, the whole Revelation of God. Each writer of Holy Scripture had, we believe, just that measure of light from Heaven, which enabled him perfectly to fulfil his appointed part in relation to the Manifestation of the Lord Jesus Christ—just that measure of inspiration, which opened his spiritual eye to discern that light, and opened his mouth to declare it to the world. Clearly in old time Lawgiver, Historian, Prophet, Psalmist saw each but a part of the full image of the

Christ to come, and of the perfect Gospel of His Revelation of God. Even Evangelists in the New Testament drew each his appointed and characteristic aspect of the great picture of His actual manifestation on earth. Even Apostles—St. James, St. Peter, St. Paul, St. John—had each, what St. Paul calls 'his Gospel' to deliver; each his own phase of the perfect truth of Christ to set forth. In respect of light, as of grace, 'Christ Himself is all in all.'

(IV) So, face to face with this Revelation centred in Christ, the two questions which Criticism has to ask are surely these, 'Is it sufficient for its avowed purpose?' 'Is it in all its aspects true?'

Is it sufficient for its purpose? This question is answered almost as soon as asked. The Bible thus viewed is, as we have already seen, first a Revelation of God, as a Living God, Creator and Sustainer of all being, Father of all men, as made in His likeness; it is, next, a Revelation of Man, as in that sonship, distinct in an essential superiority from the whole inanimate and animal world, having in him here a true spiritual life, the germ of an immortal perfection hereafter; it is, above all, the Revelation of God and Man as not only like, but really one, in that unity foreshadowed from the beginning, and perfected by the Incarnation of Godhead in humanity, which is at once its salvation from sin and death, and its regeneration by a new indwelling Life. All this Revelation, moreover, we have, not given in hard abstract form, but wrought out in relation to every phase of human thought and need, and so living to us in graphic reality.

Who can well doubt that, if it be true, it must be sufficient for all essential human needs?

We look at it in itself. It answers the three great questions: 'What is the world? What am I? What is the Supreme Power over both, in which both live?' Just where the thought of man runs up into mystery—the mystery of Matter and Life in the world around us—the mystery of our own humanity, in itself and in its struggle against sin and death—the mystery above of ultimate Eternal Being—it meets that searching of thought, and shows how all the threads, lost to reason in darkness, are gathered into the hand of a God, not unknown and unknowable, but revealed in the Lord Jesus Christ. What can man need more in respect of that knowledge, which is to him the key of life, and of that life as in communion with the Life Eternal?

We look at it, again, through the experience of faith, in all the Jewish and Christian centuries. The glorious recital in the Epistle to the Hebrews of the victories of faith may now be indefinitely extended through the higher Christian experience. For it is matter of simple historical fact, that in this Revelation of Christ, grasped by the living faith of mind and heart and conscience, men of all generations, all races, all characters—not the few only, but the many—have found the light of their whole life. To the simple—the hard workers and patient sufferers, who are, and must be, the great mass of humankind—it has presented itself in the simplicity which ignores difficulty; to the wise and thoughtful, it has revealed in fulness inexhaustible the needful light through all the difficulties and perplexities, which it is their burden to know and feel, and the key to the inner meaning of all the gleams and dawns of other knowledge which, through these, it is in measure their privilege to see. Men have disputed over certain points of its interpretation, and through disputes over these points, important but yet of secondary importance, they have divided the Christianity which should be one. But in the great essentials of the faith there is still a Creed of Christendom, and in this all who accept the one Bible, are at one still. They have grasped it as true; and of its sufficiency, as so grasped, they have never had to doubt.

We may look at it, if we will, even through the eyes of serious and thoughtful unbelief. The very sense of darkness and despondency, when it believes itself forced to give up the old faith, and go forth into the dimness of a twilight speculation, with perhaps some refracted rays from the lost sun, and some flickering gleams of earthly light—the very effort, which it often makes, to avoid the dread inevitable alternative, and to keep without a Divine Christ something of Christianity—something of Christian morality, and Christian love, and even Christian idea—they tell us pathetically how sufficient, if it could but be accepted as true, would be to them the revelation of the Gospel that they have lost.

Every way, as it seems, that first question answers itself. It is on the second—the question, 'Is it true?'—that the great division comes. What that question really means, and what is implied in the answer—it will remain for us to consider hereafter.

Meanwhile I commend to your thoughts these three processes of Biblical criticism, of which I have spoken—the study of the varied structure and unity of Scripture, which has already so largely done its work—the study of the growth of Holy Scripture, still progressive, with all the imperfection and promise which belong to progress—the study of the substance of what it is as a Revelation, and of the marvellous sufficiency of that Revelation to those who can accept it. In all these three forms of search into the Scriptures certainly the words of the text have been fulfilled. They have 'testified of Christ'—Christ as the central life of the whole organic structure—Christ as the perfection of the whole growth—Christ as the final giver of that all-sufficient Revelation. Even so, I cannot but think that they go some way to answer by anticipation the question of all questions, 'Is that testimony a splendid dream of speculation and hope, or is it a witness of the Supreme Truth?' Sternly—yet with a beneficent sternness—Criticism forces that great question upon us. It is well. For, as of the contemplation of Christ in Himself, of which we spoke last Sunday, so of the Scripture, as expressing Him to us, I cannot but believe that this study, even so far as I have already spoken of it, brings out everywhere in itself the stamp of obvious reality. No such ideal could have been created by what we can see to have been the thought and aspiration of early Christianity. No mere ideal, indeed, was ever so consistent in all its phases, so living in itself, so spiritually powerful in its effect. The more we test it, whether by deep and earnest thought, or by the energy of practical trial, or by the insight of spiritual aspiration in prayer, the more we shall feel that (to apply St. Peter's words) 'we have not followed cunningly devised fables, but are eyewitnesses of a Divine Majesty [1].'

[1] 2 Pet. i. 16.

LECTURE VIII.

TRUTH IN REVELATION.

Search the Scriptures . . . they testify of Me . . . I am the Truth.—John v. 39; xiv. 6.

(I) To the command of our Lord, addressed to all enquirers, on which we dwelt last Sunday, as at once the authorization and the guide of true Biblical Criticism, I add to-day from His later and deeper teaching to His disciples, the utterance, which determines what must be the essential characteristic of all that bears witness of Him. For truth alone can testify to Truth —truth in various forms and measures to the Truth of a Divine Perfection. We have already studied, and sought to estimate, in regard of their spiritual importance, the first two enquiries of Criticism, into the structure and the growth of Holy Scripture. In regard to its final enquiry into what is the essential and unique character of Scripture, as the ground of its claim of supreme authority, I have suggested to you that — much popular usage and language notwithstanding — it should really concern itself with the objective fact of Revelation, rather than the subjective process of Inspiration: and that the enquiry, which is at once all-important and hopeful, is whether that Scripture is, or is not, a Revelation of 'all things necessary to salvation.' Of its sufficiency for this purpose, if it can be accepted, there can be no question. But does it fulfil, in all its mingled variety and unity, the function which our Lord assigned to Himself, that He 'came into the world to bear witness of the Truth'?

This is to us above all others the question of questions. On the answer depends certainly the claim of Scripture to be in any special sense what we commonly call it, a 'Word of God.' There is a homely insight in the conclusion of the widow of Zarephath, that a Man of God must speak 'a Word of the Lord' and that this 'word in his mouth must be truth[1].' The whole meaning of Holy Scripture is in its manifestation of Christ; and in the latter part of my text our Lord expresses the central idea of that manifestation in the words, 'I am the Truth.' It is because He is the Truth, that He is also 'the Way and the Life.'

If it be asked 'What is Truth?' the general answer must, no doubt, be, that Truth is accordance with the great Laws of Being, the various expressions of the supreme 'Law Eternal.' But, in applying that answer to Scripture, we must clearly distinguish the various elements—the History, Law, Psalm, Prophecy, both of the Old Testament and the New—which, as we have seen, make up its manifold unity. For in relation to each of these the general definition of Truth has a peculiar form of significance, and our question must be 'Has each element that specific kind of truth, which properly belongs to it?' We must not evade or obscure

[1] 1 Kings xvii. 24.

that question by the consideration, important as it is, that the one great purpose of Scripture is to convey spiritual truth; that all is subordinated to that spiritual Revelation, on which we touched last Sunday, of God, of Man, and of God and Man made One; that its object is not to supersede human knowledge and discovery, but to meet and supplement these by the disclosure of what is hid from them; that its promise is to make men wise indeed, but wise unto salvation; that we may, if we venture on such rather futile speculation, conceive that this Revelation might have been given, and this Wisdom imparted, in a form less complex, and having fewer points of critical contact with human literature and history. For all this does not touch the main question. The Bible is what it is. It is actually presented to us in that complex structure, by which, as we have seen, it places itself in touch with humanity in all its phases. In all the parts of this actual structure it must be searched into, and estimated by a right criticism, on the principles appropriate to each. We must try to see clearly and resolutely what in respect of each we really mean, when we speak of the truth of the Revelation, which it thus professes to give.

(II) Thus its backbone is undoubtedly history—the history of man, and of the world as it concerns man, from the beginning to the coming of the Lord Jesus Christ, and the first establishment of His Kingdom over Jew, and Greek, and Roman, as the three great representative races of humanity. To avoid all points, on which difference of opinion may exist among those who accept the authority of Scripture, let us fix our thoughts on the continuous thread of narrative which begins with the call of Abraham.

In the earlier chapters of Genesis, which tell the story of the Creation and Primeval Man, and give brief, and often obscure, glimpses of the antediluvian world, it is true that many profoundly believing interpreters, ancient and modern, have held that we are reading simply a sublime and instructive symbolic description of a world not properly our own, designed merely to reveal, as it certainly does reveal, great moral and spiritual truths—the Creation of all things by God, the nature of man made in the image of the Divine Righteousness, the fall from it by rebellion and sin, the hope and promise of Redemption [1]. It may be so; yet the narrative itself, as distinct from such imaginations from it, as Milton has made familiar to us, paints to us in striking simplicity what we can well conceive to be an actual picture of primeval humanity. But from the Flood onwards, and still more clearly from the call of Abraham, we have what most definitely, and, if I may use the word, prosaically, declares itself to be a history of facts. History or fiction it may be; but apologue or parable it cannot be. There is an instructive distinction, which brings out this general character, between the Book of Job, avowing itself by its very form to be a magnificent Poem on a historic

---

[1] It should be allowed that the acceptance of a symbolic theory of interpretation of the narrative need in no way imply any want of faith in the absolute reality of these fundamental truths; and it is certain that it has not done so in the case of many who hold it.

basis, having all the creative freedom and right of poetry, and the Books (for example) of Exodus or Joshua or Samuel.

But what is confessedly the one requisite of History? It is well that it should be impressive, graphic, picturesque, and in its grave way eloquent; it is well that it should, as a 'philosophy teaching by examples,' bring out the great Laws of Nature and Humanity. But with all these things History may dispense, and yet be history. The one thing, which makes it what it is, is what we rightly call 'historic truth'—truth that is in record of facts, both the facts of event and action, and the facts of human character. If the Scripture narrative professes to be history, by this canon of historic truth it must be judged. The question does not now turn on the enquiries of what we have spoken—out of what materials it may have been framed, and where, as usual, it is anonymous, by what hands and in what times it may have been compiled. It is not even a question of the degree in which, under the 'inspiration of Selection,' its writers may have been left, in respect of details, to their own human care and study[1]. The question is, whether the great substance of the narrative—professing to record in human history the

[1] This consideration bears upon the discrepancies of detail, real or supposed, between parallel narratives, or those which apparently come from the incorporation in one narrative of documents independent of one another. If we may judge from the analogy of New Testament criticism, we shall (I think) find that the amount and importance of these have been much exaggerated, and we shall be also led to conclude that many of them are but apparent, and due to our imperfect knowledge of the whole facts.

special preparation in the Divine Order for the Coming of the Lord, His Manifestation on earth, and the first beginning of its proclamation to the world—is really true. It is with that question that finally Criticism must busy itself—testing the narrative by comparison with itself, and by comparison with other discoveries of historical, archaeological, linguistic, Science, and that question we must look plainly in the face.

In this view I would again remind you that we must make up our minds with plainness and decision on what is called 'the miraculous element' in the whole Scripture history. It is not indeed, as a careless reader might think, sown broadcast over the history. It has (as I have already reminded you) its own law of distribution and order. It is concentrated in its full brightness on the Manifestation on earth, from the Incarnation to the Ascension, of the Lord Jesus Christ. In the Old Testament narrative of preparation for that Coming, the record of it is almost entirely confined to two great eras of advance and expansion—the Exodus and Eisodus, which were the birth of the Nation under the Law, and the beginning of Prophecy, especially in its victorious struggle against the Baal Apostasy in the days of Elijah and Elisha[1]. In the New Testament narrative of the Apostolic Ministry proclaiming the Lord's Coming, it has been noted as appearing with

[1] I do not, of course, venture to assert that these are the only epochs in which miracle largely occurred. If we had equally minute and graphic accounts of other periods in the history and of other prophetic biographies, we might find it in them also. But still the fact remains that only in these have we records of any remarkable outbursts of miraculous power.

intermittence, and coming out in special fulness at critical periods, such as the first great era of St. Peter's preaching after Pentecost, and St. Paul's ministry in the very home of Gentile magic at Ephesus [1]. But there it undoubtedly is, inextricably woven with the history which is often unintelligible or incredible without it, recorded merely as a clear manifestation of the Divine Will of Righteousness, in the same grave and simple tone as what we call ordinary events. I cannot see how any view, which holds that Miracle is incredible, and that its records must therefore be conscious or unconscious fictions, is compatible here with historic truth, or perhaps even with historic truthfulness.

Now here the main stress of argument must be on the New Testament record of the Gospel itself—on the whole story of the Life and Death of the Lord, on the witness to the great Miracle of miracles in His Resurrection, and on the history of its proclamation to the world, in itself and in all that follows from it, to open the new era of Christianity. On it criticism has in all ages, not least in our own, turned its most searching light. For on the question whether it is a solid and Divine truth, or an ideal legend, in which human hope and aspiration cheat themselves into an imaginary fulfilment, depends the vital question whether the Creed

---

[1] See Acts v. 12–16; xix. 11, 12. In the latter passage the phrase δυνάμεις οὐ τὰς τυχούσας is instructive, as indicating what we may call an undercurrent of miraculous power, emerging into special prominence on special occasions. We may note that in 2 Cor. xii. 12 St. Paul alludes to displays of such power at Corinth, of which we have no direct historic record. Comp. also Rom. xv. 19.

of Christendom is founded on the unchanging rock of reality or on the shifting sand of imagination. We welcome that light of criticism, which, as I have already said, seems to me to dissipate all intermediate theories of a mythical type, between the two great alternatives of truth and falsehood, a 'cunningly devised fable' and 'the eye-witness of a Divine Majesty.' For it certainly makes it absolutely clear that the Christ of the Gospel record and the Apostolic preaching is not an ideal phantom, but a true Son of Man, who was born and lived a real life on earth, and died on the Cross of Calvary. But the same witness which establishes that historic reality of His earthly life, bears with equal cogency and simplicity on the supernatural character of that life, as manifested in miraculous power, and as sealed by unquestionable fact in the Resurrection. It must be taken as it is; its various parts cannot be torn asunder without destroying the life of the whole[1].

But yet, though in less degree, the same principle must apply to the criticism of the Old Testament, which for us Christians cannot be separated from the New. It is well here also to look clearly at the issue involved. By some leaders of modern criticism it is made plain enough—when (for example) leading Old Testament books are described, as not only having accretions and

---

[1] The lifelike simplicity, for example, of the narratives of John ix. and xi., which shows in every line the testimony of an eye-witness, must bear forcibly on the truth of the miracles of the healing of the blind man and the raising of Lazarus, which are the central features of these records.

corruptions, but as being themselves deliberate creations of later days[1]—when the whole history of the Tabernacle in the wilderness, of the setting apart of the tribe of Levi and the appointment of the priesthood, is represented as fabricated for the honour of the Temple and the support of the priestly dignity[2]—when the undoubted claim of the Prophets to a supernatural insight is declared to be but a fictitious investiture with Divine authority of the fallible anticipations of human sagacity, if not actually the fraud of pretended predictions made after the event. By theologians of soberer and more reverent temper in our own Church these extravagant assertions are summarily rejected. But yet we must carefully consider what is really implied in the assumption, as a main principle of interpretation, that 'in many parts of the historical books we have before us traditions, in which the original representation is insensibly modified, and sometimes

[1] See Wellhausen's *Prolegomena* (pp. 293, 294). The history, as we have it, is 'a later repainting of the original picture'... not only 'with discolouring influences in the mythical elements, but in the uniform stamp impressed on the tradition by men who regarded history exclusively from the point of view of their own principles... There was a systematic recoining of the old tradition... The old books had to be remodelled, in order to make them valuable, digestible, and edifying.' An illustrative example is given in respect of *the visit* to Ramah (1 Sam. xix. 18-24), which is 'a pious caricature— the enjoyment of the disgrace of the naked king.'

[2] See Wellhausen's *Prolegomena*. 'It may seem to have been asserted that the Tabernacle rests on a historical fiction. In truth it has been proved... as to the Tabernacle of the Priestly Code; for some kind of tent for the Ark there may have been' (p. 37). 'The statement' (he adds) 'is simply a dogmatic way of making history,' with 'the absurd consequences to which it leads.'

(especially in the later books) coloured, by the associations of the age in which the author recording it lived,' and the claim for the Scriptural historians of freedom 'in placing speeches or discourses in the mouths of historical characters,' which 'in some cases, no doubt, agree substantially with what was actually said,' in others 'develop at length, in the style of the narrator, a compendious report'; but which may also invent altogether 'what was deemed consonant with the temper and aim of a given character on a particular occasion [1].' Similarly we must estimate clearly what is the bearing on historic truth of the supposition of 'an unconscious idealizing of history, the reading back into past records of a ritual development, which was later,' representing 'the real purpose of God, and only anticipating its realization'; and whether it is consistent with what 'our faith strongly disposes us to believe, that the record from Abraham downwards is in substance in the strict sense historical [2].' In the acceptance of these principles a strong distinction is drawn, and rightly drawn, between the Old Testament and the New. But, if they are accepted as compatible with Inspiration, it is hard to be sure that this distinction is one of kind and not of degree.

Now these assertions of modern Criticism and the reasons given for them are, of course, to be met, as has

[1] See Driver's *Introduction to the Literature of the Old Testament* (Preface, p. xvii).

[2] See *Lux Mundi* (ed. of 1889), pp. 351, 353. It must be remembered that to us the main question is of Revelation rather than Inspiration, and so of the objective truth of the narrative, rather than the subjective truthfulness of the narrator.

been done in respect of the New Testament, by full and candid enquiry, and not by denunciation. But still it is well that the nature of the issue should be understood to be no less than the question between that substantial historic truth, which the whole tenour of the narrative claims, and which certainly the teaching of our Lord Himself seems to imply, and a strange heterogeneous growth of truth and falsehood, legend and history; of which it is hard to conceive how it can be accepted as a historic revelation of God's actual dealings with men, and as holding the place given to it by our Master in the historical preparation for His own coming.

(III) But, interwoven with this great historic thread, there is what we may call in the largest sense, the Prophetic element of Scripture—its teaching (that is) in God's Name of His Will, His Righteousness, His Love, in a continuous dispensation to man. What is needed here for a true Revelation of God? Clearly truth once more, but now moral truth—according with that Eternal Righteousness, which is witnessed to by the conscience within and written on the course of the world without, but revealing that Righteousness in a clear and living certainty, to inform and inspire the one witness and to explain the other.

That teaching comes to us first through Law—the Supreme Will of God (that is) declared in commandment, to guide and control human conduct, and enforced by reward and punishment in this world or in the next. Beginning in the simple Law of the old Patriarchal time, it starts, from the birth of Israel as a Nation onwards, into the full searching Law, which we call the Law of Moses; it becomes, as in the Sermon on the Mount, the Law of Christ, so far as His teaching is merely Law, perfecting (as He Himself declared) what was given to them of old time. That Law, like all other law, must adapt itself in form and detail to the various ages and conditions of the men to whom it was given; so that in its earlier stages it may allow to the 'hardness of men's hearts' what is forbidden to the later; it must, if it is to grow deeply into men's nature, take up and stamp with its own impress existing laws, customs, traditions of humankind; it must necessarily at every stage contain the rule, which is temporary in obligation, as well as the underlying principle, which is eternal; it must, so far as it is strictly law, be limited by some possibility of enforcement, and be content to rule the outward life of conduct rather than the inner life of the spirit. Therefore, in all its earlier stages, it was confessedly an imperfect preparation for a perfection in Christ, and, even from His lips, so far as it was still Law, it was but a means and guard to the higher life of the Spirit in Him. All this has been rightly impressed upon us by criticism, studying the Scriptural Law in its gradual development, tracing in it various elements of connection with other ancient laws, illustrating it by greater knowledge of history. It is well. For from errors on these points have arisen many difficulties in understanding the Law, many fatal anachronisms in applying it, many attempts to do through it what Law, even if perfect as Law, can never do.

But yet for all this, if the Scriptural Law, which, be it remembered, is a continuous development, is to have to us any sacredness or authority, it must have, through all these imperfections and limitations, accordance with moral truth; it must gradually unfold that moral truth in growing purity and harmony, until it reaches perfection, so far as law can be perfect, in the Law of Christ Himself. I do not know that we can limit this requirement to the commandments which we ordinarily call moral; although, no doubt, in them it will have its fullest development. Even in the civil and ceremonial laws, under the outward forms which have passed away, there are implied inner principles, having a distinctly moral character, which can never be obsolete. In all its branches the supreme idea of the Law is the basing of all moral duty, and the kindling of all moral enthusiasm, in the first great commandment of the knowledge and love of God. Its very purpose (as St. Paul teaches again and again) is to assert and guard what is called the Covenant of God with man, implying real moral relations of the Infinite with the finite. It brings out, therefore, in the individual, in the nation, in the Church, the supreme moral conception of Holiness—a purity (that is) of heart and mind, consecrated and sustained by conscious communion with God—as the inner secret of the life 'hid in God' Himself, and as including all its relations of righteousness and love. With a view to the attainment of such holiness, it recognises, as lying at the very root of that Covenant, the great principle of Atonement, implied in all Sacrifice, and expressed in the great Sacrifice of

Calvary. These ideas are fundamental and far-reaching in their effect: only if they are morally true, can the Law of Scripture be in any sense—what Our Lord Himself made it—a Law of God, and a preparation for His own kingdom.

But higher and deeper than all Law is the teaching of what we may call in the largest sense Prophecy—the revelation (that is) of the Will and the Nature of God in essential spiritual principle, and the writing it freely by force of its own intrinsic light and righteousness on the souls of men—implying necessarily an inspiration from on high, in those who utter it and those who receive it.

We have that Prophecy, running like a golden thread through the whole of the Old Testament. There is an element even in the Law, which as our Lord Himself says, 'prophesies.' For it enters constantly, as no human law can enter, into the free inner life of the soul; its first and great commandment is the Love of 'the Lord our God,' which no constraint of law can engender. There is in the older prophets of unwritten prophecy a gradual development of that spiritual teaching and influence, in relation to the present life individual and national, by the power of which Israel grew out of the retrograde and half-barbarous era of the Judges into a fitness for the high religious civilization of later days. It was clearly the inner life to the people of moral culture, freedom, progress, victorious against despotism of material power, against superstition and idolatry, against false worship of false gods, with a victory of which Elijah at Carmel is the glorious type. There is in the later prophets of the written prophecy a fuller development of that same teaching, not only as the life of the present, but as the earnest of the Diviner life : of the future. No unprejudiced reader can doubt that, in unfolding the working of the whole scope of God's Righteous Will, they claim power in various measures, not only to look back and read it in the past, but to look onward by the light which He gives and read it, sometimes generally, sometimes definitely, in the ages to come [1]. No student can well doubt, that in various degrees of clearness and sublimity, this onward looking of Prophecy gathers itself round a future Kingdom and a future King—One who is a true Son of Man, seed of Abraham, Son of David, yet on whom are accumulated attributes too great for any but an Emmanuel, 'God with us.'

For that Prophecy, taken as it thus actually is, still more essential than even for the Law is this requirement of moral truth—illumined, of course, as all moral truth must be illumined, by some insight into the great laws of being. That requirement must apply to all its elements—to its representation of God and of humanity —to its claim of special inspiration and prophetic foresight—to its gradually brightening conception of the Messiah to come. Necessarily by that very conception Prophecy confesses its own imperfection, as in the Revelation which it transmits, so in the Inspiration,

---

[1] Nothing surely can be more uncritical than to assert that 'the prophets did not attach primary importance to the lateral and immediate fulfilment of their prophecies' (Muir in English translation of Kuenen's *Prolegomena*, p. xxxvii). See Note I.

which gives its power to understand and declare it; and that imperfection will attach to its moral and spiritual, as well as its intellectual, character. Clearly, as we connect the prophecy with the history, and compare prophet with prophet, we note the distinction of their age, their mission, their character, which make them differ from one another in the fulness and spirituality of their message. We speak of some more than others as clearly Messianic in foresight and Evangelical in character. As we compare the Prophecy of the Old Testament with the Gospel of Christ, we may be sensible, that, as was needful for earlier and cruder stages in the life of humanity, there may be some shadow in it of the sternness of the Law, a more frequent appeal to godly fear, a less constant reliance in godly love. But yet for all there is the claim of a 'Word of the Lord,' spoken by 'the Spirit of the Lord'; and in that claim it must be implied that morally the word so spoken is true.

But from this, confessedly imperfect and preparatory, we pass on to the Prophecy of the New Testament—the Revelation of God by the great Prophet of prophets, by His own lips, or by the lips of those to whom He promised that the Holy Spirit should bring home His word, and through whom it was His pleasure to evangelize the world. Clearly for this the requirement of moral truth must be absolute and perfect, if it is, as Christian faith declares it to be, an universal and absolute guide to humanity. With that requirement, as an inseparable condition, must go the requirement of a corresponding perfection of illuminating insight into the secrets of God and of man. Whatever may have been the mysterious self-limitation of the Godhead in humanity—on which (let me say it in passing) the experience of past Christian centuries gives us but little hope of any definite and sound conclusions—however, in His humanity, the intuition into things Divine and human, may have 'grown in wisdom' by clothing itself in gradual acquisition of form and exemplification by detailed knowledge[1]—still He claims for Himself to have the word of eternal life, and 'life eternal is knowledge of God.' But it is in the requirement of moral and spiritual truth that I now speak; and this clearly implies, that in the great principles of the doctrine of Christ— as, for instance, in Mediation, Atonement, Sanctification through grace,—there must be nothing, which is not perfectly in accord with the Eternal Righteousness and Love of God, and the undying responsibility of man; that in the Christian morality of the New Testament there must be nothing false, insufficient, one-sided, inoperative, corresponding only to some of the moral conditions and needs of humanity, and not to all[2]: that in the spiritual life in Christ, both individual

---

[1] This is but the old distinction of knowledge δυνάμει and ἐνεργείᾳ.

[2] It will be, of course, easily understood, that in the New Testament special stress may be laid on some moral graces—such as humility and purity—which, in the best morality of those days, had been ignored or depreciated; while others, which were already honoured even to excess—such as manliness and intellectual enthusiasm—are taken for granted, and rather guided and tempered than enforced. Note, for example, the treatment of manliness in 1 Cor. xvi. 13, 14; where it is emphatically shown to have its root in faith, and its guiding and controlling principle in love.

and collective, there must be the full satisfaction of the highest spiritual aspirations, and the harmony, which this requires, of the Infinity of God and the true finite individuality of man. Not less than this surely is involved in the moral truth of Holy Scripture; and the conception clearly differs, not in degree but in kind, from the qualified admiration and reverence, which the world is ready to give to it, and to the moral teaching of Christ, which speaks in it.

(IV) But there is a third element of Scripture, closely connected with this, which is the response of inspired humanity to these Revelations of God in Law and Prophecy, and which expresses to us the attitude of the soul, as by meditation, by prayer, by adoration, it realizes its communion with Him. We find gleams of it interspersed through the books of history[1]; it forms again and again an element in the utterances of the Prophets, who speak alternately, as representatives of God to man, and of man to God[2]; above all, it expresses itself in its meditative and intellectual aspect in the Books of Wisdom, and in its spiritual aspect in the great Book of Psalms. It comes to its perfection in the devotional utterances of our Lord Himself, and, caught from these, the outpouring of Apostolic spirits to God.

What needs this element of Holy Scripture, that it

[1] See the Psalm of triumph at the Red Sea (Ex. xv. 1–21); the Song of the Well (Numb. xxi. 14, 15); the Song of Moses (Deut. xxxii); the Song of Deborah (Judges v); the Song of Hannah (1 Sam. ii. 1–10); the 'last words' of David (2 Sam. xxiii. 2–6).

[2] See (for example) Is. xii; Jer. xx. 7–18; Jonah ii. 1–9; Hab. iii.; Is. xxxviii. 9–20.

may be, as it has been through the ages, the ideal and the inspiration of our own devotion? Truth, we may answer still, and spiritual truth; but truth subjective, seen (as it were) on the other side from that which we have as yet considered, through the inner human consciousness. The conception of God so gained must be true in the realization of His Divine Attributes, not of Power only or chiefly, but of Wisdom and Righteousness and Love. The attitude of man towards Him must be true to the mingled dignity and lowliness, strength and weakness, righteousness and sinfulness, freedom and dependence, which mark our human nature at all times, but mark it especially in the consciousness of the Fatherhood of God. Here, also, there will be degrees in the perfection of this grasp of spiritual truth, as the spiritual education of humanity is wrought out by the increasing Revelation of God. In the simple childlike outpourings of Patriarchal faith; in the impulsive and enthusiastic communings with God of the great Lawgiver of Israel; in the pleadings, remonstrances, longings of the Prophets; even in the priceless and undying utterances of the Psalmists, which have been and are the living treasures of all the Christian ages; there must still be imperfections. There will be elements (as, for instance, in what we call the Imprecatory Psalms, or in the utterances of doubt and despondency, from time to time chequering the brightness of faith), which, though they have by the very force of sympathy their instruction of encouragement and warning to us, yet the higher consciousness of Christian faith must use, as indeed it has used them in all the centuries, with correction from the teaching and the example of our Master. They, indeed, whose whole lives are penetrated with the spirit of the life of Christ, insensibly Christianize the utterances of the older days. For only in Him is there the subjective perfection of spiritual being; as it expresses itself in the prayer of daily life, which He has given us, in the fervent prayer of the great crises and agonies of life, in the sublime Intercession[1], which enters, and carries all humanity with it, into the central mystery of the Divine Presence. Even Apostolic utterances, though they catch and reflect that perfection, yet have something of individual colouring, full indeed of force and beauty, but narrower and less universal than the clear white light of the mind of Christ Jesus. But though there be imperfections in the disclosure through Scripture of the spiritual life, still there must be substantial truth, with no falsehood, no perversion, no unworthy thoughts of God's nature, no unworthy slavishness or selfishness on the human side. All must grow, under the true relation of God to man, up to the supreme perfection in Christ. Only on that condition can it be to us the ideal revelation of our higher humanity, the unfailing and unceasing food of our devotion of thought and worship to God.

(V) But above all and through all these forms of Scriptural Revelation the supreme requirement is of what we may call Theologic truth—the truth (that is) not of God's works, but of the Nature of God Himself, a truth confirming and correcting, but transcending, all

[1] John xvii.

lower Revelations of Him. Such revelations there are. Through all philosophic questionings, and in spite of a consciousness of complexity and mystery in Nature, such as our fathers knew not, the maturest thought confirms the instinctive common-sense of mankind; it finds in Nature the working of a Supreme Will, certainly infinite in power and wisdom, possibly in righteousness and goodness. In Humanity, just in proportion as it is conscious of itself,—its own will and reason and conscience, its own capacity of truth in love —there is a Revelation of a God—as in the secrets of the soul itself, so in visible handwriting upon the history of the world—a Revelation which seems to me to be exactly the complement of the other, witnessing primarily of His moral relation to us in righteousness and mercy, and secondarily of His wisdom and power. Yet both these are crossed and painfully obscured by the great mystery of evil—the evil of suffering, pain, apparent waste and failure in Nature, and the addition to these of moral evil, vice, crime, sin, and death by sin, in humanity. Clearly a true and supreme Revelation of God must confirm and illustrate both these lower witnesses. But it must transcend both, in glimpses at least of the mysteries, lying above their ken, and in the dissipation or illumination of that heavy cloud of perplexity which hangs over both.

It is precisely this, which the Scriptural Revelation of God claims to do. The idea of God grows, widens, deepens through the whole; and we note that at each point it is at once personal in relation, yet universal in itself. The Creator of all the world is yet close, in tender care and love, to the man made in His image. The God of Abraham, Isaac, and Jacob is in covenant with His chosen servants, while yet He is always known as the 'God Almighty,' 'the Judge' and Ruler 'of the whole earth.' The Jehovah of that Mosaic Revelation, which is wrought out by the whole order of the Prophets, is the God and King of the chosen nation of Israel, close to their action and their thought at every point, and dwelling between the Cherubims, in the Tabernacle or Temple which is His chosen seat of Revelation to them; yet the very meaning of the Name proclaims Him as the One Eternal Self-existent Being, fountain of all created life, the One ultimate object of all created reverence and love. The final Revelation, in the word of the Lord Jesus Christ Himself, is of the supreme mystery of the Triune Godhead, the Father, the Son, and the Holy Ghost, stamped in Baptism on the very forefront of our Christianity; yet of the fulness of that Godhead, as dwelling bodily in the true Son of Man, whom we know, as it were, face to face, and through Him dwelling in measure in the very heart of the simplest humanity.

Everywhere the Nature of God, as Truth in Love, is brought out to us, although it seems as if the two elements were blended to our eyes in different proportions. The sterner element of Righteousness assumes a prominence in the era of the Law, unknown to the simplicity of the earlier and more childlike days; while Love is as a deep undercurrent, felt rather than plainly seen. In its turn it passes gradually from that prominence, as the free spirit of Prophecy rises above the rigour of Law; till in Christ we know, above all else, that 'God is Love'; while yet that Love has still by necessity the discriminating judgment of Righteousness, and, although it weeps over a Jerusalem, cannot take away the self-chosen doom of men.

At every point, moreover, in some degree, and with ever-increasing clearness, this Revelation of God (as we have already seen) recognises as only too real, although subordinate and unnatural, the power of evil in the world. It unmasks it in the History; it scourges it in the Law; it deals with it by remonstrance, rebuke, entreaty, in Prophecy; it confesses it, sadly and almost passionately, in the Psalm. Finally, it makes the Cross of Atonement the very badge of Christianity, because the very expression of the true Gospel for a world like this; and so it claims to be able to tell how the guilt of sin is already forgiven, its power already broken, and how it is destined in the hereafter to vanish away.

It is on the truth of this Revelation—the only alternative, as the world's experience seems to show, to a blank agnosticism as to the Supreme and Absolute Being—that the sacred authority of Holy Scripture depends. If it be what it claims to be, it must be in essence the most perfect Revelation of God which humanity is capable of receiving; there must be no secrets of God, which can be told and need to be told to man, not contained in it, and capable of being drawn out for all generations by the Spirit of God, as the inspiration of the higher life in Him.

(VI) This, and not less than this, is what is implied

in the belief in the Truth of Holy Scripture, as in all its lines of development in history, law, prophecy, devotion and meditation, expressing in different measures and forms Him who is Himself the Truth. With the examination of this, above all, criticism is concerned: it has to see in each branch of its witness, where the root of the matter lies, and then to ascertain whether it strikes deep down into the eternal foundation. The task is a great one, and in some sense a formidable one to every thoughtful and reverent mind. Yet it must be done. It is vain to deprecate or denounce such criticism. The mind of man must think for itself, even on that which is presented to it by the very highest earthly authority; even on the Scripture, witnessed to as in a special sense a Word of God by the Church of Christ, following in this, as closely as she may, the teaching of her Master. For it has in this a moral responsibility, not a mere intellectual interest. It has to make truth, as we say, 'its own,' to realize it subjectively, as a part of itself and of its life. If it is to do this, it must not only know in whom it believes, but in measure know what is the real meaning and essence of that which is received in faith. And, indeed, the whole tenour of Holy Scripture itself implies, not only permission, but command, so to do. Of it the famous words, on which we have already dwelt, are typical, 'Prove, or test, all things: hold fast that,' and that only, ' which is good.'

But it is nevertheless well that we should understand clearly what is really at issue, and consider thoughtfully what is involved in critical conclusions or speculations, which we may be called upon somewhat hastily to accept. For this consciousness breathes into our judgment the needful spirit of caution, gravity, reverence. It may even guide that judgment in no small degree. For, just as we should distrust a train of ingenious intellectual reasoning, which landed us in a plainly immoral result—just as we should hesitate to believe what might seem a plausible consensus of evidence against a character, which we have learnt to trust, as we should trust ourselves—so it is not wrongful prejudice, if those who by faith and by experience have come to recognise a Divine Spiritual power in Holy Scripture, take with them this conviction, as one important element of consideration, in examining critical speculations, which may even seem to ascribe to it qualities inconsistent with that known character.

Then, if only these conditions be fulfilled, we need certainly have no ultimate fear of Criticism. We cannot, of course, without shutting our eyes to facts, be free from anxiety as to its immediate effect upon the faith of individuals, especially when it takes from them old conceptions and interpretations, which are not unnaturally mistaken for the truth, round which they have grown. We cannot be unaware, that there may well be some general effect of unsettlement on the whole tone of mind of the many, who do not, perhaps who cannot, study and understand the criticism itself, but who are obliged to know vaguely that it exists, and that it professes to change much which has in days past been accepted without hesitation. But for the truth itself of the Revelation in Holy Scripture we are

Y

taught, not only by a rational faith, but by much past experience, the sure conviction that the mere speculations and inventions, which are but the nebulous accompaniments of solid and true criticism, will spend themselves and mostly pass away; but that the effect of its proper distinguishing and testing power will be to clear up for us what is confused and doubtful in our faith, to remove some accretions which have gathered round it, and some theories of our own about it, which change like ourselves, and so to bring out its truth—historical, moral, spiritual—not only more clearly and surely than ever, but in closer living relation to Him, who is the Truth itself.

(VII) And so, with this reference to that aspect of the subject which is now so greatly occupying thoughtful minds, I draw to an end the argument, which I have desired to submit to your consideration, and which is, after all, simply this—that the key, which, in view of our advancing search into the secrets of Being, opens so many doors in the Palace of Truth, must surely be the master-key of the Great King.

I am, of course, aware that the very plan of such argument precludes the working out of each element with that thoroughness of mastery, which has so often distinguished the treatment from this pulpit of more special subjects. But I would venture to suggest the importance, even at this cost, of attempting from time to time some comprehensiveness of view, especially in days like our own. For we live in an age of which an exhaustive specialism, if it be a glory, is also a danger

Plea for comprehensiveness of view.

—gaining, no doubt, much depth of special insight, but apt to lose the right proportion of the parts of the great whole, and, in relation to faith, to rest the whole stress of thought and aspiration on one strand, and not the whole, of 'the threefold cord which is not quickly broken.' True indeed it is, that in the great life of humanity these various specialisms will by degrees find their right place; if each contributes its single note, all, even through some apparent discords, will blend more or less in the harmony of the collective Wisdom. But truth, and especially moral and religious truth, concerns the individual, as well as the race; it is his life, as in its right vividness, so in its right proportion. So every man, while, if he is wise, he will accept from experts the results of their special and often lifelong study, will yet for himself stand (so to speak) further back than they are apt to stand from the picture of the whole, and look at it through the eyes of the simple humanity within him.

For let me remind you, that in this view the cumulative force of various testimonies is far greater than the sum of these testimonies themselves, and that it increases with immense rapidity, as their number and variety grow. It is so familiarly in the forensic evidence of the 'two or three witnesses': the effect of the second far more than doubles the first: the addition of the third mostly turns probability into moral certainty. It is so in historical or scientific coincidence, especially if the testimonies yielded are of different kinds; as when internal evidence suddenly gains support of external; when the conclusions of mechanical science are confirmed by the study of life or mind; when deductions from some general principle are met by coincident results of observation and induction. It is true in matters admitting of demonstration, that no number of probabilities can make a certainty: but that saying is not true in relation to the moral certainty, on which so much of our life and the life of the world depends. And I may add that this strength from coincidence, while it must apply primarily to the evidence, in which all agree, yet secondarily, by establishing the credibility of each witness, attaches even to that on which each speaks alone. It were well that this fact, so well known in our law-courts, were more often recognised in the courts of philosophical investigation.

Hence, I think, the importance of the view, which our consideration has brought before us, of the various relations to multiform Science of the one Gospel of Christ, which is indeed Christ Himself. On their variety, as well as their number, their aggregate force depends. Each, as it seems to me, has its special lesson, yet all these lessons are to be read into one.

Thus we considered, first, the striking relation of the scientific discoveries in Heredity to the Christian doctrine of Mediation, and of the scientific principle of Evolution to the doctrine of the Incarnation, as at once the consummation, ordained from the beginning, for which all the natural order of the world of humanity was the preparation, and the beginning of a higher Supernatural Order, to pass hereafter into the yet higher perfection which we call heaven. That relation, which is perhaps the most modern form of the great truth of Analogy, tells us (I think) chiefly of the reality of the Christian truth. It shows it now to our fuller knowledge—substantially as our first great Anglican theologian showed it to the knowledge of three hundred years ago—as the supreme element of the Law Eternal, of which the order of all human life and history is the expression. It is the perfection, and not the contradiction, of 'the Reign of Law'; which, if we are to take the word 'Law' in its only proper sense, is the Reign of Supreme Will, the Reign of God.

Then, next, we passed from this to the elucidation by increasing knowledge of certain elements of the doctrine of Christ, which remained comparatively in obscurity, if not in abeyance, in earlier times—as in the new light thrown by our knowledge of the vastness of the universe on the Apostolic teaching of the Headship of Christ, not only over humanity, but over all created being in heaven and earth, and by our Social Science, alike in its discoveries and its problems, on the doctrine of the unity of all human society, as One Body in Christ. The idea suggested here is rather of the expansiveness of the Gospel, to meet new lights and new needs; which is the sure sign of a rich vitality in it, capable of indefinite growth in a true development, as distinct from the dead and inelastic symmetry of an artificial system, which must necessarily have its day, long or short, and then cease to be.

Lastly, the critical attitude of our modern science, chiefly in its historical and literary aspects, towards the

Gospel, although at first sight it may appear to be unsympathetic, even antagonistic—in respect both of the Supernatural character of the Gospel itself, and of the supreme authority of the Scripture, which expresses it—yet has its function of distinction of what is of the essence of both, and of examination of the evidence, external and internal, on which it is based. Its effect here is to bring out the solid simplicity, in the true sense of the word, of the Gospel, as it is centred in Christ Himself. Whatever is unreal, unsubstantial, uncertain in our popular Christianity, it may well destroy. But the merely negative and destructive action of criticism is at best secondary, and only preparatory for the higher positive duty of discovery and test of the real inner truth. We who believe in our heart of hearts that He, who is Himself the Truth, is in the Gospel, must welcome the most searching criticism, which may bring us to rest on Him, and on Him alone.

It is in the combination of all these various forms of investigation—each approaching the central object on a different side—that the force of the resultant witness lies. And that combination—to dwell once more on that which has been touched again and again—depends on the directness with which all lead us through Christianity to Christ Himself—to His Manifestation, as the crown of all revelations of God in the visible Law and Order of His Creation—to the Light of His Gospel, as that which, when the barriers of ignorance are gradually thrown down, illumines more and more all the breadth and length, and all the height and depth of Being—to His Person as the Eternal Word of God, in Himself the truth, and in His Gospel and His Church the Giver of truth to men. Each line of light converges to Him; and all unite to form the brightness which encompasses Him. So they guide us to Him; they claim for Him our homage. When they have done this, their function is over.

For the rest we must have the guidance of Faith. In His Face there is a glory above all else, spiritual, transcendent, Divine. If it be as we believe, the Revelation through the Incarnation of Godhead of all the mysteries of heaven, it claims true Faith as its due. The alternative to that Faith, as human thought more and more clearly sees, is not Science, but Nescience—the confession as to all ultimate Being of the unknown and unknowable. To that Faith (be it always remembered) we are drawn, not only by the understanding, but by the conscience in its hunger and thirst after righteousness, by the heart in its inexhaustible capacity of reverence and love, by the spirit in its ineradicable aspiration after the Infinite and Eternal. Science, even were it complete, could satisfy and develop but one part of our nature, leaving the rest to an unsatisfied atrophy; while the knowledge, which is our life because it comes from the Life Eternal, must appeal to and develop all. We, who realize this character of the true knowledge, have necessarily a twofold position in relation to Science. If Science, as we ordinarily understand the word, claims to be the sole and all-sufficient knowledge of God and Man, then, like the Law in St. Paul's days, claiming that absolute devotion which is worship, it will become an idol; and against idolatry Christian thought utters continual and effective protest. To do this is a good and a needful, if a painful, work. But if Science confess its imperfection and limitation, as insufficient to meet all the needs and capacities of humanity, it will be—as I trust we have in some aspects seen that it is—a Schoolmaster to lead us to Christ; and I contend that to welcome it in this its true character is not only a higher and gladder work, but the one most urgently needful in these our days.

The cry of Science is that, which escaped on the eve of death from the lips of one of its great masters, for 'Light, more light.' Is there any loss here, men ask, in these our days, of the force of the answer to that cry, which is embodied in the motto of this ancient University—*Dominus illuminatio mea*—the confession of faith in Him who said 'I am the Truth,' 'I am the Light of the World'?

I trust not: I believe not. There is much change, no doubt, in the form and tone, in which that answer is given now. It may be less plainly and soberly expressed than in days gone by, in the law and order of the common life, and in the good old conventions which at once express and influence opinion. Men may speculate (especially in the sanguine hopefulness and unconscious self-confidence of younger days) more freely— nay, if you will, more wildly,—on great questions, which the inherited life of past centuries once accepted, or seemed to accept, as settled in themselves for ever, and therefore only needing to be visibly represented in the venerable beauty of this place, and embodied in its institutions. Perhaps we of the older generation may be pardoned, if we sometimes think that in the growing tendency to specialism of study, even from early academic days, there is some risk of being content with partial and broken lights of truth, instead of recognising the full Light, in which all are blended. But if it be true, as they testify who best know, that, with a growth of intellectual activity and culture, there is also at least as high a standard as of old, not only of moral life, but of free spiritual interest in the light and grace of God in all their workings for humanity—then we, who are confident that these things can come only from One Divine Source, must see in them still not only the reality, but the recognition, of the old truth—freer perhaps, and therefore with all the inevitable irregularities, but therefore also with the intensity and reality, of freedom. For the sake of all who have part in the life of this place—for the sake of the country and the Church, on which that life must be a leading influence for evil and for good—God grant that this our belief and hope may be justified by the reality! If freedom of thought, feeling, action, grow from more to more, yet the word of Christ remains, 'I am the Truth,' 'In My Word ye shall know the Truth,' and it is 'the Truth' only, which 'shall make you free.'

NOTES.

Note A, p. 3.

It is important to emphasize this sense of personal relation to a Supreme Personality as of the very essence of Christian faith. For the word 'Faith,' like other words which have their true home in the religious sphere, is now apt to be loosely used of all intuitions of truth short of demonstration, and especially of the inference, from things visible and tangible, and so within the reach of observation, of the invisible principles underlying these, which cannot be discovered by observation and are incapable of logical proof, but which are the necessary guides of observation and thought and are continually verified by results.

Now, it is notable that, in the one passage of the New Testament, which gives us an abstract definition of faith (Heb. xi), the first opening of that definition corresponds to this wide generality; for it speaks of it as 'the substantiation of things hoped for, and the test of things not seen' ($\dot{\epsilon}\lambda\pi\iota\zeta o\mu\acute{\epsilon}\nu\omega\nu$ $\dot{\upsilon}\pi\acute{o}\sigma\tau a\sigma\iota s$, $\pi\rho a\gamma\mu\acute{a}\tau\omega\nu$ $\ddot{\epsilon}\lambda\epsilon\gamma\chi o s$ $o\dot{\upsilon}$ $\beta\lambda\epsilon\pi o\mu\acute{\epsilon}\nu\omega\nu$). This is simply what in modern language would be called 'the realization of the Invisible,' in the present and in the future. In this sense it might include all the highest actions of our complex nature, through its intellectual and aesthetic, through its moral and spiritual faculties—all, in fact, which constitutes the true humanity in us, as superior to the capacities working within the sphere of sense, which are plainly shared by us with the animal creation. The inclusion is deeply significant; for it implies that this general action of our humanity is (so to speak) the raw material of the true faith, which is to be unfolded in the following verses; so that this faith is emphatically natural to man as man, an integral element of his spiritual nature.

But starting from this general definition, the whole chapter goes on to stamp upon faith its own proper impress, bringing out, in relation both to the visible world and the course of human history, the reference of all these invisible principles to a Divine Personality; and this closer and more definite conception of faith, implied in every line, comes out explicitly in ver. 27, where it is described as seeing not merely the Invisible (Τὸ ἀόρατον) but Him who is Invisible (Τὸν ἀόρατον). Except in the consciousness of this personal relation, all the glorious description of Faith and its fruits would be unmeaning and unintelligible.

When we pass from this particular passage to examine the general use of the word faith in the New Testament, especially in the writings of St. Paul—tracing it through the phases of the *Credo Deum* and *Credo Deo* up to the *Credo in Deum*—it is obvious that this essentially personal character continually grows in clearness and intensity. It is the one means of the living consciousness of God as our God; it is not the idea of Christ, but it is Christ Himself, who 'dwells in the heart by faith.' Necessarily it perfects itself in the love which can attach only to personality: for 'he, that loveth not, knoweth not the God who is Love.'

Nothing less than this is faith in the Christian sense. We may accept the vaguer meanings given to the word, so far as they are preparations for this higher and more definite meaning. But such acceptance must be under protest, so that it may not obscure the nature of the real crucial difference between faith and unbelief—that the one realizes, and the other denies or ignores or doubts, the Divine Personality, as having 'covenant' of relation, or rather of unity, with the personality of man. For it is just this characteristic of faith, which opens it, on the one hand, to the most childlike simplicity, and makes it, on the other, the rest of the maturest thought.

NOTE B, p. 6.

Law (says our first great Anglican theologian), is 'That which doth assign unto each thing the kind, that which doth moderate the force and power, that which doth appoint the force and measure of working . . . for some foreconceived end for which it worketh' (Hooker's *Eccl. Pol.* Book I. c. ii. sect. 1). Properly (as he goes on to say) it is imposed by a superior Will: but he chooses to use it, with due explanation, of that which is self-imposed with a view to a fore-ordained end; as in 'the Law Eternal, which God before all ages set down for Himself to do all things by,' or, as in what St. Paul calls for men, 'the law of liberty,' 'the law which they are to themselves.'

But in any case it is essentially the expression of Power, Purpose, Will. To use it for a mere formula, declaring, without explaining, a recurrence of facts in simple antecedence and consequence, is not only theoretically improper, but practically delusive—transferring to what is a mere description of mode something of that idea of Cause, secondary or primary, which attaches to the word 'Law' in its proper sense. Many difficulties and controversies would have been spared, if it had been always remembered that, for instance, the 'Law of Gravitation' is simply the enunciation of an universal fact, and the 'Law of Evolution' a description of order and method. Behind the Law, so understood, lies the investigation of Cause. But even to use the word in reference to a First Cause, recognised as a merely Impersonal Power, whether a material force or a diffused life, is, to say the least, an ambiguous and questionable use. The fact is, that in both cases the instinctive and universal conceptions implied in human language, and apparently incapable of eradication from it, bear testimony against the ambiguities or negations, which seek to express themselves in that language.

NOTE C, p. 59.

A Theology, which starts practically from Original sin, and not from Original righteousness, overborne in man but never lost, cannot well claim to be in a true sense Scriptural, however it may press into its service certain passages from Scripture. But yet, as all men, who study human life and nature, incline to Pessimism on the one hand, or Optimism on the other, so, in different minds and under different conditions, Christian Theology, however orthodox, has been coloured by predominance, now of the deep sense of sin and the misery which it brings on humanity, now of the still deeper sense of the ineradicable good in that humanity, in spite of its acknowledged imperfection and corruption.

Accordingly, although the truth of Christ must be seen by all to rest foursquare, as in the Apostles' Creed, on the Incarnation, the Passion for us, the Resurrection and the Ascension to the right hand of God, yet it may be said that, in the one case, Theology tends to a Gospel primarily of the Atonement, going back to the Incarnation as a preparation for it, and in the other to a Gospel of the Incarnation, implying a Mediation in which the Atonement is included as the leading and determining element. To this division, moreover, of speculative Theology there corresponds, as always, a certain practical distinction—in preaching between a preaching mainly of Conversion and Justification, and a preaching of Sanctification and Edification—in view of life, between the view, ascetic or Puritan, which flees from the world, as sinful and so antagonistic to God and to redeemed humanity, and the view, which embraces all knowledge and culture, all social affection and duty, all joy and brightness in the world, as parts of man's original birthright, never wholly lost, and now restored to man in the Kingdom of Christ.

In the earlier centuries, as we see by the great Catholic Creeds, and by the controversies out of which they emerged, it is this latter Theology which is distinctly predominant. It is on the mystery of the Incarnation, as the manifestation of the Godhead in the true Son of Man, and the union of the two Natures in Him, ἀληθῶς, τελέως, ἀδιαιρέτως, ἀσυγχύτως, that, as in the Nicene Creed, the whole stress is laid. Of the Atonement it is held sufficient to say, that 'for us men and for our salvation, He came down from Heaven, and was incarnate . . . and was crucified for us.' It was in the West—struggling for conversion of the Empire and the barbarians, and in this struggle painfully conscious of the engrained power of sin, both in its subtler and its cruder forms—rather than in the more thoughtful and philosophical East, that, through the Pelagian Controversy and the Augustinian Theology, the Gospel of the Atonement assumed a prominence, which for centuries it retained, and which was certainly (as all the various Articles of the Sixteenth Century bear witness) brought out with fresh strength and intensity at the Reformation. But in our own days it seems plain that in this, as in some other points of faith, we are forced to go back—not, of course, without important modifications, embodying what the later forms of Theology have taught us—to the older Theology of the First Centuries, and so to the Gospel of the Incarnation, in all the breadth and fulness of its meaning.

We observe that the course of the Christology of the Apostolic age is from the first proclamation of the risen Christ, as the 'Lord and King,' to the 'Christ crucified,' whom St. Paul preached at Corinth, glorying in the Cross, which was a stumbling-block to the Pharisaism of the Jew, and foolishness to the intellectuality of the Greek; and next, from the Christ crucified to the Christ incarnate, the Eternal Son of God, tabernacling in human flesh, who is the great subject of the later Epistles of St. Paul and the writings of St. John. The progress was natural; for the spiritual meaning of the Resurrection to humanity at large depended on the reality of the Atonement, as the conquest of sin for all mankind; and the possibility of the one Atonement for all rested on the Incarnation of Infinite Godhead in the Great Sufferer. So only, it may be, could the stupendous truth of God made man, the Infinite incarnate in the finite, be grasped through gradual development of Christian faith. We, 'on whom the ends of the world are come,' have to enter upon the fulness of this development. While we use all these forms of the proclamation of Christ, we must rest ultimately on that which is at once largest and deepest. In relation to all practical and social life, we still claim all the kingdoms of the world to be the kingdom of the risen Christ. In our struggle against sin and misery, we still preach the doctrine of the Cross, as the one only truth which can light up its darkness—the measure of the sinfulness of sin and the measure of redeeming Love. But, if we have to go down to the foundation of all truth, claiming all the thought and will of humanity for God, we have to teach beyond all else the doctrine of the sublime opening of the Fourth Gospel—the doctrine (that is) of the Eternal Word, taking to Himself our human nature, and making it in Himself one with God.

Note D, p. 60.

It is impossible not to note the profound psychological truth, underlying the simplicity of the narrative of the Book of Genesis, when we look at it in itself, rejecting all the fabric of unreality, which human speculation and imagination have raised upon it, and putting aside for a time even the fuller Scriptural treatment of the subject in subsequent revelations.

The origination of evil in the race, as there described,

corresponds most closely with what our daily experience discloses, as the ordinary process of its origination in the individual. It is shown, first, as using appeal to desires innate in man, both physical and spiritual—desires natural in themselves, but apt to break their proper subordination to the control of a supreme Law of righteousness in the Divine Will. It is described, next, as receiving its first impulse by temptation from a spiritual power of evil, deliberately using this perverted force of desire, and denying or misrepresenting the Law, which should restrain it. Such power over the individual is familiar to us as exercised by evil men; in the origination of evil in the race, it is described as coming from some supernatural power, impersonated in the false wisdom of the serpent. Its essential character is then shown as the claim of a false independence of God—the desire in man to be 'as a god' to himself. In it he assumes the right to know both good and evil—obedience (that is) and resistance to the Divine Will—as distinct principles of conduct, and to choose between them as by an inherent right, instead of knowing and loving only what is good as his true life, and recognising evil simply as the unnatural and monstrous negation of that good. In respect again of the penalties of sin, the narrative dwells only on its plain physical penalties, of labour and weariness and fruitlessness on the one hand, of suffering and subjection to bondage on the other—both shared by all humanity, though apportioned in predominance to the two sexes—and the natural end of these in physical decay and death. The heavier spiritual penalty is but implied in the sublime irony of the passage, 'their eyes were opened, and they knew that they were naked'; for the sense of shame is the instinctive cowering of the sinful from the sight of God, in conscious helplessness and guilt, awaiting His righteous judgment. In accordance with the true order of God's Word, what is here only implied, is left to be wrought out explicitly in the more advanced stages of His revelation; in which death physical, in the withdrawal of the breath of life, is seen as a symbol of the death spiritual, in the loss of the higher life of the Spirit of God. From all, finally, there is given a promise of deliverance, not without struggle and suffering, by 'the seed of the woman'—obviously clear as to its reality, while absolutely mysterious as to the character and method of its fulfilment—again a *Protevangelium*, to be developed hereafter.

It would be difficult to find a more striking exemplification, first of the 'double sense' of Holy Scripture—the profound teaching to the maturity of human thought in the fulness of times, through the simplicity capable of being in measure understood in the childhood of the race, and, next,—in comparison with human mythologies and philosophical speculations as to the origin and character of evil—of what St. Paul means when he declares that 'the foolishness of God is wiser than men.'

Note E, p. 75.

The text of these Articles is an instructive illustration of the ruthless dogmatism, to which the resolute uncompromising logic of a religious Determinism can lead. Even as somewhat timidly softened by the Bishops, they run thus:—

1. Deus ab aeterno praedestinavit quosdam ad vitam, quosdam reprobavit ad mortem.

2. Causa movens praedestinationis ad vitam non est praevisio fidei, aut perseverantiae, aut bonorum operum, aut ullius rei quae insit in personis praedestinatis, sed sola voluntas beneplaciti Dei.

3. Praedestinatorum definitus et certus est numerus, qui nec augeri nec minui potest.

4. Qui non sunt praedestinati ad salutem necessario propter peccata sua damnabuntur.

5. Vera, vera, et justificans Fides, et Spiritus Dei justificanter non exstinguitur, non excidit, non evanescit in electis, aut finaliter, aut totaliter.

6. Homo vere fidelis, i.e. fide justificante praeditus, certus est, plerophoria fidei, de remissione peccatorum suorum et salute sempiterna sua per Christum.

7. Gratia salutaris non tribuitur, non communicatur, non conceditur, universis hominibus, qua servari possint, si voluerint.

8. Nemo potest venire ad Christum, nisi datum ei fuerit, et nisi Pater eum traxerit. Et omnes homines non trahuntur a Patre, ut veniant ad Filium.

9. Non est positum in arbitrio aut potestate uniuscujusque hominis salvari.

Those, who read these terrible utterances in the light of earlier theological speculation, will see how they deliberately close every loophole of escape from the absolute iron Determinism, which, in the sense of the Sovereignty of God, utterly loses and abjures the true individuality of man. It is no wonder that those who believed them, or thought that they believed them, were dissatisfied with the Lutheran doctrine of 'Justification by faith,' which, if it rightly places the origin of salvation in God's Love in Christ, yet by the very requirement of faith evidently implies some fellow-working of human will, asserting itself that it may surrender itself. Still less is it surprising, that they should have been utterly discontented with what have been ignorantly called our 'Calvinistic Articles' (Art. XVI, XVII).

For the XVIIth Article, while, closely following the very words of Holy Scripture, it dwells on the whole process of salvation, from the Supreme Will and grace of God, through all the steps of call, obedience to that call through grace, justification, adoption, conformation to the image of Christ and religious walking in good works; yet (*a*) is resolutely silent as to reprobation to death, (*b*) continually implies the fellow-working of man, (*c*) positively declines to make Election a fundamental Article of the Faith to be pondered by all, and (*d*) declares that we are to receive God's promises, as they are set forth *generaliter* (that is to all mankind) in Holy Scripture, and not to presume to enter into the secret Will of God. The XVIth Article expressly acknowledges that, 'after we have received the Holy Ghost, we may depart from grace given and fall into sin, and by the grace of God, we may arise again and amend our lives.'

NOTE F, p. 126.

St. Augustine, *De Genesi ad Litteram*, c. xxiii, has a remarkable passage (referred to but not quoted by Mr. Moore), curiously anticipating the course of evolutional speculation. He first traces the gradual growth of a tree, in stem and branches, in leaves and fruit, from the seed, in which (he says) 'illa omnia fuerunt primitus, non mole corporeæ magnitudines, sed vi potentiaque causali.... Quid enim ex arbore illa surgit aut pendet, quod non ex quodam occulto thesauro seminis illius extractum atque depromtum sit?' He then proceeds to draw out substantially that analogy between the growth of the individual being and the evolution of the sum of all beings, with which we are now familiar: 'Sicut in ipso grano invisibiliter erant omnia simul, quæ per tempora in arborem surgerent, ita ipse mundus cogitandus est, cum Deus simul omnia creavit, habuisse simul omnia quæ in illo et cum illo facta sunt ... sed potentialiter et causaliter, priusquam per temporum moras ita exorirentur.' This opinion of St. Augustine is referred to in the passage from St. Thomas Aquinas, of which Mr. Moore gives a translation: 'Alii enim expositores dicunt quod plantæ productæ sunt actu in suis speciebus ... secundum quod superficies litteræ sonet. Augustinus autem dicit quod causaliter tunc dictum est produxisse terram herbam et lignum, id est producendi accepisse virtutem ... Ante ergo quam orirentur super terram, factæ sunt causaliter in terra. Confirmatur autem hoc etiam ratione, quia in illis primis diebus condidit Deus creaturam originaliter vel causaliter, a quo opere postmodum requievit, qui tamen postmodum secundum administrationem rerum conditarum per opus propagationis usque modo operatur.... Non ergo in tertia die productæ sunt plantæ in actu sed causaliter tantum' (*Summa Theologiæ*, pars prima, quæst. lxix. Art. ii).

NOTE G, p. 162.

The original of this remarkable passage (*Oratio contra Gentes*, sect. xlii.) is here subjoined:—

Αὐτὸς γοῦν ὁ παντοδύναμος καὶ παντέλειος ἅγιος ὁ τοῦ Πατρὸς Λόγος, ἐπιβὰς τοῖς πᾶσι καὶ πανταχοῦ τὰς ἑαυτοῦ δυνάμεις ἐφαπλώσας, καὶ φωτίσας τά τε φαινόμενα καὶ τὰ ἀόρατα πάντα, εἰς ἑαυτὸν συνέχει καὶ συσφίγγει, μηδὲν ἔρημον τῆς ἑαυτοῦ δυνάμεως ἀπολελοιπώς, ἀλλὰ πάντα καὶ διὰ πάντων καὶ ἕκαστον ἰδίᾳ καὶ ἀθρόως ὁμοῦ τὰ ὅλα ζωοποιῶν καὶ διαφυλάττων· τάς τε ἀρχὰς πάσης αἰσθητῆς οὐσίας αἵπερ εἰσὶ θερμὰ καὶ ψυχρὰ καὶ ὑγρὰ καὶ ξηρὰ εἰς ἓν συγκεραννύων... μίαν καὶ σύμφωνον ἀποτελεῖ ἁρμονίαν... Οἷον γὰρ εἴ τις λύραν μουσικὸς ἁρμοσάμενος καὶ τὰ βαρέα τοῖς ὀξέσι καὶ τὰ μέσα τοῖς ἄκροις τῇ τέχνῃ συναγαγών, ἓν τὸ σημαινόμενον μέλος ἀποτελοίη· οὕτως καὶ ἡ τοῦ Θεοῦ Σοφία, τὸ ὅλον ὡς λύραν ἐπέχων, καὶ τὰ ἐν ἀέρι τοῖς ἐπὶ γῆς συναγαγών, καὶ τὰ ἐν οὐρανῷ τοῖς ἐν ἀέρι, καὶ τὰ ὅλα τοῖς κατὰ μέρος συνάπτων καὶ περιάγων τῷ ἑαυτοῦ νοήματι καὶ θελήματι, ἕνα τὸν κόσμον καὶ μίαν τὴν τούτου τάξιν ἀποτελεῖ, καλῶς καὶ ἡρμοσμένως. αὐτὸς μὲν ἀκινήτως μένων παρὰ τῷ Πατρί.

NOTE H, p. 208.

The portion of the Sermon on the Mount, which is usually known as its Law, is the second section (Matt. v. 17-48). It begins with the famous declaration that in it our Lord does 'not destroy the Law and the Prophets'—the moral element of the old Covenant, as expressed both in the sternness of the Mosaic Law, and the freer and more spiritual teaching of the Prophets—'but perfects' it by His own higher authority. It ends in the sublime ideal of our moral life, as an imitation of God: 'Be ye perfect, as your Father, which is in heaven, is perfect.'

But this perfecting of the Law shews itself under different aspects. First, in relation to the sixth and seventh Commandments, it simply strengthens and spiritualizes the Law, as still Law. It carries into far stronger and wider development the prohibition of evil and selfish passions, both of violence and of lust, extending that prohibition from action to word and thought, and enforcing it with a far greater sternness than that of the Law of old time. Next, in relation to the third Commandment it more distinctly idealizes the Law. From the prohibition of false swearing, which 'takes God's Name in vain,' it rises to the command of that pure, instinctive truthfulness, which needs not the sacredness of the oath to sustain it, and which reverences all that marks the presence of God too much to invoke it rashly. Lastly, in relation to the law of retaliation and to the recognition of friend and enemy in the battle of life, it leads the disciples of Christ to rise above law and its stern unvarying justice, in all that concerns their own interest and rights—to decline to accept the protection or vengeance against evil, which all law, which has to keep together an imperfect human society, must offer—to refuse to meet evil by evil, and to be ready by forgiveness, love, blessing of our enemies, to overcome evil with good.

Of this threefold application of the principle of this perfection of the Law, no difficulty can be felt in theory, although infinite failure is confessed in practice, as to the first and second elements. The first is felt simply to enforce, in the usual sense of the phrase, obedience to the spirit rather than the letter of the law; the second bears merely a striking witness to the truth, that one great function of law is to foster the growth of character, and that character, when fully and rightly developed, goes beyond all legal requirement. These two truths come home to us without difficulty; the verdict of conscience upon them is but clenched by a Divine authority. But it is on the third—the law of absolute self-sacrifice, in non-resistance and unlimited forgiveness of evil, that serious thought often does feel difficulty, not because the law is too hard for flesh and blood, but because it seems to ignore justice, and accordingly to tend to the disintegration of society.

Of course it belongs to individual action, in that region of our experience, which is beyond and above law. The old command of retaliation properly (see Ex. xxi. 24, Lev. xxiv. 20, Deut. xix. 21) applied to the national enforcement of law, and to those who were charged with it. They cannot put it altogether aside, although they may make punishment, not a matter of crude and simple retribution, but a deterrence from crime and a chastisement of the criminal for his reformation. When San Carlo Borromeo, the great Archbishop of Milan, was fired at in his own chapel by a villain whom he had had to punish ecclesiastically, he forgave the assassin, and dismissed him with kindness. But the Government of the day seized him, and punished him. It could not do what in his own individual person the saintly Archbishop felt himself free to do. For the authority which rules a people is, as has been well said, simply the trustee and guardian of the rights and welfare of the nation at large, and of its individual citizens. Even the community of one generation is similarly placed in charge of the whole of the national mission and life. Each nation, again, has a trust of responsibility for the peace and order and welfare of the world. All must, if need be, defend this trust against wrong. To surrender it would be to give up that which is our own.

But, even in regard of individual action, we must still beware of the error of resting on the letter, which, under changed circumstances, must change, and not on the principle, which is unchanging. As to the letter—that Our Lord intended His command of non-resistance to evil and absolute self-sacrifice to be literally obeyed by His immediate disciples, we cannot well doubt. By that simple manifestation of love, as in Himself so in them, a new commandment was to be established, a new witness for peace borne to the world. That still by those who take up directly His Divine mission to men, this same witness has to be borne, and is borne effectively, exactly in the same way, the whole tenour of our missionary enterprise and the special witness of its martyrdoms most plainly show. As to the spirit—that His command applies to all time in the principle of an unlimited forgiveness and sacrifice, so far as it can be, of our own pride, our own interests, even our own rights, if by such sacrifice we can serve and win others, is equally certain; and the more in our own life we can carry it out, the better will it be for us and for humanity.

In the practical obedience, however, to that command, there is a grave consideration, which cannot be put from us, that, while we can unreservedly sacrifice self if we will, we cannot disregard the good of others—the good of the offender himself, for whom it may well be better that he should be restrained and punished for evil-doing—the good of society, which certainly and mainly depends on the maintenance of law and justice.

The consideration extends beyond even this immediate subject. It clearly applies to all individual self-assertion and self-defence, in relation to others and in relation to society at large. This may for the same reasons become in right measure a duty; it may even be a needful contribution to the true welfare of the whole. Just as unhappily in the England of the nineteenth century we cannot literally 'give to every man who asks,' lest we should do evil, instead of good, to him and to the world, so an absolute sacrifice of self, not to the service of God, but to the service of men, may unwittingly infringe the great laws of freedom and righteousness, by which He is pleased to govern humanity.

The right discrimination in this matter is difficult at all

times; and in a complex civilization like our own, it is far more difficult than under the simpler conditions of earlier days. It is but too easy, moreover, to cheat ourselves into the belief, that we are yielding to this larger sense of duty, when we are really shrinking from self-sacrifice. But yet the difficulty and the danger of self-delusion have to be faced. There are times, when, in order to keep our Lord's command in the spirit, we have to break it in the letter. Happiest are they, to whom such times come but seldom.

Note I, p. 311.

The present tendency of criticism as to the predictive element of Prophecy, shews an extreme reaction from that older opinion, which, as is seen in common parlance, identified Prediction with Prophecy (even pressing into its service a false etymology of the word 'prophet'), or at least held Prediction to be its all-important element, and which was accordingly inclined to trace fulfilments of prophecy everywhere without sufficient ground. It has been rightly seen that the Prophet is simply one who speaks for God, because 'the Word of God comes to him,' and 'the Spirit of God is upon him'; that his true mission is to set forth the eternal Law of Righteousness and Love, in relation to the present at least as much as to the future; that some of the greatest prophets, such as Elijah and St. John Baptist, foretold (so far as we know) little or nothing; that even the great Prophet of prophets Himself made prediction but a small part of His prophetic office; that many of the supposed fulfilments of Prophecy have been on critical investigation found to be arbitrary or at least uncertain. Accordingly there has been a tendency to ignore, if not to deny, the predictive element of Prophecy altogether, so far as it involves anything of supernatural foresight. That tendency has been sometimes expressed with great boldness, as for instance by critics of the school of Kuenen; even where it is not unhesitatingly accepted, it has shown itself in some inclination to deny prediction or to explain it away, at least in the great mass of the instances, which were once familiarly known and accepted.

It is necessary, therefore, for those who accept the authority of our Lord and His Apostles on this matter, to remind themselves, that, although prediction is but a subordinate element in Prophecy, it is a real, and, if we may so say, a natural, element in the prophet's Mission. The Prophet claimed to be able to enter, in the measure granted him, into the mind of God, to whom past, present, and future are all one. The power of prediction, especially where no visible miracle was wrought, was one unmistakeable sign that this claim was a true claim; and it should be noted that, so far as the prophets formed a recognised succession, the fulfilment of the prediction of an older prophet might in this respect give authority to the utterances of his successors. But, beyond this, since the prophet had to show clearly to men the working of the righteous Will of God in human history, and since 'the mill of God grinds slowly, though it grind exceeding small,' it might often be that the present generation was not sufficient to display that working adequately, and that accordingly he who interpreted the mind of God, might need to see in measure, as He sees perfectly, the germs of the future in the present, and to extend his view, and the view of his hearers, to the ages to come; and this, moreover, definitely or indefinitely, as God might give him power. Lastly, if this predictive power is natural in itself to those, who speak for God, it was certainly specially appropriate to a religion, which, like that of Israel, 'had its golden age in the future,' and in which all the various elements were avowedly preparatory and anticipatory of that future perfection. Since, moreover, this future undoubtedly centred round a Messiah to come, all prophetic predictions would appropriately gather, in greater or less degree, round Himself and His kingdom, either as distinctly 'Messianic' in personal reference to the King, or 'Evangelical' in anticipation of the spiritual character of that kingdom. Given, we may say, the reality of Prophetic Inspiration and of the Messianic anticipation, the reality of this power of prediction becomes, so to speak, natural in the supernatural sphere.

It is, therefore, no wonder that the prophets of old time did undoubtedly assert this power; that our Lord Himself and His Apostles as unquestionably took it for granted, and appealed to it in them; and that, as in His discourse on the eve of the Passion, He plainly exercised it Himself. It is unnecessary to quote special instances on this matter. The whole tenour, both of Old Testament Prophecy, and of the New Testament teaching, is unintelligible without it; the plainest declarations would have to be taken in a singularly 'non-natural sense.' Every instance in detail of the apparent non-fulfilment of this or that prophecy constitutes a difficulty, which must be fairly and candidly met. Of such difficulties some may be, and have been, solved; others to our present knowledge remain insoluble. But, if it is true that, for the supernatural reality of predictive power in general, we have the authority of Him, who 'expounded to His disciples in all the prophets, the things concerning Himself,' and 'to whom,' as the Apostolic testimony declares, 'all the prophets bear witness,' these difficulties will be in a literal sense 'trials of faith.'

The criticism, which holds to the opinion that prophecy is but 'fallible anticipation' of what wise and good men think likely to be under God's dispensation, protests (as through Kuenen) against what it calls 'the absolutism' of the view, that 'it must either abandon its idea of the work of the Israelitish prophets, or deny all value to the twofold testimony of the New Testament, and even to the life and the word of Jesus.' But it is hard to see what third course is really open. No doubt there are cases of what the writer calls 'application' as distinct from 'interpretation,' and 'homiletic employment of the Old Testament' as distinct from 'exposition.' But these are very far from covering the whole ground; and the only way of setting aside the many cases, which are plainly interpretations and expositions, is avowed to be by questioning 'the authority of the New Testament'—which, if our records be genuine, is that of our Lord and His Apostles—'in the domain of Exegesis.'

Here, as in the cognate sphere of visible miracle, it is well to see that the real issue is of the existence of the supernatural in the whole dispensation, of which the Incarnation is the centre.

www.ingramcontent.com/pod-product-compliance
Lightning Source LLC
Chambersburg PA
CBHW020228240426

43672CB00006B/456